S0-AHK-761

# Visual Basic.NET Debugging Handbook

Jan Narkiewicz
Thiru Thangarathinam
Benny B. Johansen

® Wrox Press Ltd.

# Visual Basic.NET Debugging Handbook



First published December 2002

Published by Wrox Press Ltd,
Arden House, 1102 Warwick Road, Acocks Green,
Birmingham, B27 6BH
United Kingdom
Printed in the United States
ISBN 1-86100-729-9

# Trademark Acknowledgments

Wrox has endeavored to provide trademark information about all the companies and products mentioned in this book by the appropriate use of capitals. However, Wrox cannot guarantee the accuracy of this information.

# Credits


**Authors**
Jan D. Narkiewicz
Thiru Thangarathinam

**Additional Material**
Benny B. Johansen

**Commissioning Editor**
Benjamin Hickman

**Technical Editors**
Benjamin Hickman
Christian Peak

**Indexer**
Michael Brinkman

**Project Manager**
Beckie Stones

**Technical Reviewers**
Kevin Baker
Damien Foggon
Sean Medina
Dan Maharry
John Maletis
Mark Horner
Eric Lippert
David Schultz
Chris Winland

**Production Coordinator**
Sarah Hall

**Proof Reader**
Chris Smith

**Cover Design**
Natalie O'Donnell

**Managing Editor**
Emma Batch

# About the Authors

## Jan D. Narkiewicz

Jan is Chief Technical Officer at Software Pronto, Inc. (jann@softwarepronto.com). Jan began his career as a Microsoft developer thanks to basketball star, Michael Jordan. In the early 90's Jan noticed that no matter what happened during the game, Michael Jordan's team won. Similarly, no matter what happened in technology Microsoft always won (then again this strategy is ten years old and may need some revamping). Clearly, there was a bandwagon to be jumped upon.

Over the years, Jan managed to work on an e-mail system that resided on 17 million desktops, helped automate factories that makes blue jeans you have in your closet (trust me you own this brand) and kept the skies over Abu Dhabi safe from enemy aircraft. All this was achieved using technologies such as COM/DCOM, COM+, C++, VB, C#, ADO, SQL Server, Oracle, DB, ASP.NET ADO.NET, Java, Linux, and XML.

In his spare time Jan is Academic Coordinator for the Windows curriculum at U.C. Berkeley Extension, teaches at U.C. Santa Cruz Extension, writes for ASPToday, and occasionally plays some football (a.k.a. soccer).

Jan contributed Chapters 1-4 and Chapter 6.

### Thiru Thangarathinam

Thiru works as a Consultant at Spherion Technology Architects, an international technology consulting company, in Phoenix, Arizona. He is an MCSD. During the last two years, he has been developing Distributed n-Tier architecture solutions for various companies using latest technologies such as VB, ASP, XML, XSL, COM+, and SQL Server.

*I would like to dedicate this book to my family and friends who have been providing constant motivation and help all these years.*

Thiru Contributed Chapter 5.

### Benny B. Johansen

Benny is V.P. of Software Development at Sound ID, a Palo Alto based startup using innovative technology to "enhance the appreciation of sound". He has a B.Sc. in Computer Science, an MBA in Corporate Strategy, and most importantly of course an MCSD.

When not cracking the whip at Sound ID, or teaching ASP.NET at UC Berkeley Extension, he enjoys running, cooking, and trying to improve his piano playing. He can be reached at bjohansen@soundid.com or bennynet@etvoila.com.

*I would like to thank my wife Dorthe and my two daughters Michelle and Nicole for filling my life with joy and delight.*

Benny contributed to Chapter 5.

VB.NET

Debugging

Handbook

Table of Contents

# Table of Contents

VB.NET

# Debugging

Handbook

## Introduction

# Introduction

Like any worker, to be really effective the developer must intimately understand the tools at their disposal, Visual Studio and the .NET Framework provide many tools and options to aid you in your quest to track down bugs. This book aims to take you through those tools, showing you what they are capable of and where they are applicable.

## Who is this Book For?

In a sense this is a book for all Visual Basic developers; after all no one is perfect and all code has to be debugged. In fact for many developers spend the majority of their time debugging code so even a few tricks and tips can save a huge amount of time.

This book does assume that you are primarily developing Visual basic Application using one of Microsoft's integrated development environments, be that one of the several versions of Visual Studio or Visual Basic .NET Standard edition. Fortunately there is little difference in the core debugging functionality offered by their various IDEs.

While mainly aimed at Visual Studio developers this book still contains much information useful to those just using the command-line tools provided with the .NET Framework SDK, for instance, the coverage of the .NET Framework's `Debug` and `Trace` classes.

## What does this Book Cover?

This book takes a progressive walk through the debugging functionality offered by Visual Studio .NET. We start with:

- **Chapter 1 – Configuring Visual Studio**
  Visual Studio .NET is a highly configurable development environment, this chapter looks at all the feature relevant to debugging in Visual Studio .NET and how they can best be set up to aid effective debugging.

- **Chapter 2 – Debugging with Visual Studio**
  This chapter actually gets into the real work of debugging in Visual studio, setting breakpoints, running the debugger, and evaluating breakpoints. We also look at the large array of windows that are available for viewing all sorts of information about managed applications.

- **Chapter 3 – Exceptions, Threads, and Processes**
  Although exceptions may at first seem most relevant to release code they are a powerful aid to debugging. It is possible to configure Visual Studio so it launches the debugger when a specific exception is thrown. Using chained inner exceptions, it is possible to follow the path of an exception through an application collecting data along the way.

  Debugging multithreaded applications can be tricky so Visual Studio .NET offers several features to help navigate between threads and isolate problems. Finally, this chapter looks at debugging running process, which is vital for debugging applications such as Windows services that can't be started from Visual Studio and in a production environment.

- **Chapter 4 – Logging and Programmatic Debugger Interaction**
  Collecting and persisting information about the state of an application at various stages is crucial to tracking bugs. This approach to debugging is particularly important for deployed code; it is often undesirable to install development tools on a production system or attach a debugger to live applications. Using logging techniques, you can make an application easy to debug even in the most restrictive of environments.

- **Chapter 5 – Debugging Web Applications**
  This chapter looks at the specific issues that you will encounter when debugging applications hosted in the ASP.NET runtime. We look at setting up visual studio for debugging all types of web application and tracing for ASP pages. In this chapter, we also look at debugging SQL server code and Windows Forms controls hosted in Internet Explorer.

- **Chapter 6 – Advanced Debugging Scenarios**
  This chapter takes you through several realistic debugging scenarios, in including remoted applications, debugging VB.NET to legacy VB6 code, and debugging VB.NET to unmanaged C++ code. These scenarios give us a chance to examine client-server debugging, multithreaded debugging, and mixed-mode debugging in detail.

# What do you Need to Use this Book?

Although it is possible to develop Visual Basic .NET applications using a text editor and the command-line tools that come free with the .NET Framework SDK any serious developer should have access to one of the Integrated Development Environments available:

- Visual Basic .NET Standard Edition
- Visual Studio .NET Professional Edition
- Visual Studio .NET Enterprise Developer Edition
- Visual Studio .NET Enterprise Architect Edition
- Visual Studio .NET Academic Edition

All versions of Visual Studio .NET are suitable for all the examples in this book; Visual Basic .NET Standard edition, however, has some fairly severe limitations that mean not all the code in this book will be usable. The most relevant limitations are that you can't develop class libraries, and as the name indicates, you can only develop Visual Basic .NET code.

One example involves interoperability with a VB6 application, if you wish to build this example from scratch then you will require a Visual Basic 6 IDE.

To debug web applications and some remoted applications you will need an operating system that come with Microsoft's Internet Information Server (IIS). Suitable systems include Windows XP Professional, Windows 2000 (all versions), and .NET Server (all versions). It is possible to Install Visual Studio .NET on Windows XP Home edition but as this operating system does not support IIS it will not be possible to develop web applications and web services.

VB.NET

# Debugging

Handbook

1

# 1

# Configuring Visual Studio

This chapter presents an overview of how to enhance debugging and speed development with Visual Studio .NET. This will be achieved without actually debugging applications (single stepping, setting breakpoints, viewing the contents of variables, etc.). Better tools organization, project/solution management, and use of help will be discussed. Features for maintaining a "to do" list, marking code, better clipboard management, and viewing more code for the same amount of screen real estate will be presented.

Also discussed will be what features are in each specific version of Visual Studio .NET (Academic, Profession, Enterprise Developer, and Enterprise Architect), what flavor of .NET are installable, what operating systems are supported by the .NET Framework and Visual Studio .NET, and the location in which tool, solution and project configuration information is configured and stored.

## Runtimes, SDKs and Debuggers

Some developers have a tendency to think that every machine out there (including those used by mom, dad, and clients) all have Visual Studio .NET installed. Developers need to recognize that the amount of debugging support they can take advantage of is in proportion to what is installed on a given machine (Visual Studio .NET, the .NET Framework SDK, or just the .NET Framework). To further expand on this idea consider the following downloads available to subscribers at http://msdn.microsoft.com/:

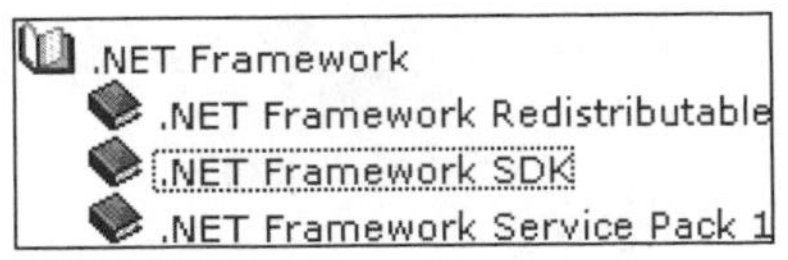

The previous screenshot should make it clear that there is .NET without Visual Studio .NET. The specific .NET configurations an application can be debugged under include:

- .NET Framework Redistributable – this environment corresponds to how customers (non-developers) using .NET applications will be configured. By installing the .NET Framework, a customer can run .NET applications but will likely not develop .NET applications (even though the .NET Framework ships with compilers for C#, VB.NET, JScript.NET, and C++). A customer will probably not have a debugger installed, just the .NET Framework, but there is some debugging functionality built into the framework itself.
- .NET Framework Software Development Kit (SDK) installed – the .NET Framework Software Development Kit contains .NET's development infrastructure (API's, documentation, etc.). The purpose of the SDK is to allow development shops that do not use Visual Studio .NET (such as rival compiler vendors or shops developing their own JIT compilers for their own flavor of CPU) to work and develop with .NET. The SDK ships with a variety of tools including an extremely versatile debugger, `CorDbg.exe`. Customers who are not themselves developers will not be likely to have the .NET Framework SDK installed.
- Visual Studio .NET installed – developer machines and typically only developer machines will have Visual Studio .NET installed. The .NET Framework and .NET Framework SDK are installed when Visual Studio .NET is installed. This is true, regardless of the version of Visual Studio .NET installed (Academic, Professional, Enterprise Developer, or Enterprise Architect).

This may sound obvious but developers should never assume that they will have Visual Studio .NET at their disposal while visiting a customer site. I have actually attended meetings where some fresh-out-of-school developer is explaining to an IT manager at a Fortune 500 company why Visual Studio should be installed on their $100,000 servers running in production. Fortune 500 guard their server like Colonel Sanders guarded his secret recipe for Kentucky Fried Chicken, so it is unlikely they (IT managers and not Colonel Sanders) will ever put non-sanctioned code on their high-end machines to help some poor developer debug an application. Applications deployed in the field must have debugging techniques built in that do not require a debugger (such as using configuration files to modify the information logged by the application and the destination of such log output).

The operating systems on which the .NET Framework Redistributable can be installed are:

- Windows 98 Second Edition
- Windows ME
- Windows NT 4.0, Service Pack 6a or later
- Windows 2000, Service Pack 2 or later

- Windows XP Home
- Windows XP Professional
- .NET Server (in all its guises)

Each of the previous operating systems does require that at least Internet Explorer 5.01 and Windows Installer 2.0 is installed. Windows 95 and 98 are not supported. The .NET Framework SDK and Visual Studio .NET can be installed on:

- Windows 2000, Service Pack 2 or later
- Windows XP Home (with limitations)
- Windows XP Professional
- .NET Server

Using Visual Studio .NET (or even the .NET Framework SDK), managed code can be developed for Windows 98 and Windows ME, but there is no debugger support provided for these operating systems. The challenges faced when debugging applications developed for Windows 98 and Windows ME will be discussed as part of this text, but clearly, Microsoft is making it quite clear move off Windows 98 and Windows ME in the longer term.

## Versions of Visual Studio .NET

There are multiple flavors of Visual Studio .NET. The specific version purchased dictates what functionality (including debugging functionality) is available. It is possible to get an academic version of Visual Studio .NET or just a single language edition (VB.NET, C# or C++ standard edition). These versions of Visual Studio .NET can be purchased quite inexpensively and are ideal for people taking a night class or attending university part time. It is recommended that a full version of Visual Studio .NET be purchased rather than just the VB.NET version as these standard editions do have considerable limitations, such as not supporting the development of DLLs.

The academic version of Visual Studio .NET is fundamentally the same as the professional version. The functionality included with these versions is quite comprehensive. With respect to applications, the following types can be developed: XML-based web services, web applications (ASP.NET including server-side controls), Windows applications (Windows Forms including controls), Windows controls hosted in Internet Explorer, Windows Services, and database applications.

Upgrading to Visual Studio .NET Enterprise Developer provides better database support, such as trigger design, stored procedures, and user-defined functions. Source code control is provided with Visual Studio .NET courtesy of Visual SourceSafe. From a debugging standpoint, Visual Source Safe is a godsend. As an application is developed it can be checkpointed and different versions checked in. If a mistake is made or for some reason code is lost (hard drive crash or human error) Visual SourceSafe contains a backup.

Visual Studio .NET also provides an Enterprise Architect edition. The features for this edition are less debugging-centric and are more architecture and design specific. It contains enterprise application templates for more rapid design, and includes Visio for software and database modeling. The software modeling features are not quite Rational Rose (a popular object-oriented development tool) and the database modeling is not quite Erwin (a popular database development tool) but Enterprise Architect edition does handle a significant number of object-oriented development and database development scenarios.

**When installing Visual Studio .NET make sure that you install the complete help and do not rely on using CDs/DVDs in order to access documentation. There is nothing more frustrating than sitting at a developer's machine when the Internet is down (no msdn.microsoft.com to retrieve help from) and being told; "Oh, I left the CD's at home so we cannot access help".**

**If your hard drive at work is not large enough to hold the entire distribution of Visual Studio .NET, maybe you should think about getting a new job.**

## *Web Servers*

Microsoft's flagship web server, Internet Information Server (IIS), is needed in order to develop web services, ASP.NET applications, ASP.NET server-side controls, applications that remote using HTTP, and serviced components that use HTTP. Developers who insist on using Windows XP Home Edition need to recognize they are forgoing IIS which is included in every other operation system that supports Visual Studio .NET. IIS is not enabled by default on Windows XP or .NET Server; therefore remember to enable it before installing Visual Studio.

IIS is not the only reason to use the Professional version of Windows XP. For instance, Windows XP Home lacks full support for Access control lists used in Windows role-based security.

## *Web Matrix*

Microsoft has produced another IDE aimed at ASP.NET web development called Web Matrix – this is available free from http://www.asp.net. Although more limited than Visual Studio it can be used for developing web services, mobile applications, ASP.NET pages, and database applications. However many features that are supported in VS.NET such as web form control development are not supported. What this tool does provide beyond Visual Studio .NET Professional (as opposed to Enterprise Developer or Architect) is the ability to edit and modify stored procedures for SQL Server and MSDE. It also includes a lightweight web server against which to test your ASP .NET code, which means you don't need IIS to use Web Matrix

What Web Matrix does not provide is any extra debugging functionality over that provide by the .NET Framework SDK. Features such as development of multiple projects and Intellisense are not supported. As a tool, Web Matrix is nifty but a lack of debugging support is clearly a major detriment.

# Configuration Locations

As a tool Visual Studio .NET manages solutions. A solution is just a container for projects – these can be console applications, Windows forms applications, web services, Windows services, etc. One of the solution's primary duties is to maintain dependencies between projects and dictate the build order of projects within the solution. When configuring and using the debugging features made available with Visual Studio .NET it is important to distinguish between debugging features that are:

- Configured for a particular user running Visual Studio .NET
- Configured for a particular solution
- Configured for a particular user of a solution
- Configured for a particular project
- Configured for a particular user of a project

## *Visual Studio .NET Configuration*

Using the Tools | Options menu these are many possibilities for configuring Visual Studio .NET; here we'll look at how to use the options to best facilitate debugging. Per-user Visual Studio .NET configuration information is stored in the Windows registry (see the following screenshot) which means such customizations are not available to a developer working at someone else's workstation or even when a developer logs in as different user:

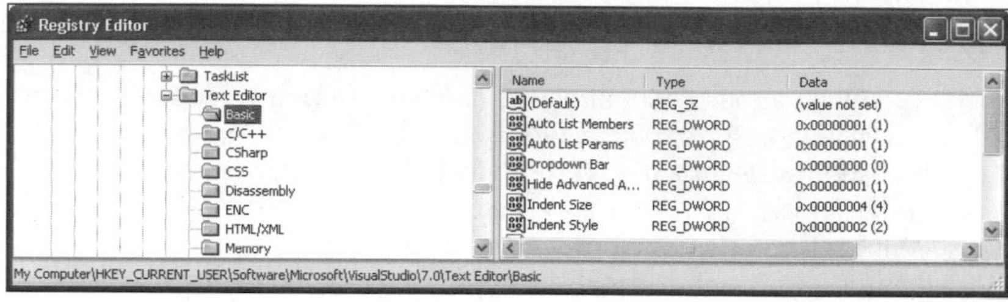


The screenshot above shows RegEdit, a Windows utility used to view the contents of the Windows registry, specifically here a key (`HKEY_CURRENT_USER`) associated with the currently logged in user. The key examined is for Visual Studio .NET and it configures the basic settings associated with the text editor (hence, Text Editor\Basic). The Insert Tabs key is set to zero. This means that spaces are used and not tabs in the source editor. More importantly, this setting and others set with Tools | Options will not miraculously be configured just because a developer sits down at a particular workstation with Visual Studio .NET installed. A user has to set up (customize) each instance of Visual Studio .NET separately.

*The per-user settings are being emphasized because a large number of developers just assume that* Tools | Options *is part of a project. I once worked on a project with three engineers who were revered as object-oriented gurus. They were gods in their field. They developed for months but no one else could ever build their projects because they configured all their directory paths and settings using* Tools | Options *rather than with per-project or per-solution settings. Remember that if you make your code dependent on settings in your Windows registry, coworkers may not be able to build your code.*

## Solution Configuration Files

As was previously mentioned, a solution is used to manage projects. A solution is composed of the following files:

- `SolutionName.sln` – contains a list of projects in the solution and the dependencies between projects.
- `SolutionName.suo` – contains per-user solution configuration settings such as breakpoints, bookmarks, and user-defined tasks. This file need not be present in order to load and run a project. If such a `*.suo` file does not exist, Visual Studio .NET creates one.

The solution file (`.sln`) is checked under source code control when using Visual SourceSafe while the solutions options file (`.suo`) is not checked under source control. You should find it logical that the `.suo` file is not placed under source code control. When another developer pulls the code to be built (including the `*.sln` file) they probably do not want to inherit such debugging entities as breakpoints, bookmarks, and user-defined tasks.

## Project Configuration Files

A project consists of various document files (source files, resource files, application configuration files, etc.) and project configurations contained in files that behave similarly to a solution's `*.sln` and `*.suo` files:

- `ProjectName.vbproj` – contains a list of files built as part of the project and information with respect to how to build these files.
- `ProjectName.vbproj.user` – contains per-user project configuration settings such as the working directory used when the project is debugged, the executable or URL used to debug the project, and the command-line arguments passed to the debugger when the project is run and debugged. Like an `*.suo` file, Visual Studio .NET recreates the `*.user` file if does not exist.

The project file (`.vbproj`) is checked under source code control when using Visual Source Safe while the project options file (`.vbproj.user`) is not checked under source control. When another developer pulls the code to be built (including the `.vbproj` files) they do not want to inherit such debugging entities as command-line arguments, working directory, or remote host for debugging.

The extensions discussed (`.vbproj` and `.vbproj.user`) apply to VB.NET projects only (hence the `vbproj` portion of each project name). For instance, C# projects are specified by `ProjectName.csproj` for the project administration and `ProjectName.csproj.user` for user configuration of a project.

# Visual Studio .NET Setup

The goal is not just to debug using Visual Studio .NET but to debug efficiently. The faster you debug, the faster you can get out of work (and maybe have a social life). One aspect of debugging that is often overlooked by many developers is how their environment is set up. Having taught a debugging lab on Visual Basic for a decade it is surprising how many developers never tweak their environment to make it behave more efficiently. This section makes some suggestions with respect to how to best configure your development environment for optimal debugging.

# Standard Profiles

Developers using Visual Studio .NET come from diverse backgrounds, VB6, Visual C++ 6.0, Visual Interdev, scripters and so on. For this reason, Visual Studio .NET allows developers to select a profile (which sets things like hot keys and menu short cuts) based on their legacy IDEs. When Visual Studio .NET is launched for the very first time, the Start Page is displayed with its Get Started tab selected. This is the first decision a developer needs to make with respect to the behavior of their debugger. A screenshot of the Start Page's My Profile tab is as follows:

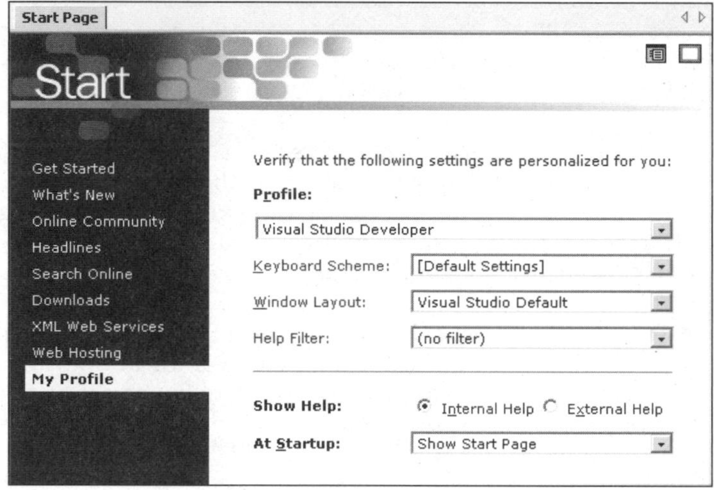


Notice that Visual Studio Developer is selected under Profile. Subordinate aspects of the Profile such as Keyboard Scheme, Window Layout, or Help Filter can also be changed if required.

The following screenshot shows the contents of the Debug menu when a project is loaded within Visual Studio .NET Profile:

Based on the Visual Studio Developer profile, the F5 key executes the projects in a Visual Studio .NET solution that are marked to start when the solution is debugged. The F10 key allows the code to be debugged one statement at a time (stepping over methods) and the F11 key allows the code to be debugged one statement at a time (stepping into methods).

Changing the profile on the Start Page to Visual Basic Developer results in the following:

Notice that now F8 performs debugging a single statement at a time (while stepping into methods) and Shift+F8 performs debugging a single statement at a time (while stepping over methods). As a VB.NET developer moving from Visual Basic 6.0, the Visual Basic Developer profile will feel quite comfortable (familiar). Former ASP developers can select the Visual Interdev Developer profile and achieve the same level of familiarity. However, this text was written using the Visual Studio Developer profile in attempt to remain profile-neutral.

The Start Screen allows certain aspects of a profile to be customized. For instance, it is possible to set the keyboard behavior (for example. F10 to single step) using the Keyboard Scheme setting or the layout of the windows in Visual Studio .NET using the Windows Layout setting.

**Once you have configured the look and feel of your Visual Studio .NET (using Tools | Options) do not change your profile. Changing your profile causes the configuration to revert to default settings. This in turn erases the effort put in to getting a look and feel for Visual Studio .NET that you are happy with. For example if you had set each tab within source code to be represented by four spaces, changing profiles would cause this to revert back to tabs being represented as the tab character (the default).**

### Using Multiple Accounts

One place where profiles can bite you is the case of a coworker sitting at your machine to help you with a bug. There is nothing more frustrating than being used to F10/F11 to single-step through the debugger and having to remember F8/Shift+F8. One trick to make your machine more coworker-friendly (without erasing your configurations) is to have multiple accounts. On my laptop, there is an account with the Visual Studio .NET's profile is set to Visual Basic Developer. This is because one of my places of employment uses Visual Basic .NET for the product under development. When developers sit at my machine, they get to work in their preferred profile – when I code, I log in as myself, and the profile is set to Visual Studio Developer.

This same trick (creating extra users on your machine) is also useful when developing and testing internationalized software. You can set up accounts with say German, Egyptian, and Chinese users, to test how characters in different languages are displayed.

You can also set up accounts with different levels of permissions (administrative, guest, and standard user) so that the security aspects of different applications can be debugged and tested.

## *Toolbars*

Visual Studio .NET provides a plethora of toolbars to aid in development (each icon on the toolbar represents a command in Visual Studio .NET). Toolbars are named for the types of commands handled by the icons displayed. For example, the Debug toolbar contains icons that handle debugging (run, single stepping into methods, etc.). By default, Visual Studio's toolbars are as follows for a project currently being debugged:

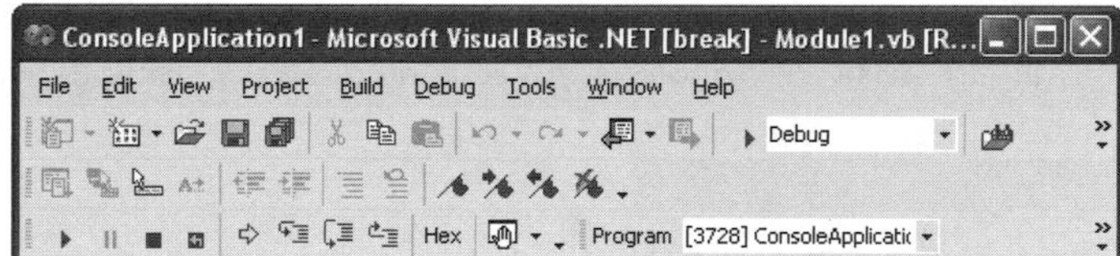


There are three lines of icons displayed given that the Standard, Text Editor, Debug, and Debug Location toolbars are displayed. Most developers use only a few icons per-toolbar. This means that the rest of the icons are just wasted real estate. This real estate would be better used to show source code (so you can see what you are debugging). There is no law requiring that these toolbars be used. Left mouse-click on the left edge of any toolbar and simply drag it off and then it can easily be closed (or moved to the side). A right mouse-click on any toolbar or on the top border of the main window, displays a context menu that lets toolbars be enabled or disabled. A snippet from this context menu is as follows where the Debug and Debug Location toolbars are currently displayed (enabled) but Data Design and Database Diagram are not displayed (disabled):

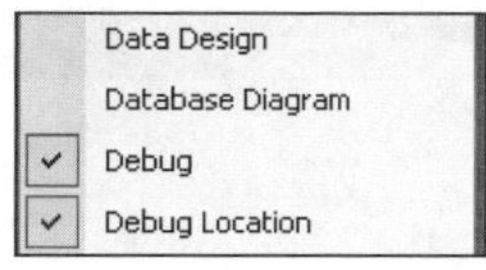


At the bottom of the toolbar context menu is the Customize menu item. When this menu item is selected the Customize dialog appears. Selecting the Toolbars tab on this dialog lists all available toolbars. Regardless of the tab selected, icons can be dragged off (commands removed from) or added to (commands added to toolbar) toolbars as part of customization.

Using the Commands tab of the Customize dialog, icons can be dragged onto toolbars. One nifty trick is to drag the most commonly used icons and to place them on the menu bar, the line along the top were the menus are displayed. Icons placed on the menu bar take up no screen real estate because the menu bar was going to be displayed anyway. An example of this is as follows:

In the screenshot above the Standard toolbar's project configuration icon is displayed indicating that the Debug version of the project is presently being used (built, run, and debugged by Visual Studio .NET). The Debug Location toolbar's program icon is being displayed to show which program (process) is presently being debugged. As Visual Studio .NET can debug multiple processes in the same instance of Visual Studio .NET, displaying the program being debugged is a godsend when debugging both the client and server of a client-server application inside a single instance of Visual Studio .NET.

The Customize dialog allows the menu, to be customized (changed, new menus added, etc.) and the keyboard shortcuts to be customized. Be warned though, if you over customize your Visual Studio .NET, no one on your team will want to sit at your machine and help you debug!

> *A developer at I knew recognized that coworkers did not like his hardware (as opposed to Visual Studio .NET) setup because he was a lefty and put the mouse on the left. To make his workstation friendlier to coworkers, he purchased a wireless mouse so you could just toss the mouse to the right or the left side without tangling any wires. Then again, he could have just purchased the mouse because it was cool.*

## Specialized Options

Profiles provide broad configuration settings for Visual Studio .NET, but there is a finer level of granularity (specialization) to Visual Studio .NET configuration. This is achieved using the Tools | Options menu item. Selecting this menu item displays the Options dialog (Tools | Options | Environment | General in this case):

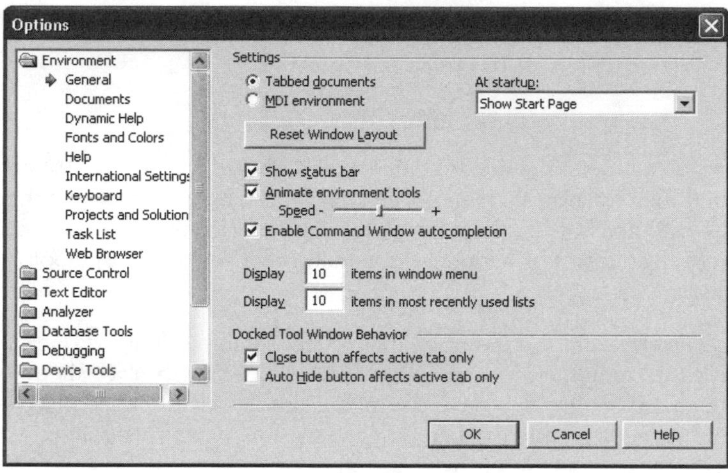


There is an awful lot of productivity to be gained by tweaking the options for your tools. For example the following settings are handy to tweak:

- Environment | General folder – Change Display 4 items in most recently used list to contain a value of ten. This lets you select from the last ten files accessed or the last ten projects accessed.

- Environment | Fonts, and Colors folder – a lot of times a group of developers gather around a monitor to look a problem. Setting the Text Editor font to Lucida Console with a size of 16 will make the code visible to all.

  *At a Xerox spin off this was called Otto-izing Visual Studio (where Otto was the name of a brilliant engineer with Coke-bottle glasses).*

- Source Code | SCC Provider folder – if your Source Safe login name differs from your Windows login name, you can specify your Source Safe login name here. Over time this will save a tremendous amount of unnecessary typing.

- Text Editor | All Languages | Tabs folder – enable Keep Spaces so if you need to place source code into a document (such as a design document or a book written for Wrox Press) the code aligns properly and not with the tab settings of the word processor being used.

> **Do not trivialize the importance of Text Editor | All Languages | Tabs. This dialog can be used to standardize how code is laid out (tabs versus spaces, etc.). I once worked for a shop where half the developers used tabs and half used spaces. When a developer using one editor would check out the code it would change tabs to spaces. When the code was checked in, every line in the file was modified. An unrelated bug was introduced with this change so an attempt was made to compare the old version with the new file. The problem was every line of the file had changed so no one could figure what the two or three new lines of code were. The changes had to be rolled back because of space/tab foolishness. If you are working in a team set a standard stick to it.**

The previous list is just a miniscule subset of all the configuration tweaks that can be made with the Tools menu Options menu item. For most settings, the familiar adage, "If it isn't broke, don't fix it." is probably wise.

# Efficient File Manipulation

A huge chunk of any project's development time is spent doing rather boring things like managing files, accessing the contents of files, etc. A bit of debugging attention should therefore be paid to Visual Studio .NET's File menu. Yes, this menu allows files, projects, solutions, and source code control to be managed.

For example, the File | Open | File menu item conceals a rather under-utilized debugging tool. Selecting the aforementioned option displays the Open File dialog that contains an Open button. Clicking on the downward pointing arrow to the right of the Open button reveals the following:

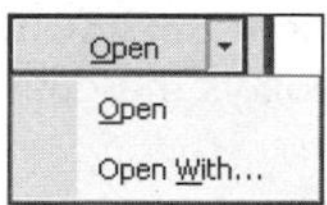


Basically Open With specifies that you can open up a given file type but you are not obligated to use the default application associated with that file's extension The Open With dialog can also be display by right-clicking on a file within the Solution Explorer window. This displays a context menu complete with an Open With menu item to display the Open With dialog. When Open With is selected an Open With dialog is displayed such as the following:

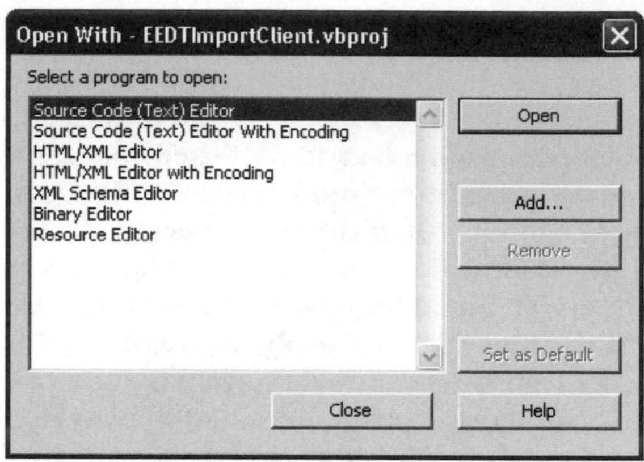


It should be clear from the Add button in the previous dialog that third-party editing tools can be added to Visual Studio .NET for access through File | Open | File. It would also be possible using the Open With dialog to open the solution file (`.sln`) associated with a variety of projects using the Source Code (Text) Editor rather than the default (loading the solution in Visual Studio .NET). It would be possible to load the project file (`.vbproj`) associated with a VB.NET project using the HTML/XML Editor. Why would you want to manually edit such files? To solve problems such as when a set of projects is created with the word "Recieve" in their names. The tired developer (henceforth referred to as c'est moi) had to go back and rename everything to the correct spelling (Receive) and editing the solution and project files directly was the fastest way to remedy the rather pervasive spelling error.

## *Editing Binary Files*

The option in the Open With dialog screenshot that is particularly intriguing is the Binary Editor selection. Those who work with binary files will find such an editor indispensable. When developing Lotus's flagship e-mail system (back before Lotus was acquired by IBM), a binary editor was used to view the administrative, data, and index pages of the propriety database used to store e-mail. An example of the binary editor exposed by Open With is as follows where the left hand column displays the byte offset within the file, the middle column displays the data in hexadecimal form, and the right hand column displays the data as text:

```
0001cf60  02 00 08 00 EF 08 00 FF  FE 53 61 6D 61 74 68 61  .........Samatha
0001cf70  FF FE 4B 61 68 58 00 FF  FE 34 35 36 20 45 6C 20  ..KahX...456 El
0001cf80  43 61 6D 69 6E 6F 20 52  65 61 6C FF FE 53 75 6E  Camino Real..Sun
0001cf90  6E 79 76 61 6C 65 43 00  41 00 FF FE 39 35 34 33  nyvaleC.A...9543
0001cfa0  32 3C 00 35 00 31 00 26  00 26 00 12 00 10 00 0B  2<.5.1.&.&......
0001cfb0  00 02 00 08 00 EF 08 00  FF FE 53 75 73 61 6E 57  ..........SusanW
0001cfc0  00 75 00 58 00 FF FE 31  32 33 20 4D 61 69 6E 20  .u.X...123 Main
0001cfd0  53 74 72 65 65 74 FF FE  53 74 6F 63 6B 74 6F 6E  Street..Stockton
```

It is possible to use the binary editor to modify a binary file. Quite often while debugging what is written to and read from a binary file, mistakes in the data can be seen using a binary editor. By editing the file on the fly, debugging can continue even if the data was initially written improperly. When working with a binary file, data cannot be deleted or inserted, so do not bother with the delete key or the backspace because a specific memory location cannot be deleted. To modify data, simply typing in a new value can overwrite a memory location and hence change the memory locations for the binary file.

## Recently Used Lists

The File menu contains a list of most recently used files (Recent Files submenu item) and recently accessed solutions (Recent Projects menu item). Recall that the number of items in the recently used list is set using Tools | Options, and the Environment folder:

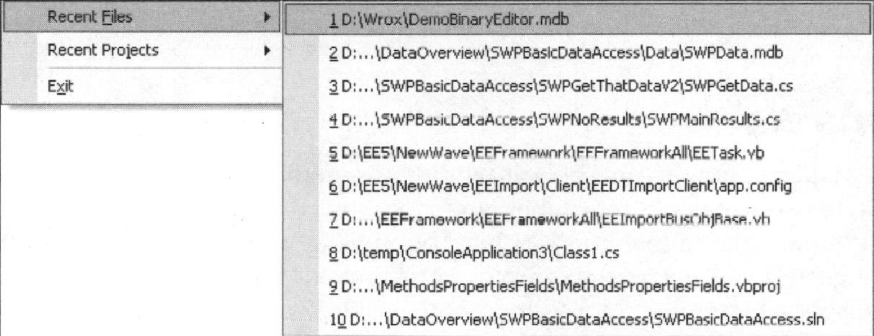


What is particularly useful about the most recently used file list is that it remembers how you lasted opened a file. The screenshot of the binary editor showed a Jet database file (a binary file of type `*.mdb`), `DemoBinaryEditor.mdb`. Using File | Open this file would have been opened using Microsoft Office's Access application. Actually, the file was opened with Open With and the binary editor. Specifically, the recently used file list is cognizant of this and subsequently opens the file using Visual Studio .NET's binary editor.

# Managing Text within Files

When managing a solution's files the File menu was the focal point. It only makes sense that when manipulating the contents of files, the Edit menu plays a key role. It includes a variety of elegant features that can simplify development and hence preempt bugs:

- Find and Replace
- Bookmarks for moving between locations in files
- Outlining regions of code so they can be collapsed or expanded
- Clipboard management

## Find and Replace

The Edit menu's Find and Replace menu item exposes some time-saving features that will leave you more time to fix bugs. Selecting the Find and Replace menu item displays a subordinate menu with some old favorites: Find, Replace, and Find in Files. A new favorite is also available on this subordinate menu, Replace in Files. Using this option, text to find and replacement text can be specified. This replacement can span multiple files and does not require the files to be opened in VS.NET.

The Find and Replace submenu also provides a Find Symbol menu item. This allows you to search for a symbol, such as a namespace, class, structure, or interface. Within these constructs Find Symbol can also locate properties, methods, events, variables, constants, and enumeration items. The entities searched can include a project's source files or the assemblies (binary entities) referenced by a project. The search of assemblies includes the global assemblies such as `System`, `System.Windows.Forms`, `System.Data.SqlClient`, and `System.Xml`. Again, this feature is not debugging-related but its usefulness and potential to save time should be obvious.

## Bookmarks

Ever had to add a feature to an application that required changes to eight different locations in the source code? Inevitably, you make seven of the eight changes and that takes a few hours. After a few hours of hard debugging you completely forgot the eighth change and hence spend the rest of your time tracking down the bug because of the lone spot where you forgot to modify the code. Addressing this problem is the Edit menu's Bookmarks submenu:

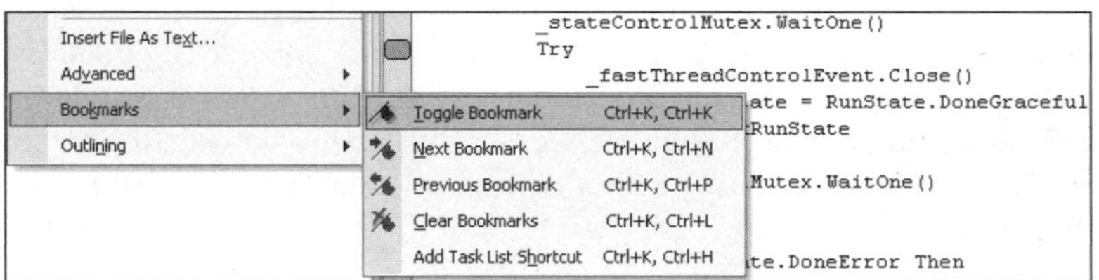


The idea is to put bookmarks at the eight different locations (before you get engrossed in fixing the problem) and then it becomes a snap to jump between them to make the necessary changes. The bookmarks also serve as a reminder of what you had to do and where you had to do it. What is a bookmark? Actually the previous screenshot shows a bookmark inside the code (the octagonal "dot" to the left of the `Try` in the source code). The idea is simple. Rather than attacking the eight areas of code spread out of the project, bookmarks would first be placed at each location (*Ctrl+K, Ctrl+K*). The *Ctrl+K, Ctrl+N* key sequence can be used to move the cursor to the next bookmark and *Ctrl+K, Ctrl+P* can be used to move the cursor to the previous bookmark. This really cuts down on the time it takes to jump between disparate regions in the code. As the changes to the code are completed for a particular region, the bookmark can be toggled off (*Ctrl+K, Ctrl+K*) or all bookmarks can simply be cleared at once (*Ctrl+K, Ctrl+L*).

There is one final menu item in the Bookmarks submenu, namely Add Task List Shortcut. A better name for this menu item might be "Toggle Task List Shortcut". The task list is a list of things that need to get done – for example if your code contains a compilation error or warning, it is added to the task list. This list can be viewed courtesy of the View menu (more on this later). It turns out that you can also add items to the task list using the Add Task List Shortcut menu item. An example of this is as follows:

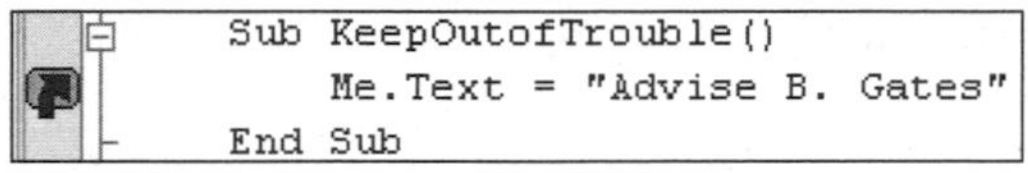

```
Sub KeepOutofTrouble()
    Me.Text = "Advise B. Gates"
End Sub
```

The crooked arrow that looks like a sign you would see while driving (right turn ahead) represents the task-list short cut. When the task list is viewed each such shortcut will appear in the task list as in the following screenshot:

Task List - 2 tasks

| ! | | ✓ | Description | File | Line |
|---|---|---|---|---|---|
| | | | Click here to add a new task | | |
| | ↱ | ✓ | ~~Me.Text = "Advise B. Gates"~~ | ~~C:\Documents and ...\Form1.vb~~ | ~~68~~ |
| | ↱ | ☐ | Me.Text = "Hang with Steven Hawkings" | C:\Documents and ...\Form1.vb | 68 |

This screenshot shows a task list that contains two task-list short cuts created with *Ctrl+K, Ctrl+H*. One of the tasks is checked off as being completed (the task at the line where `Me.Text` is set to `"Advise B. Gates"`). When an error or warning is removed from a program, the corresponding error/warning is removed from the task list. There is no checked off task with a line drawn through it.

On the surface Visual Studio .NET's organizational features, such as bookmarks and the task list do not seem closely related to debugging. They are – the best way to debug is to be preemptive. Organize development in such a way that you reduce the bugs inside your code, by jotting down friendly reminders to yourself (using bookmarks or the task list) you can reduce the number of bugs before the debugger is even fired up.

## Outlining and Directives

The Edit menu contains the Outline submenu. To understanding outlining consider an application where you are debugging two methods simultaneously in the same source file, `Method0()` and `Method1000()`. The problem is that there are 999 methods between `Method0()` and `Method1000()` so it takes some work to see both methods on the screen at the same time. Sure you could use bookmarks to jump between the two methods but you could also collapse (hide) the entire set of methods (`Method1()` through `Method999()`) in one fell swoop using the `#Region` directive (a feature of VB.NET) and outlining (a feature of Visual Studio .NET). C# developers have their own directive, `#region`, so they can make use of this feature as well.

Why this preoccupation with how source code is viewed on the screen? Why do we care about outlining? Why do we suggest you do not leave a billion toolbars exposed in Visual Studio? To paraphrase Obi-Wan Kenobi's advice to Luke Skywalker in Star Wars (concerning debugging), "Use the source, Luke." As a Jedi Master, Obi-Wan recognized (as most of us do) that the best way to debug is to read your source code before running it, and hence effort should be placed into organizing source code within Visual Studio .NET and ensuring that as much a possible of the relevant source code is visible on the screen at any one time.

Back to our original problem, namely, how do we use the `#Region` directive in order to aid in debugging `Method0()` and `Method1000()` simultaneously? To facilitate this debugging we place a `#Region` directive before `Method1()` and a corresponding `#End Region` directive after `Method999()` (as is shown below):

```
    Sub Method0()
    End Sub

#Region " Hide these for now while debugging Method0 and Me
    Sub Method1()
    End Sub
    ' Rest of methods 2 through 998 here
    Sub Method999()
    End Sub
#End Region

    Sub Method1000()
    End Sub
```

Notice that Visual Studio .NET recognizes VB.NET's `#Region` directive and places a minus sign in a box to the left of `#Region`. Clicking on this minus sign, causes the region to be collapsed (hides the code from the user) and hence it becomes simpler to debug the elaborate algorithms exposed by `Method0()` and `Method1000()`.

Notice also that next to each method a minus sign is available so individual methods can be collapsed and expanded. The same is true for namespaces, classes, properties, multi-line comments, and the accessors within properties (the individual `Get` and `Set` clauses). In Visual Studio .NET terms, we can collapse an outline region (as is dictated by the `#Region` directive or by the presence of a namespace, class, method, property, etc.) or expand an outline region (a.k.a. outlining can be toggled). In support of this is the Edit menu's Outline submenu.

The Outline submenu will not win a Nobel Prize for usefulness in debugging but it does allow outlining to be turned on en masse (Collapse to Definitions) and off en masse (Stop Outlining). Notice in the previous screenshot that a `#Region` is collapsed (named, `Windows Form Designer generated code`). Windows Forms applications (and other application types within Visual Studio .NET) automatically take advantage of outlining in order to keep Visual Studio .NET generated code from cluttering up a developer's view of the source code.

## Compilation Constants

The `#Region` directive is not the only directive supported by VB.NET. Also implemented by the language are:

- `#Const` – specifies a constant (`#Const ConstantName = Expression`) used at compilation time with the `#If/#Else` construct. This constant cannot be used programmatically at run time (only at compilation). The `#Const` directive can be used as follows:

```
#Const NumberOfNinjasItTakesToDefeatMe = 50
#Const IAmBetterAtSoccerThan = "Ronaldo"
```

- `#If Then #Else` – facilitates conditional compilation. `#Region` hides code but the code is still compiled, the `#If Then #Else` directives allow code to be compiled or not compiled based on evaluating the `#If` expressions. This is a great way to disable large regions of code within an application.

```
#If IAmBetterAtSoccerThan = "George Best" Then
        MessageBox.Show("I am dreaming")
#Else
        MessageBox.Show("I am awake")
#End If
```

There is one more directive, the `#ExternalSource`, which maps between lines in an external file and the present file. This directive is useful for reporting errors when one file is used to generate another.

An example of where this is useful is an environment that uses SQL embedded directly in the code (not the way ADO.NET does it). An embedded SQL environment uses a processor to convert from a source file containing SQL and a destination file containing some process generated code. There is a correlation between the destination file generated and the source file used to seed the generated code. This correlation can be maintained using `#ExternalSource` in order to map an error in the generated code back to the line number in the original code. However, most developers will never encounter this esoteric compilation constant.

### Standard Compilation Constants (#Const)

The Project | Properties | Configuraiton Properties | Build dialog contains two checkboxes that specify conditional constants (Define DEBUG constant and Define TRACE constant):

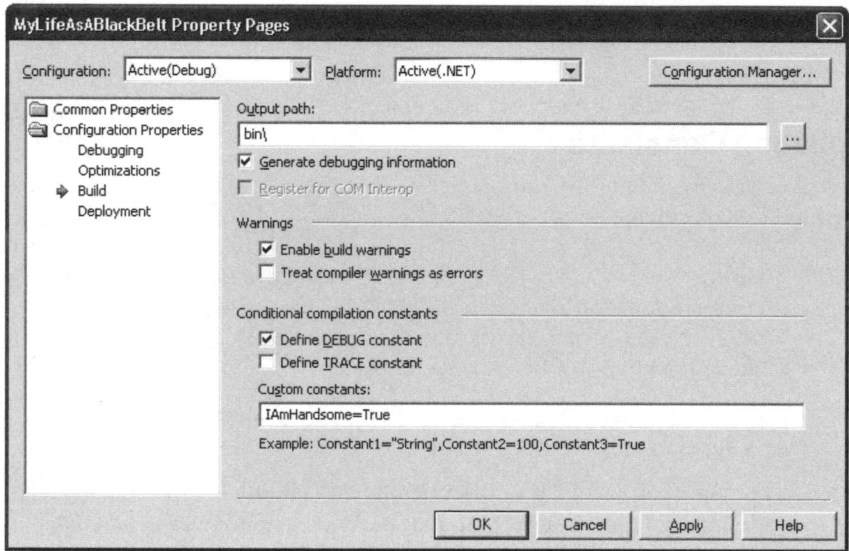


The purpose of the checkboxes found under the Conditional compilation constants section in the previous screenshot are:

- Define DEBUG constant – when this checkbox is checked the DEBUG conditional constant (type, `Boolean`) is set to `true`. By default, the DEBUG constant is enabled for debug builds and disabled for release builds.

- Define TRACE constant – when this checkbox is checked the TRACE conditional constant (type, `Boolean`) is set to `true`. By default the TRACE constant is enabled for both debug and release builds.

The `System.Diagnostics.Trace` and the `System.Diagnostics.Debug` classes are (among other things) used to generate logging output. If TRACE is defined then the `Trace` class's write methods generate output. If DEBUG is defined then the `Debug` class's write methods generate output. The default location for the output from both `Debug` and `Trace` is the Output window of Visual Studio .NET. The `Trace` and `Debug` classes are covered further in Chapter 4.

### Constant Scope

Each `#Const` specified is limited in scope to the file in which it is specified. Project-wide compilation constants are superseded by per-file `#Const` declarations. For example, if the following were specified in a file then the `TRACE` constant would be set to `False`. A setting of `False` is not the default behavior for either the debug or release builds:

```
#Const TRACE = False
```

#### Custom Compilation Constants

It is also possible using Project | Properties | Configuration Properties | Build to set custom project-wide compilation constants. The aforementioned dialog, which is the same as the previous screenshot, contains a Custom Constants textbox that can be used to specify one more project-wide compilation constants such as:

```
ValidateAllParameters=True, UpperVersion="8.1", DebugLevel=4
```

Within a specific file is it possible to disable a compilation constant. The rationale for doing this would be in order to override the behavior of a project-wide compilation constant. Disabling a compilation constant is achieved by using `#Const` and setting a previously defined compilation constant to `Nothing`:

```
#Const ValidateAllParameters=Nothing
```

At this point you might be thinking of creative ways to make use of this feature, however, .NET has XML-based application configuration files, which are a better way to accomplish most configuration tasks. See Appendix A for an introduction to .NET configuration files.

#### Debug versus Release Configuration Settings

The previous screenshot of Project | Properties | Configuration Properties | Build contained a very important feature that should not be overlooked. Namely, the upper left corner of this dialog contained a drop-down list that enabled the settings to be specified for the Debug build only, Release build only, or All Configurations (both Release and Debug). Using this it would be possible to specify that the DEBUG constant is defined for Release builds or All Configurations when by default this is not the case.

Choosing between Debug, Release, and All Configurations is not solely the domain of Configuration Properties | Build. Each property page displayed using Project | Properties can make use of these per-configuration settings.

#### #If Then #Else

As was previous discussed, the `#If Then #Else` construct allows regions of code to be included in compilation or excluded from compilation. In the VB model, the `#If Then #Else` construct is terminated by an `#End If`. This construct also supports `#ElseIf` so that conditional compilation expressions can be evaluated in else clauses. The formal definition of `#If Then #Else` is as follows:

```
#If expression Then
   statements
[ #ElseIf expression Then
   [ statements ]
...
#ElseIf expression Then
   [ statements ] ]
[ #Else
   [ statements ] ]
#End If
```

One typically use of `#If Then #Else` is to specify one set of code for debug builds and another set of code for release builds. For example, consider a class library, for debug builds (`#If DEBUG Then`) extra error checking could be performed to such a level that application performance could be affected. Under release builds (the `#Else` case) more practical and realistic (less detrimental to performance) error checking could be performed.

## Better Cutting and Pasting

Ever want to move several different regions of a source file into a different source file or files? The process has been quite tedious given that each Edit menu Cut/Copy was matched to a single Paste (one item in the clipboard at a time). More to the point, has juggling a single clipboard every caused you to make a mistake (inject a bug into you code) or to lose code because you overwrote the code in the clipboard? Coming to the rescue is the clipboard ring – basically a jazzed up version of the clipboard with fifteen slots.

Each time code is cut (Edit | Cut) or copied (Edit | Copy) it is placed in the next location in the clipboard ring. Once all fifteen slots are full, the slots get reused. Retrieving the item copied to the current clipboard ring slot is a matter of pasting (Edit | Paste). The Edit menu also provides a way past the next entry in the clipboard ring, the Cycle Clipboard Ring menu item. Each time this menu item is selected the next item in the clipboard ring is pasted from the clipboard into the document. If the item pasted is not the desired item stored in the clipboard, simply selected the Cycle Clipboard Ring (*Ctrl+Shift+V*) menu item until the desired selection is pasted.

Clearly the Edit menu's Cycle Clipboard Ring menu item is a bit of a guessing game. The Toolbox window provides a more visual way to view the contents of the clipboard ring. The aforementioned window is displayed using the View | Toolbox menu item. In order to see what is contained in the clipboard ring, simply select Clipboard Ring from inside the Toolbox windows such as is shown next:

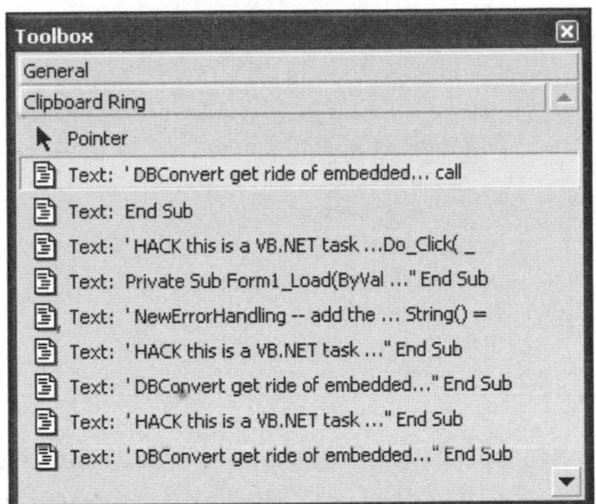


Clicking on any of the clipboard ring slots displayed in the Toolbox window causes the current clipboard ring location to advance to the slot clicked on. Any Edit | Paste operation performed will copy the contents of the selected clipboard ring location into the location marked by the cursor's current location. The contents of a selected clipboard ring location can also be placed at the current cursor by double-clicking on the clipboard ring slot. The clipboard ring won't debug invalid data or corrupted memory, but the clipboard ring is a better development tool and using better tools should serve as a way to preempt the inclusion of bugs in the code.

# Viewing Project-Related Windows

There is a huge amount of information that can be discerned during the debugging and development of a .NET project. The number of windows that can be accessed and made use of may seem daunting. To manage these windows and display them when a developer needs, there is Visual Studio .NET's View menu.

If you are using Visual Studio .NET and you need a Window that you do not know how to display, go to the View menu. Some of the windows can display the classes in a project (via the Class window), properties, associated files, and controls (via the Properties window), and the files associated with a project along with the projects associated with a solution (via the Solution Explorer window).

## *Solution Management*

Solutions, their projects, and those project's files are managed using Solution Explorer. An example of the Solution Explorer window is as follows:

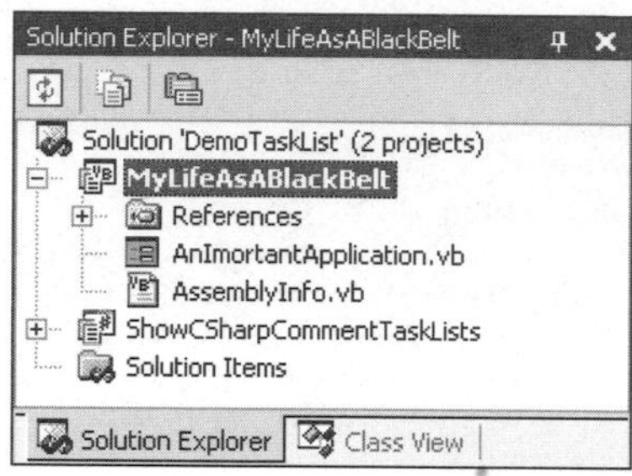


This screenshot contains a solution (DemoTaskList) (which can be downloaded with this book's code) and two projects (MyLifeAsABlackBelt and ShowCSharpCommentTaskLists). Double-clicking on any source file (such as `AnImportantApplicaction.vb`) within the solution opens that file in the editor. The real excitement with Solution Explorer comes when entities (the solution itself, projects, the References folder, and source files) within the solution hierarchy are clicked on thus revealing a context menu germane to the entity clicked on. For example the context menu displayed when References is clicked on contains the Add Reference and Add Web Reference menu items.

## Viewing as Much Code as Possible

Obi-Wan Kenobi (Jedi Master) is a big proponent of the View menu's Full Screen menu item (*Shift+Alt+Enter*). Obi-Wan's rationale for this is because when Full Screen is toggled on, only document windows are displayed rather than tools windows. Document windows are things such as source code while tools windows include Solution Explorer, Task View, and Properties. By only displaying document windows (no toolbars, no tools windows, etc.) more source code can be displayed on the screen without the clutter of Visual Studio .NET's infrastructure (remember, "Use the source, Luke"). When in Full Screen mode an icon entitled Full Screen is displayed:

Clicking on this icon disables full screen mode and brings back the pleasantly familiar clutter of Visual Studio .NET's tools windows and toolbars.

## Much Ado about ToDo Lists

When we discussed bookmarks, the concept of tasks was introduced. This was because the Edit menu's Bookmarks submenu allowed in the task list entries of type shortcut to be created. There is a great deal more to task lists than just shortcuts. One way to demonstrate the features associated with the task list is via the View menu's Show Tasks submenu:

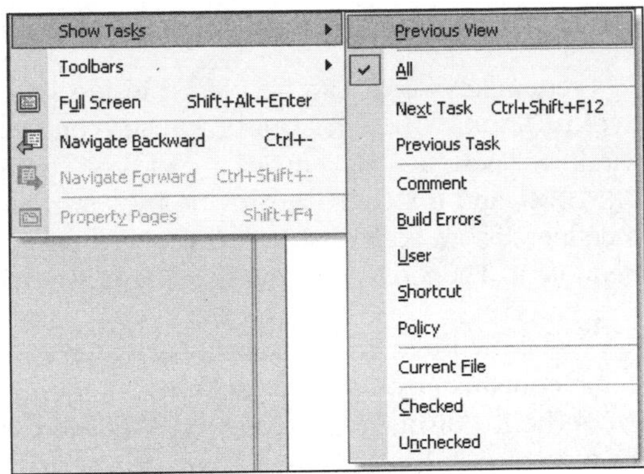


The tasks in the task list are categorized by type (Comment, Build Errors, User, Shortcut, and Policy). The menu items under the Show Tasks submenu allow all tasks to be viewed or a subset of the tasks to be viewed in the Task List window. For example, the All menu item is selected in the previous screenshot indicating all tasks should be visible in the Task List window. An example of the Task List window displaying all tasks is as follows:

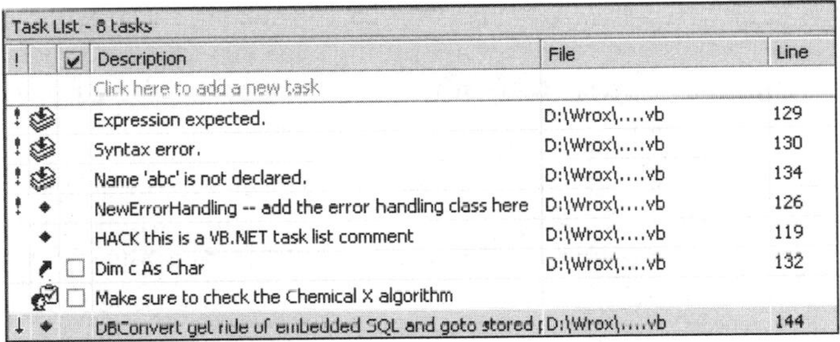


The entries in the previously demonstrated Task List window can be thought of as a hyperlink. Double-clicking on a task list entry causes the specific source file to be opened and moves the cursor to the line specified by the task list entry. Certain tasks are not associated with a file (user-defined task list entries) and therefore such tasks do not behave as a hyperlink.

An icon prefixes each task in the previous screenshot. This icon serves to specify the type of a task list entry. For example, the icon that looks like a down arrow plunking into a stack of papers indicates a build error. Is this because when developers visualize building an arrow striking a stack of papers comes to mind? Actually, this icon is used because on the Build toolbar the arrow hitting the stack of papers is associated with the task of building a project. The icon still makes little to no intuitive sense, but at least there is some consistency in the lack of intuition exhibited.

The menu items of the Show Tasks submenu dictate which tasks are displayed in the Task List window. These menu items are defined as follows:

- All – displays all tasks in the task list indiscriminately.
- Comment ◆ – certain keywords can be placed inside source code comments. These keywords (HACK, TODO, and UNDONE) cause entries to show up in the Task List window. These task list entries are of type comment. The token values HACK, TODO, and UNDONE are provide by Visual Studio .NET but it is possible to define custom comment task list tokens using the Tools menu Option's menu item. The icon prefixing these task list entries is a diamond.
- Build Errors – show build errors in task list. After a build has been performed that contains errors, the Show Tasks submenu is automatically set to Build Errors (hence displaying the errors associated with the build). The icon for this type of task list entry is a down arrow striking what appears to be a stack of papers.
- User – displays user-defined task list entries. Such task list entries are created manually using the Task List window. The icon prefixing this type of task list entry looks like a head that is about to be struck by a massive clipboard containing a check mark.
- Shortcut – displays only the task list shortcuts. These are created using the Edit menu's Bookmarks submenu and the Add Task List Shortcut menu item. The icon prefixing this type of task list entry is an arrow pointing up and to the right.
- Policy – Visual Studio .NET Enterprise Developer and Enterprise Architect editions support a language called the Template Definition Language (TDL). This language is used to architect enterprise-level applications. Errors in the policies specified by TDL show up in the Task List window when the Policy menu item is selected.
- Current File – displays only the task list entries associated with the currently displayed source file.
- Checked – displays only task list entries that have their checkbox checked.
- Unchecked – displays only task list entries whose checkbox is unchecked.

There is one more type of task list entry, for some reason this is not listed on the Show Tasks submenu:

- IntelliSence – these entries point to code that is causing IntelliSence validation errors

## Task List Comments and Custom Comments

Task list entries of type comment are managed using Tools | Option and the Environment, Task List folder as is displayed in the following screenshot:

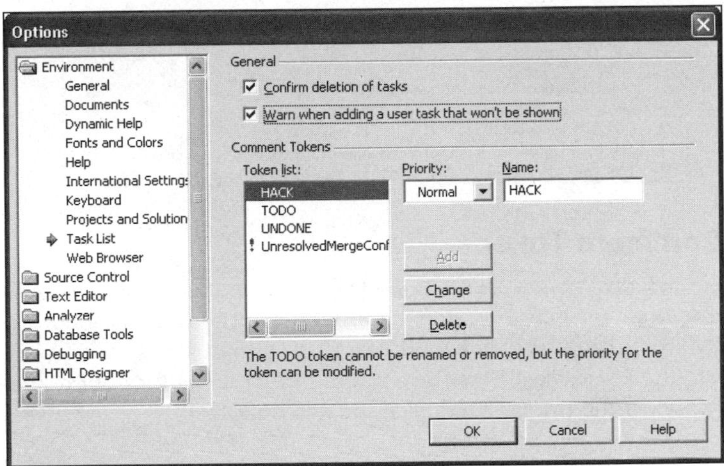


As can be seen in the screenshot, Visual Studio .NET provides predefined tokens (HACK, TODO, and UNDONE) which when placed in a comment will show up in the task list:

```
' HACK this is a VB.NET task list comment
// TODO this is a C# task list comment
/* UNDONE this is another C# task list comment */
```

What precisely HACK, TODO, and UNDONE mean is up to the user. A piece of code that works but is ugly and could be fixed could be marked as HACK, while the location where a feature needs to be added is marked in a comment as TODO. A piece of code started but not finished can be marked in a comment as UNDONE. The task list police will not arrest you if you do not rigorously adhere to these definitions, but if other people are working on the same code it makes sense to use them in an intuitive manner. The UnresolvedMergeConflict task list comment token is provided by SourceSafe and is placed in source code when a conflict takes place during a SourceSafe merge.

Each task list comment token is associated with a priority: Low, Normal (HACK, TODO, and UNDONE), and High (UnresolvedMergeConflict). The priority associated with a task list comment token dictates how the task list entry is displayed within the Task List window and each High priority entry in the task list is prefixed by an exclamation point. Following the high priority task list entries, the normal priority entries are listed without any prefix character. Following the normal priority task list entries are the low priority task list comment entries that are prefixed by an arrow pointing downwards.

An example of comment entries in the task list follows:

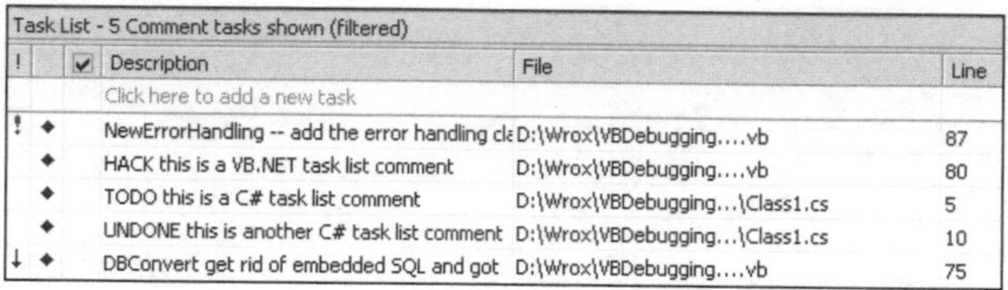


## Custom Comment Tokens

In the previous screenshot *two* user-defined task list comment tokens were included. The NewErrorHandling user-defined token is of high priority, while the DBConvert token is of low priority. To create user-defined tokens, display the Options dialog (Tools | Option), and navigate to the Environment | Task List folder. Type a name for your token in the Name: textbox, select the priority, and click the Add button.

Once the database conversion process is complete, the DBConvert user-defined token can be removed using the Delete button just as the NewErrorHandling token can be removed once the new error-handling infrastructure is in place.

## User-defined Task List Entries

The Task List window contains an entry Click here to add a new task. You may find this impossible to believe, but if you click on this entry you can add a user-defined task such as is shown in the following screenshot:

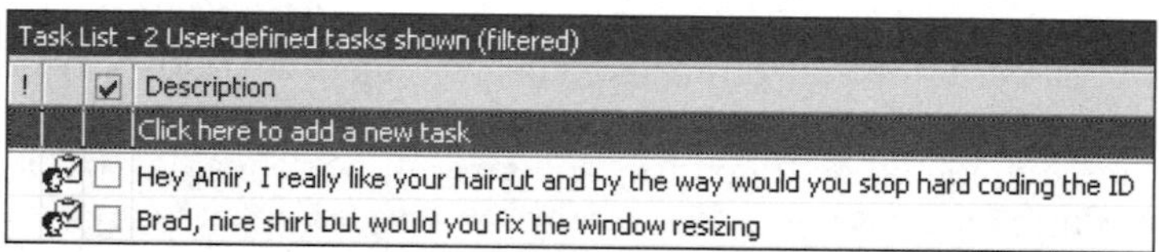


Notice how the user-defined tasks can be used as gentle hints not only to yourself, but also to other developers working on the project.

# *Viewing Extraneous Information*

In the next chapter, the windows that display information most directly applicable to debugging will be reviewed (Watch, Memory, BreakPoints, etc.). Such windows are associated with the Debug | Windows menu item. Still there are some other interesting windows within Visual Studio .NET that are applicable to applications being debugged. This category of windows are found under View | Other Windows. Selecting this menu option displays the following list of additional windows, some of which fall under the category of "useful to the art of debugging":

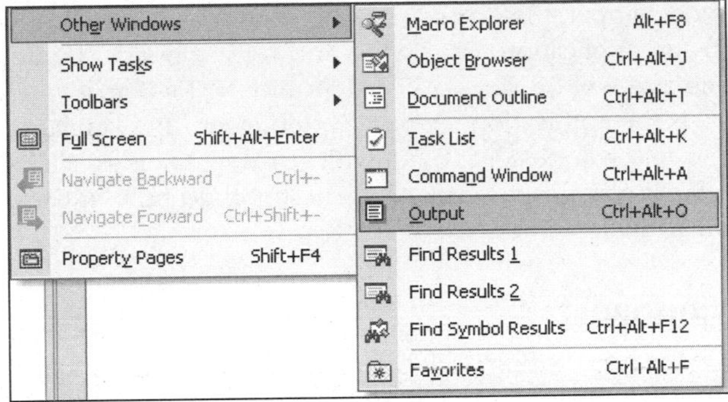


The previous screenshot contains a slew of windows (Object Browser, Find Results 1, Favorites, etc.) but these windows do not directly pertain to debugging. The windows that are directly germane to debugging include Output and Command Window.

## Debugger Output Window

When an application is being debugged it can attempt to log information to the debugger, Visual Studio .NET falls under the category of debugger. The Output window does have direct implications on debugging. Recall from our discussion on compilation constants (`#Const`) that the DEBUG and TRACE compilation constants were used by the `System.Diagnostic` namespace's `Trace` and `Debug` classes. Specifically the `Debug` and `Trace` classes wrote (logged) information that was useful while debugging. This information should not be construed as earth shattering. The information logged is a text string and it is up the application performing debugging to ensure useful information is logged.

By default, the `Debug` and the `Trace` classes write their output to the debugger. By "to the debugger", we mean that the application debugging an application receives the strings written by `Debug` and `Trace`. Visual Studio .NET displays the output generated by `Debug` and `Trace` classes' write methods in the Output window. Many third-party applications can pick up the strings output by the debugger. `DBMon.exe` is an example of such an application that Microsoft used to ship as part of MSDN, but as of .NET, this has been removed. There are plenty of copies of `DBMon` floating around the web or similar tools that allow debugger output to be viewed without an application as cumbersome (two gigabytes of disk space) as Visual Studio .NET.

One bit of confusion developers sometimes have is between the console windows (the window displayed by console applications) and Visual Studio .NET's Output window. To demonstrate, consider the following:

```
Console.WriteLine("To the application's console window")
Trace.WriteLine("By default - to Visual Studio .NET's Output Windows")
Debug.WriteLine("By default - to Visual Studio .NET's Output Windows")
```

In the previous code snippet, the `Console.WriteLine()` text is sent to the console window created by an application. For debug and release builds (by default) the `Trace.WriteLine` text will be sent to Visual Studio .NET's Output window provided Visual Studio .NET is the application serving as debugger. In a similar manner, `Debug.WriteLine` text will be sent (by default) to Visual Studio .NET's Output window for debug builds. We'll cover the use of `Trace` and `Debug` fully in Chapter 4 (*Logging and Programmatic Debugger Interaction*).

### Command Window

Visual Studio .NET's Command window allows interaction with the debugger via commands entered from a command prompt. To put this in perspective, we need to step back in time. Development used to take place at the command line with a separate build (make files) and debug steps. This was before GUI-based IDE's such as Turbo C and Visual C.

The command-line debugging tools (such as UNIX's `gdb` and `dbx`) provided a way to single step, run, watch variables, and set breakpoints all via the command line. Using View | Other Windows | Command it is possible to visit this bygone era by entering commands that cause the debugger to run to the cursor (rtc), single step (p) or stop debugging (q). Most developers will forego the Command window and stick to controlling Visual Studio .NET with mouse clicks, shortcuts, and hot keys. However, this feature could be useful if you are using a machine with an unfamiliar setup, as these commands remain constant.

# Configuring Projects

The menu items for a given menu differ depending on the current context of Visual Studio .NET. For example, if there is a project selected (highlighted) in the Class View or Solution Explorer windows then the Project menu contains a Set as start project menu item. Notice this menu item speaks in the singular and not in the plural. Since a project was selected in Class View or Solution Explorer the Set as start project means that the currently selected project will be the only one started (executed) when debugging is initiated. If the solution were selected in Class View or Solution Explorer then Set as start projects would be available as a menu item. This menu item allows one or more projects within a solution to be selected as the project or projects started when debugging is initiated. Set as start project versus Set as start projects is just one example of how the contents of the Project menu (or any menu for that matter) changes with context.

## *Project Properties*

The most important location of debugging settings for a project is the Property Pages dialog (Project | Properties). This dialog allows the per-project properties to be specified. There are alternative ways to display the dialog; the context menu displayed when right-clicking on a project in Class View or Solution Explorer also contains a Properties menu item.

## Compiler Options

When it comes to debugging and facilitating debugging, compiler options play a critical role. Within the Properties dialog, the Common Properties | Build settings can be configured. Among the per-project features that can be specified are the compiler options:

- Option Explicit – this option requires that all variables in the code be declared before being used.

  ```
  IAmUndeclared = 10 ' Legal with "Option Explicit OFF"
                     ' Illegal with "Option Explicit On"
  ```

  By default, this option is set to On.

- Option Strict – when this is Off (the default) VB.NET implicitly converts between data types. When this option is On, a compiler error is generated when an implicit type conversion may result in data loss. For instance, as a `Short` has more possible states than a `Boolean`, so converting between these types results in a so-called *narrowing* conversion and data may be lost.

  ```
  Dim IAmTypeful As Short = 1
  Dim IamBoolean As Boolean

  IamBoolean = IAmTypeful  ' Legal with "Option Strict OFF"
                           ' Illegal with "Option Strict OFF"
  ```

  With Option Strict On, you must explicitly declare that you want to perform a narrowing conversion, using one of the CType functions:

  ```
  IamBoolean = CShort(IAmTypeful) ' Right way for Option Strict ON
  ```

  A side effect of this is that all variables must also have their type declared. For those new to VB.NET, it is actually legal to declare a variable generically as an object rather than being explicit with respect a variable's type:

  ```
  Dim IAmTypeless ' Legal with "Option Explicit On"
                  ' Illegal with "Option Strict On"
  Dim IAmTypeful As Integer 'Right way with "Option Strict On"
  ```

The Option Explicit and Option Strict project properties correspond to statements that can be placed inside source files before any code is specified:

```
Option Explicit On
Option Strict On
```

These statements allow you to control this behavior on a file-by-file basis.

### Type Safety vs. Legacy Code

Clearly Option Explicit set to On (the default) is a wise debugging move so that variables must be declared before they are used. Option Strict should also be set to On (the non-default option) so that implicit type conversions do not result in data loss. The point of the previous example is to show that the default (Option Explicit On but Option Strict Off) is not sufficient for safe development. This is because later in the code `IAmTypeless` could be used as a `Short` then as a `Boolean` and then as a `SortedList`. Applications whose variables are type-ambiguous are subject to more errors and incur certain performance penalties as the runtime determines at the last minute exactly which variable is of which type.

So, if it is better to write code with these options on, why can they be turned off? This is mainly to support migrating legacy code to VB.NET. Consider a rush project where a legacy VBScript file is converted to a VB.NET source file. By setting `Option Explicit Off` and `Option Strict Off`, the file can be more quickly converted to VB.NET. Clearly, this will increase the chances that bugs will be manifested in the converted code. Again, such a choice should be made only when time is vastly more important than coding safety.

## Configuring a Project's Interaction with the Debugger

How a project interacts with a debugger is critical to debugging. For example, when developing a class library it is important to be able to select the executable that will load and run the class library (a DLL). Manipulating project and debugger interaction is the purview of Configuration Properties | Debugging folder:

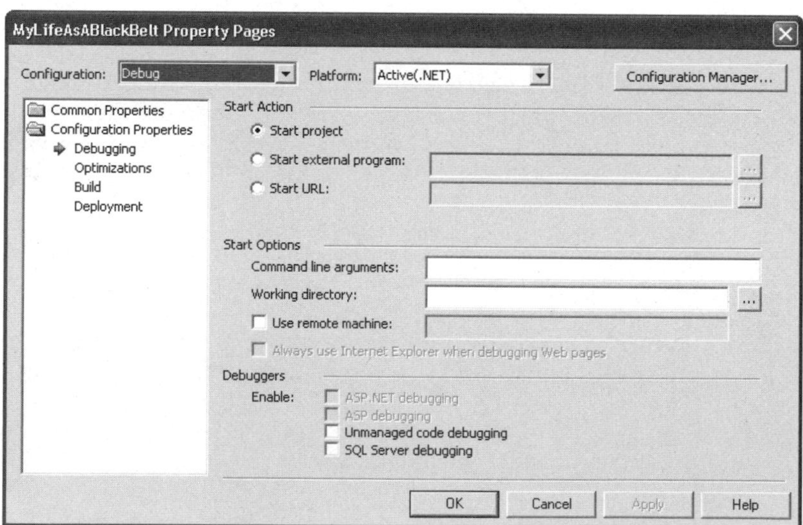

### Configuring a Project's Behavior when Debugging is Started

The Start Action region of the Configuration Properties | Debugging property page specifies how the project will start when being debugged. For example if the project is an executable (Windows Forms application, console application, etc.) or an application that behaves like an executable (ASP.NET application) the Start Action is set to Start Project. This means simply run the executable associated with the project when performing an action such as Debug | Start or Debug | Step Into.

There are times when a project (such as a Class Library or a Windows Forms Control) is run within an executable. Under this scenario, the DLL can be specified as the start project and the executable can be specified in the Start external program textbox. To the right of this textbox is a browse button (...) that allows you to browse for the executable. When debugging is initiated, the executable will run and the DLL will be loaded by the executable. This is particularly useful for debugging a DLL when no source code is available to debug the executable.

A URL can also be specified as the application used to begin debugging a project, hence the radio button labeled Start URL. This is handy when debugging a Windows Forms control that is hosted by internet explorer (an assembly of type DLL). A Windows Forms control can be displayed in a web page, so the Start URL for the control's project should be the URL of the page in which the control is used.

### Settings Options for a when a Project is Started within a Debugger

Thus far, the discussion has centered on the different ways in which a project can be started by the debugger. Still further information (compiler options) can be specified to coordinate the start of debugging. The property page that handles this is also Configuration Properties | Debugging. This property page for example allows command line parameters to be passed to the application being executed via the Command line arguments textbox.

Within the Command line arguments textbox it is possible to configure how a console application interacts with the:

- `stdin` – the location from which console applications receive input or where users can enter input (`System.Console.In` within the .NET Framework).
- `stdout` – the location where a console application displays general output (`System.Console.Out` within the .NET Framework).
- `stderr` – the location where a console application displays errors (`System.Console.Error` within the .NET Framework).

Clearly `stdin`, `stdout`, and `stderr` are not applicable to Windows Forms applications or ASP.NET pages because the aforementioned application types do not contain console windows. For applications that do utilize `stdin`, `stdout`, and `stderr`, entities can be placed in the Command line arguments textbox in order to control `stdin`, `stdout`, and `stderr`:

- <FileName – Reads the contents of FileName as `stdin` (`Console.In`).
- >FileName – Writes `stdout` (`Console.Out`) to file FileName.
- >>FileName – Appends text written to `stdout` to file FileName.
- 2>FileName – Writes `stderr` (`Console.Error`) to file FileName.
- 2>>Filename – Appends text written to `stderr` to file FileName.
- 2>&1 – Sends text written to `stderr` (value 2) output to same location as the text written to `stdout` (value 1).
- 1>&2 – Sends text written to `stdout` (value 1) output to same location as the text written to `stderr` (value 2).

The current Working Directory of the application can also be specified in the provided textbox. A browse button is provided so that you can browse for the working directory. Programmatically the current working directory is found using `System.IO.Directory's` `GetCurrentDirectory()` method or `System.Envionrment's` `CurrentDirectory` property. When a file is opened by an application, the current working directory specifies the location in which the file to be opened is searched for.

**Remote debugging**

When the Use remote machine checkbox is checked, the textbox to the right of this checkbox is enabled (no longer grayed out). The remote machine textbox is used to specify the remote machine on which an application runs. Examples of where this is useful include:

- Debugging a client-server application – it is possible to run a client-server application on a lone machine. More realistically, a client-server application should be run on two machines. It is possible to debug the client on one machine and to specify the remote machine as the server in order to debug the server on the client host.
- Debugging an application running on a headless workstation – rack mounted servers often do not have monitors and in fact such machines may be deployed in ultra-secure server rooms that are off limits to developers. For example, such a machine could reside at in a web-hosting company in another country. Under this scenario, the remote machine textbox is set to the name of the headless workstation.

*I worked for a company once that was going to move its machines from New Jersey to California. A paperwork snafu left them locked out of their own machines for a week (while stuck in New Jersey) because the hosting company refused to allow access until the identities of those entering the facility to move the machines could be validated. There was no way "dangerous" equipment such as laptops could be brought into the pristine and sterile, server-hosting room.*

On a lighter note, debugging both client and server in a single instance of Visual Studio means that a developer's cluttered desk needs only contain a single monitor while still affording the developer the ability to debug across multiple machines.

The topics remote debugging and using an external application to load the project being debugged are fairly advanced. Rather than providing a trivial (non-real world) example, demonstrating these features has been deferred. In Chapter 6, a remoting (client-server) example will be demonstrated. It will show how the API exposed by the server (a DLL) can be loaded by the client or the sever executable where this executable acts as the external application. Since the example is a client-server example it will be straightforward (and real-world practical) to show the client and server being debugged on one machine while the server itself is actually running on a remote machine.

#### Configuring which Debuggers are Supported

Visual Studio .NET can debug just about anything you can throw at it. When unmanaged code debugging is specified by checking the Unmanaged code debugging checkbox, it is possible to debug code that does not run inside the .NET runtime. Such applications are compiled natively to x86 form and are hence classified as unmanaged code. This includes C++ code developed with Visual Studio .NET or Visual C++ 6.0 or Visual Basic code developed with Visual Basic 6.0.

It is also possible to debug SQL code by checking the SQL Server debugging checkbox. This includes stepping through SQL Server stored procedure calls. This is an extremely impressive feature of Visual Studio .NET and will be presented in Chapter 5.

Notice also in the Configuration Properties | Debugging property pages that both ASP.NET and ASP applications can be debugged. Visual Studio .NET can debug both legacy web applications (ASP applications typically originally created with Visual InterDev) and contemporary web applications (ASP.NET applications typically developed with Visual Studio .NET). Under the oppressive, totalitarian, regime of Visual InterDev it was nearly impossible at times to get applications to run under the debugger. It is actually simpler to debug a legacy ASP application with Visual Studio .NET rather than the "impossible to configure" Visual InterDev.

Debugging the previous scenarios is handled via the ASP.NET debugging and ASP debugging checkboxes. These checkboxes are disabled (grayed out) in the previous Configuration Properties | Debugging property page because the application being debugged is of type Windows Form.

Clearly, the permissible debuggers are quite diverse. Again, each of the project types and corresponding debuggers will be presented in detail in the relevant chapters.

**If for some reason you cannot debug ASP.NET with Visual Studio .NET, it is possible to reinstall ASP.NET using the `aspnet_regiis.exe` utility. This utility is a real lifesaver because sometimes (in Version 1.0) ASP.NET cannot be debugged right out of the box. Thanks to Jennifer C. of PeopleSoft who pointed me to `apsnet_regiis.exe`.**

## Build Optimizations

Debugging includes the ever-pervasive bug known as "application runs too slowly". Some people might argue this isn't really a bug but it is a problem that needs fixing, at that level any difference from debbugging is just semantics. Handling build optimization is the project property page displayed when Configuration Properties | Optimizations is selected. This property page includes a checkboxes labeled:

- Remove integer overflow checks – by default this checkbox is not checked, which means that integer overflows result in an exception being thrown
- Enable optimization – turns compiler build optimizations on.
- Enable incremental build – build soution incrementally; compilation is faster but it may result in less optimized code

### Integer Overflow Checks

We'll demonstrate the difference Integer Overflow Checks make using a simple Windows Forms application, `WXIntegerOverflow`; for clarity we have omitted the Windows form designer code the full code for this application is available as part of the book's code download, see Appendix C.

```
' WXIntOverflow.vb

Public Class WXIntOverflow
  Inherits System.Windows.Forms.Form

  ' Windows Form Designer generated code Omitted

  Private Sub ButtonExit_Click(ByVal sender As System.Object, _
                               ByVal e As System.EventArgs)
                               Handles ButtonExit.Click
        Application.Exit()
End Sub
```

`WXIntegerOverflow` contains a method triggered when the Run button is clicked. The code for this method is as follows:

```
Private Sub ButtonRun_Click(ByVal sender As System.Object, _
                            ByVal e As System.EventArgs) _
                              Handles ButtonRun.Click
  Try
    Dim blowOut As Integer = Integer.MaxValue

    blowOut *= 2
    TextBoxResults.Text = _
    String.Format("Integer.MaxValue ({0:N0}) * 2 = {1}", _
                  Integer.MaxValue,
                  blowOut)
  Catch ex As Exception
     TextBoxResults.Text = ex.ToString()
  End Try
End Sub
```

Notice that in the highlighted code an integer is declared, `blowOut`, which is assigned to the maximum value associated with an integer. The value of `blowOut` is then multiplied by two. This arithmetic action results in an integer overflow. The exception this action (clicking the Run button) generates is caught (`Catch ex As Exception`) and displayed to a textbox as follows:

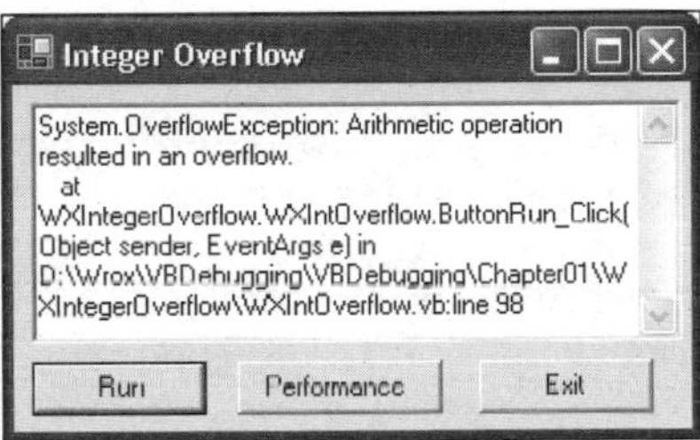


When the Remove integer overflow checks checkbox is checked, integer overflows do not generate an exception and therefore the textbox would simply display the following:

Integer.MaxValue (2,147,483,647) * 2 = -2

Clearly two billion multiplied by two is not -2 – unless of course you are an accountant for one of several large US. corporations.

Why would this checkbox ever be provided? The hint comes in the name of the specific property page: Configuration Properties | Optimizations. Clicking the Performance button in the `WXIntegerOverflow` application runs the following code:

```
Private Sub ButtonPerf_Click(ByVal sender As System.Object, _
                             ByVal e As System.EventArgs) _
                               Handles ButtonPerf.Click
  Dim i As Integer
```

```
        Dim upperBound As Integer = (Integer.MaxValue / 2) - 1
        Dim a As Integer = 0
        Dim start As DateTime = DateTime.Now

        For i = 0 To upperBound
            a = 2 * i
        Next
        TextBoxResults.Text = _
          String.Format("Execution time: {0:N0}", _
          DateTime.Now.Subtract(start).TotalMilliseconds())
    End Sub

End Class
```

In the previous code, one billion integer multiplications are performed. Running this code with integer checks enabled and disabled results in the following performance numbers being generated:

- Integer checks disabled: 2.814 seconds to execute one billion multiplies
- Integer checks enabled: 5.528 seconds to execute one billion multiplies

Remember that these performance numbers are for a specific machine (1.2 GHz Pentium III with 1 GB of RAM). Regardless of the machine's specific configuration, enabling error checking for integer overflows degrades performance (provided the bulk of the code performs integer arithmetic). Clearly if a large number of arithmetic operations are to be performed (billions of operations) and no overflow is guaranteed, then integer overflow checks should be disabled. How many VB.NET programs fall into this category? Very few, hence the default setting (overflow checks enabled) should usually be left in place. Remember, if the application has a user interface (GUI), then performance is probably even less important, as the application will likely spend millions or billions of cycles just waiting for user input.

The Debug | Windows submenu contains a Disassembly menu item. This menu item displays the x86 disassembly window associated with the code. By x86 we mean code compiled natively to run on the x86 instruction set rather then code disassembled to run as .NET intermediate language (IL). Why would we resort to using assembly code in order to determine performance? Recall what Obi-Wan says, "Use the source!" and in keeping with this theme consider the following VB.NET code (`a = 2 * 1`) and its corresponding dissembled code. The disassembled code includes the assembly associated with the integer arithmetic complete with overflow checks (the default setting):

```
                 a = 2 * i
00000060  mov         eax,ebx
00000062  imul        eax,eax,2
00000065  jno         0000006E
00000067  xor         ecx,ecx
00000069  call        75D710E7
0000006e  mov         dword ptr [ebp-0Ch],eax
```

Without breaking down the assembly in grotesque detail, there are six assembly language instructions in the code snippet above associated with the statement, `a = 2 * i` when checking for integer overflow is enabled. When integer overflow is disabled, the assembly code associated with `a = 2 * i` is as follows:

```
                a = 2 * i
00000060  mov          eax,ebx
00000062  add          eax,eax
00000064  mov          dword ptr [ebp-0Ch],eax
```

This time the code snippet only contains three assembly instructions; that is why not checking for overflow is faster than checking for overflow.

**Optimizations**

A checkbox that enables and disables the integer overflow check is not the only optimization afforded VB.NET applications. There is also a checkbox labeled, Enable Optimizations. For those new to compiled languages, the term optimization needs a bit of definition. When code is compiled a set of instructions are generated in the underling low-level language. This generated code often contains redundancies such as unneeded temporary variables, extra arithmetic operations, etc. Optimization removes the excess and leaves functionally equivalent code with fewer and more efficient assembly instructions and a smaller assembly that should run fatser.

So why would you ever need to disable optimizations? Disabling optimizations does mean that code compiles more quickly, but this is rarely a significant time saving on a modern desktop machine. The legacy reason for removing optimizations is that they can sometimes inject errors into the code. Hopefully, as compiler deign has come a long way in recent years, this should be a very rare problem for .NET code.

**Incremental Build**

It is also possible to decrease the time it takes to build an application while still leaving optimization enabled. This is achieved by checking the Enable Incremental build checkbox. This builds the code in sections, which requires less memeory and is faster, but as not all the code is inspected in one go some of the possible optimizations will be missed.

When it comes to optimization settings that is all there is. In previous languages using different compilers, optimizations could be fine-tuned. This allowed performance bottles necks to be overcome, not through perfect coding but by specifying the correct compiler settings. At the same time, it was possible for developers to use such convoluted optimization settings that their code broke on different platforms. In .NET the compiler optimization settings are not precise enough to be radically useful but they are simple enough so that developers cannot sabotage their own code.

## Build Configuration

How a build is configured (whether it contains debug information, whether warnings are treated as errors, etc.) is managed using the Configuration Properties | Build property page. Aspects of this property page have already been discussed, namely the DEBUG and TRACE compilation constants. Still, the following screenshot demonstrates there is a bit more to build configuration:

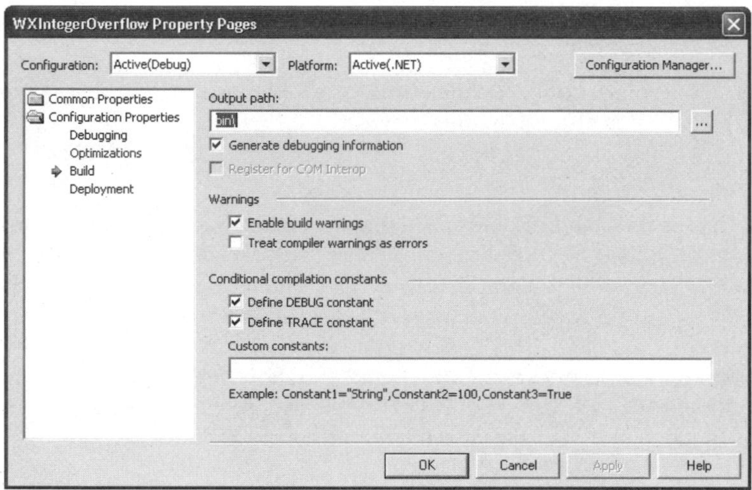


By default, compilier warnings are displayed in the Output window and are not generated as build error entries in the Task List window. It is possible to disable build warnings but it makes little sense to do this from a debugging point of view – Warnings at compile time can easily translate into exceptions at run time.

Warnings can be ratcheted up a notch by checking the checkbox labeled Treat compiler warnings as errors. Most typically, this is enabled for release builds. Recall from previous discussions, that the settings for release versus debug builds can be configured separately using the drop-down list in the upper left corner of the dialog.

It is possible to create debugging information for a release build by selecting the Generate debugging information checkbox on the Project | Properties | Configuration Properties Build page for the Release configuration. It is also possible via this property page to build a Release build with debug information.

Debugging release builds was quite in vogue using Visual C++ 6.0 as a development tool. This is because C++ could generate exceptions that crashed a program and enabling the debugging of release builds allowed better reverse engineering of errors. Under .NET (VB.NET, C#, managed C++, etc.) the specific location where an error took place is known and the state of the call stack is known. Given that this information is available under both debug and release builds of managed applications there is less impetus to enable debugging for release builds.

# Help Menu

Having taught debugging for many years, it is stunning to see reputed Staff Engineers and Architects stumble through using the help. Visual Studio .NET probably has one of the most extensive help facilities available for any application. It might not be perfect but learning to use it effectivly can save you a huge amount of time.

Within Visual Studio .NET, help can be displayed inside Visual Studio or externally (as specified by the profile information on the Start Page). You can also view help for Visual Studio .NET (and a lot of other Microsoft products) at http://msdn.microsoft.com/.

What follows is an example of help (MSDN for Visual Studio .NET) displayed outside the confines of Visual Studio .NET:

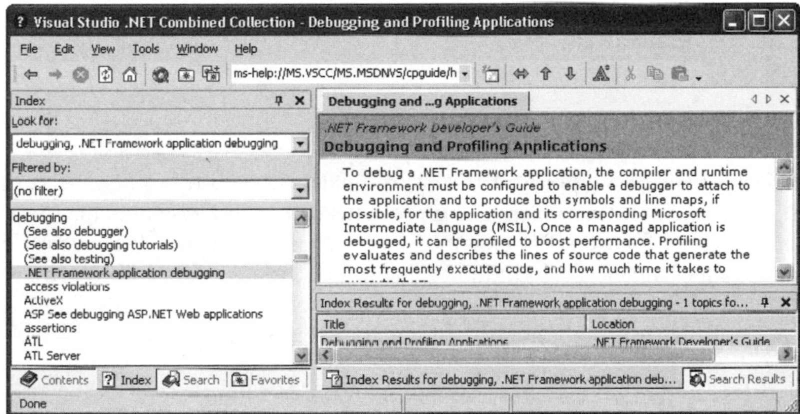


In this screenshot, the left panel contains four separate tabs:

- Contents – think of this like the table of contents for a book (a really big book). After working with MSDN for a while you will feel comfortable attacking help from the table of contents perspective.
- Index – think of this tab like the index in the back of a book where the entries in the index (ordered alphabetically) correspond to entries in the table of contents. The index is the best starting point for retrieving the help you need with .NET.
- Favorites – displays your Internet Explorer web favorites. Entries in MSDN are reference by URL even if they are available on your local machine, so refences to useful articles can be stored this way.

- Search – too many developers needing help head straight for Search. If a term such as socket is entered under Look for and a search initiated then the contents of every help article will be searched for the term, socket. This will result maximum number of search items (500 results) being returned. Use search when a reasonable number of key terms are used that will result in a manageable search. Also used Search in conjunction with Filter (described below).

In the event that a search returns an unmanageable number of entries, there is a quick way to wrangle the entries into a controllable form. The Search results window contains three columns: Title, Location, and Rank. The Rank column allegedly is how accurate a match the search result is – more useful than Rank is the Location column. Click on the Location column and the results are sorted by location. For example if Array was searched on, the Location could be used to see only Titles related to VB.NET arrays or .NET arrays in general. Locations such as Foxpro, VBA, J# or C++ could be ignored en masse since they are all clustered.

## Filter

New to MSDN for Visual Studio .NET (OK it originally showed up in SQL Server help) is the Filter by drop-down list, which in the previous screenshot contains (no filter). This lets a search be more focused. For example, if knowledge of VB.NET arrays is needed do not simply select the Index tab and put Array under Look for. This will return array information concerning J#, FoxPro, VB Script, C++, etc. Using Filter by the quest for information on arrays can be honed to only include VB.NET.

The toolbars below the menu hold some key features of Visual Studio .NET. The URL for the particular help article is displayed in the toolbar:

ms-help://MS.VSCC/MS.MSDNVS/cpguide/

This is extremely handy when someone asks you to look up a particular article (here is the URL, so go read it yourself) and of course the said URL can be stored under favorites using the icon, which adds the presently accessed article's URL to the favorites folder.

## Sychronsing Help View

Besides the Add to Favorites icon, the icon is extremely useful. Consider a case where the `Socket` class (namespace, `System.Net.Sockets`) was looked up using the index tab. Clicking the icon with the left and right point arrows synchronizes the article presently being read with the table of contents. This means that the cousins of the `Socket` class will be visible (and when coding with the `Socket` class you will likely end up coding with the cousins of this class: `TcpClient`, `TcpListener`, and `UdbClient`):

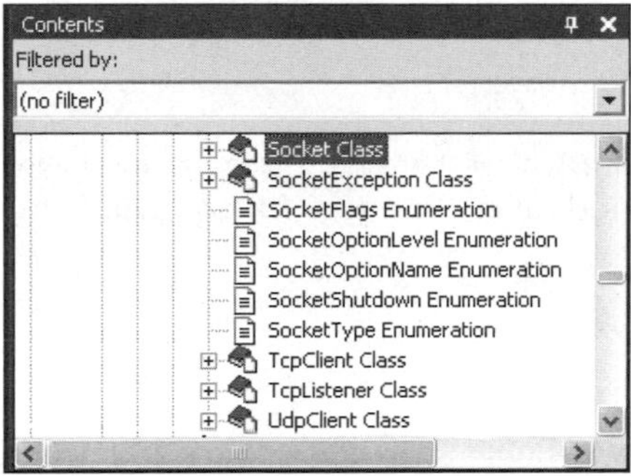


## References and Imports

Since people first discovered fire, they have often asked, "Is this data type supported by my operating system? How do I know if my project requires a reference be set up? How do I determine what namespace a data type belongs to?" Every developer should know how to quickly answer these questions using help, because it is a huge time saver. This tasty bit of information is found by typing in the name of the data type (such as Thread class) within the Look for textbox of the Index tab. This will reveal an about section for the data type, such as about Thread class. At the very bottom of the about section is some of this critical information:

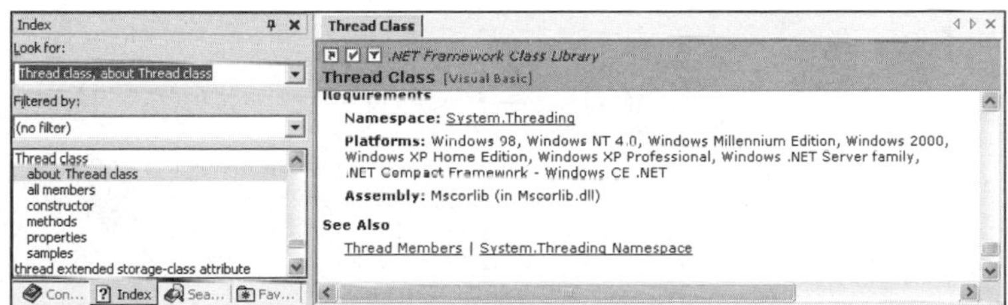


From this screenshot it should be clear that, the `Thread` class works on all .NET Platforms, it is found in `System.Threading` Namesapce and resides in `Mscorlib.dll` Assembly. Every .NET project intrinsically references the `Mscorlib.dll` assembly; therefore there is no need to set up a reference to this assembly.

### Useful Sections

A wise and venerable developer has a perused the table of contents and knows what treasures lie beneath. For example, if you need a bit of Sample code, look to:

```
Visual Studio .NET
  .NET Framework
    Samples
```

If you want to peruse free development periodicals and texts, look at:

```
MSDN Library
  Development (General)
```

Under this section, there are Technical Articles, Columns, and Periodicals. Included here is MSDN Magazine. This periodical is a key tool for any Windows/.NET developer.

# Summary

Many developers just view debugging as breakpoints and watching variables. Clearly, there is a lot more to debugging, much of it preemptive. Given the diversity of what is offered, it is better for a developer to have a good, well-rounded knowledge of the tool rather than just jumping into the basics (breakpoints and viewing the contents of variables). Understanding the full power of Visaul Studio .NET, in itself, should help your code more effciently and therefore reduce bugs. At the very least, knowing how to properly configure you develpoment enviroment should speed up your bug hunting. The next chapter discusses using Visual Studio .NET to actively debug (setting breakpoints, watching variables, managing threads, displaying call stacks, etc.).

VB.NET

# Debugging

Handbook

2

2

# Debugging with Visual Studio

The previous chapter covered nearly every debugging feature of Visual Studio .NET except the functionality associated with running applications under the debugger, viewing program state (variable values, memory, the assemblies loaded, etc.), breakpoints, exceptions, threading management, and process management. As it turns out, the Debug menu provides this functionality.

Using the Debug menu, you can get the Visual Studio .NET debugger to navigate through an executing program, execute a single instruction at a time, breaking at specific locations given a specific criterion, halt execution, and detach the debugger from an application. Various aspects of a program can be examined using the Debug menu including the position within the code of breakpoints, memory locations, variables from a variety of different perspectives (per-instance, per-function and user-specified variables), the modules used by a program (including assemblies and unmanaged modules), and the state of the call stack. Each of these areas can be quite intricate, for example break points can be associated with functions, can be associated with a specific line in a source file, can be launched after data has been modified and/or can be launched after code has been executed some number of times.

## Starting the Debugger

The epicenter of debugging and managing the debug process is Visual Studio .NET's Debug menu. The aforementioned menu has two distinct modes of operations:

- The Debug menu displayed when not debugging an application
- The Debug menu displayed while debugging one or more applications

While not debugging, the Debug menu displays those menu items for initiating the debugging of projects. When an application or applications are being debugged, the Debug menu displays menu items used for debugging of the present application or debugging additional applications (multiple processes).

When no solution is loaded, Visual Studio .NET does not display a Debug menu. However, the Tools menu does contain the Debug Processes menu item this menu item; was introduced in Chapter 1 with respect to debugging processes that were currently running (either locally or remotely) using Visual Studio .NET.

## The Debug Menu

Visual Studio .NET's Debug menu appears as follows when a solution is loaded but it is not currently debugging anything:

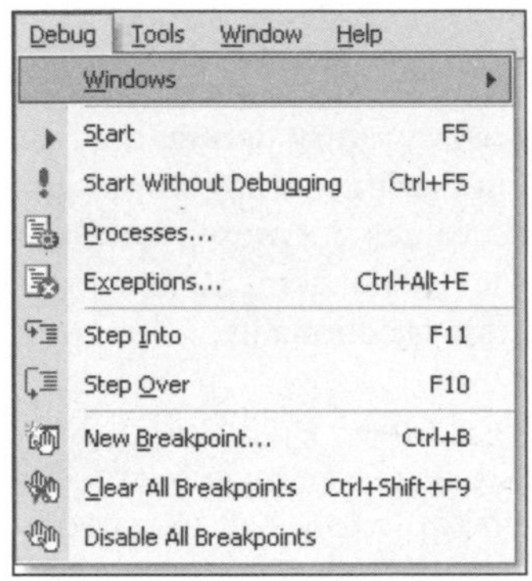


The Debug menu provides a set of options that control the execution of a program. These options include:

- Start – this starts execution with Visual Studio .NET acting as a debugger. Once the code breaks execution (say by encountering a breakpoint) then you can view the values of variables and so on. Once debugging has started, the menu items for the Debug menu change and the more appropriate Continue (continue execution after stopping) replaces Start.
- Step Into – like Start this starts a program executing with VS.NET acting as the debugger but in this case, execution proceeds a single statement then stops. Using this command repeatedly, you can single-step through the execution of a piece of code. If the source code is available (VB.NET, C #, etc.) then a single, line of the source language is stepped. If only disassembled code is available, then a single machine instruction (line of assembly code) is stepped at a time. If a method or property is initially encountered, Step Into will move the execution pointer to the first line within it but will not execute any statements.

- Step Over – This option behaves identically to Step Into save for when a method or a property is encountered. In this case, the method/property executes to completion, and execution halts at the line following the method or property.

The context menu displayed for solutions within Solution Explorer provides an alternative way to start debugging a project. This Debug menu item displays a submenu that contains:

- Start
- Step Into

## Step Into vs. Step Over

Why Step Into and Step Over? The answer is precision. You perform these actions when you need to check one line at a time precisely, to be sure what is going on in a region of code. Step and examine the state of variables. Step again and see if the resultant changes are what you expected. For regions of code that you don't need to examine in such detail, use Start to run over them; obviously execution won't stop until it hits a breakpoint though. Of course, it is nice to have a breakpoint set at the next crucial area where single-stepped debugging should resume.

The Step Into option would not work for a case where the method or property contained native code and the project (a managed application) is only configured to debug managed code (the Project | Properties | Configuration Properties | Debugging dialog's Unmanaged code debugging option is not checked). By default, this option is off – for performance reasons. Under this circumstance Step Into behaves as Step Over because the user of the debugger has decided to prevent stepping into the type of code in question. To look at the difference between Step Over and Step Into, using the following snippet of code from the WXGetOwnModules solution:

```
14    Shared Sub Main()
15
16        Try
17            Display()
18            Console.WriteLine("Done displaying")
19        Catch ex As Exception
20            Console.Error.WriteLine(ex)
21        End Try
22
23    End Sub
```

Notice in the previous piece code that line seventeen is marked by an arrow and the `Display()` method is highlighted – on screen these would both be yellow. This marking indicates the location of the execution cursor; `Display()` has not yet been executed but it is next up to bat. Selecting Step Over would move the execution cursor to line eighteen in the program stepping over the `Display()` method; remember the `Display()` method still gets executed and any results are returned. Selecting Step Into would move the execution cursor into the `Display()` method. Step Into works because the source code for the `Display()` method is available; not surprising in this case since it is part of the same class.

### Initiating Per-Project Debugging

The context menu displayed by right-clicking on a project within Solution Explorer contains a key debugging menu item, Set Startup Project. Invoking this menu item causes the project to be displayed as boldface thus indicating that when debugging is initiated this is the sole project started. If the solution at a later time is configured (as was discussed previously) to debug multiple projects then the lone start up project ceases to be displayed in bold since it is no longer the one-and-only startup project. The Set Startup Project menu item is also available if a project is right-clicked (displaying a context menu) within the Class View window.

This context menu also contains a Debug menu item. This Debug menu item displays a submenu that contains:

- Start new instance – begin debugging the selected project
- Step Into new instance – begin debugging the project specified by single-stepping into the selected project

Actually, the previous options (including the Debug menu item) are available by right-clicking within the Class View window. This right click displays a context menu that allows debugging to be initiated from the Class View window in the form of Start new instance or Step Into new instance.

### Start without Debugging

The one menu item of the Debug menu that doesn't actually control the debugger is Start Without Debugging. This launches the application to be debugged but the application runs without a debugger attached (outside of Visual Studio .NET). What is the purpose behind Start without Debugging? Imagine a client-server application where only the client needs debugging. Launch the server with Start Without Debugging then use Debug | Start to launch the client once the server is ready to accept client connections.

## Configuring Debugger Startup

The context menu displayed by right-clicking on the solution within Solution Explorer contains a key debugging menu item, Set Startup Projects. Selecting this menu item displays the following dialog:

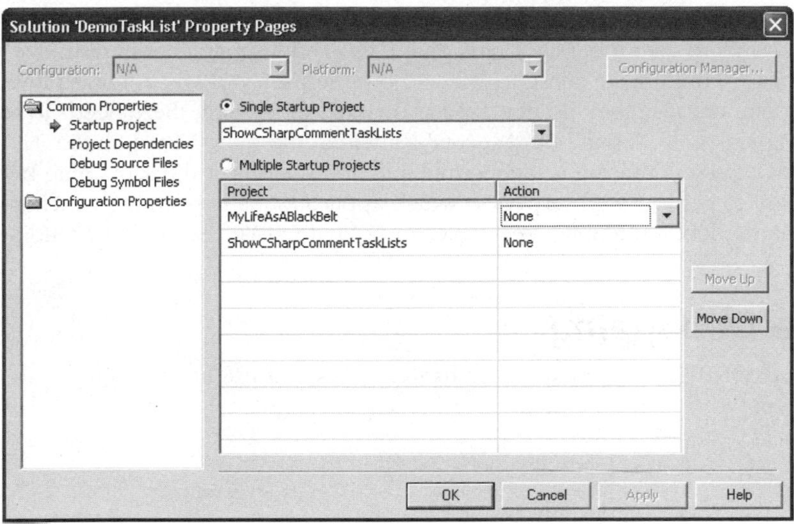


The menu item that displays this dialog is a plural not a singular, Set Startup Projects. In the screenshot above, there are two radio buttons (you can only select one at a time):

- Single Startup Project – specify the lone startup project that executes on the initiation of debugging. The drop-down list below the Single Startup Project radio button provides a list of available projects.
- Multiple Startup Projects – specify one or more projects that that execute on the initiation of debugging.

Next to each project listed underneath the Multiple Start Projects radio button is an Action column. The available actions are:

- None – do not launch the project
- Start – launch the project (with a debugger attached)
- Start without Debugging – launch the project (with no debugger attached)

It might seem a good idea to start the various parts of a client-server application at the same time using Multiple Startup Projects, but this may cause problems. If the client relies on the server already being running then there might not be time for the server to set up before the client makes a call to the server. It may be better to launch each part separately as shown in the previous section.

So when would the Multiple Startup Projects option be useful? Consider a solution where there is a standard user tool (say for reading data) and a separate administrative application. It would make sense to launch both the user tool and administrative tool at the same time because they do not depend on each other. Still, there needs to be a compelling reason to debug both executables within the same Visual Studio .NET instance. It can be confusing to debug multiple applications at the same time because it is quite easy to get lost with respect to which application is performing which task. It is often easier to debug multiple executables in separate instances of Visual Studio .NET.

## Active Debugging

Visual Studio .NET's Debug menu contains the core set of useful debugging menu items when:

- A solution is loaded
- A project is currently being debugged
- Execution for each project within the solution is currently halted.

The Debug menu displayed under the previous conditions is as follows:

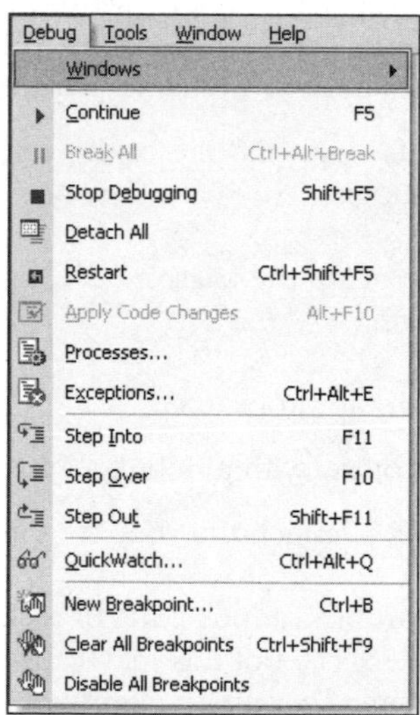


Within the flavor of the Debug menu displayed while debugging is active, the following options are available with respect to the overall execution of the application:

- Continue – the Continue menu item is displayed when at least one thread of execution is stopped (due to either a breakpoint or that we are single-stepping the application). Selecting Continue resumes execution of the application by restarting all stopped threads. Of course, they start from the location where they stopped execution.
- Stop Debugging – ceases debugging the application (execution ceases).
- Detach All – the Detach All feature is new to Visual Studio as of Visual Studio .NET. This menu item allows the debugger to detach itself from a process.
- Restart – begins execution of the application from the entry point of the application (the location at which the application starts). If the application was presently being debugged (presently executing) the application is restarted.

The Detach All is a great enhancement. Imagine a Windows service begins to behave oddly so we debug the process (Tools | Debug Processes). If after some investigation, the process actually appears to be running OK the debugger can be detached. Once the debugger is detached, the Windows service can merrily execute without the encumbrance of the debugger. Before Visual Studio .NET this option was not available so the choices were to leave the process running in the debugger or stop the process and restart it without the debugger running.

> *This is another reason to use Visual Studio .NET to debug Visual C++ 6.0 applications. If you have a server that runs as a service you can attach and detach the debugger – even though the service was built with an earlier version of Visual Studio, that didn't offer this functionality.*

## Step Out

The Step Out menu item is great for situations where you step into a method/property but then decide that you would prefer to fully execute the method/property and resume single stepping at the line of code following where the method/property was invoked. This case arises when you end up selecting Step Into by mistake (a rather common occurrence experience by overworked and tired developers) or if you only need to single step through a portion of a method/property.

Going back to the `Display()` method of the WXGetOwnModules solution:

```
5   Shared Sub Display()
6       Dim self As Process = Process.GetCurrentProcess()
7       Dim procMod As ProcessModule
8
9       For Each procMod In self.Modules
10          Console.WriteLine(procMod.FileName)
11      Next
12  End Sub
13
14  Shared Sub Main()
15
16      Try
17          Display()
18          Console.WriteLine("Done displaying")
```

The execution cursor is at line ten within the `Display()` method. The `Display()` method was called from line seventeen of the file. Selecting **Step Out** causes the `Display()` method to be executed to completion and then advances the execution cursor to line eighteen.

## Editing Code while Debugging

The **Debug** menu shown previously contained a disabled menu item, **Apply Code Changes**. This feature harkens back to a feature of VB 6.0 and Visual C++ 6.0, namely **Edit and Continue**, which allowed developers to modify code while debugging continued uninterrupted, the application being rebuilt in the background as and when required. For unmanaged C++ code, this feature is the same as before. However, for managed code it is not available, you must halt debugging, and rebuild the before the changes are made to the executing process. There are rumors that a proper **Edit and Continue** feature may be available for managed code in future versions of Visual Studio .NET but for now this must count as one of the few downgrades when moving to VB.NET from VB6.

By default (unlike C #), you cannot even modify code while debugging in VB .NET. To enable this feature check the **Allow me to edit VB files while debugging** checkbox found under **Tools | Options | Debugging |Edit and Continue.**

The .NET version of edit and continue definitely is not as useful as the old version but it can come in handy. If you spot something that needs changing in a section of code not on the current execution path, you can make the changes then just click **Continue** and carry on debugging rater than having to note down the changes needed and come back later.

If you modify some .NET code (either VB.NET or C#), upon attempt to resume execution of the modified code the **Unable to Apply Code Changes** dialog pops up:

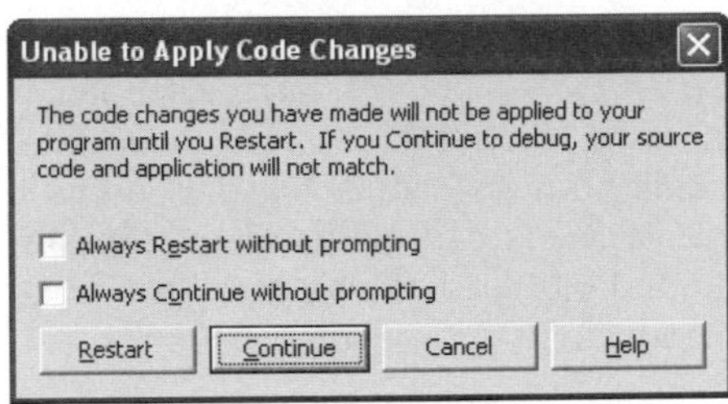


The Unable to Apply Code Changes dialog can be broken down as follows:

- Restart – stops execution of your application, builds a fresh version of the application complete with the code changes, and restarts the application under the debugger.
- Continue – continues or steps, depending on the last command chosen.
- Cancel – cancels the Continue or Single Step command specified. It was the Continue or Single Step command that caused the Unable to Apply Code Changes dialog to be displayed. What Cancel does not do is reverse the modifications made to the code. In order to back out of the change, Edit | Undo is the way to go.
- Always Restart without prompting – checking this causes the debugger to automatically restart when the cursor attempts to enter a section of modified code during debugging. If this checkbox is checked, it behooves developers not to inadvertently modify their code by erroneously hitting a key while debugging.

  *By default VB .NET developers cannot erroneously modify their source code so they are immune to the syndrome of "Profanity! Profanity! Profanity! It just restarted debugging from the beginning because I bumped my keyword!" Still, the* Allow me to edit VB files while debugging *option checkbox in conjunction with* Always Restart without prompting *is a dangerous combination.*

- Always Continue without prompting – checking this causes the debugger to continue execution without applying the changes to the executing code. it does keep the changes to the source code though. Be cautious when using this feature; it can get very confusing when the source code shown is different from the executing code.

# Breakpoints

Those of us who survived the break dance craze of the early 1980's are leery of any terminology containing the term "break". However, **Breakpoints** are invaluable as they allow execution to be halted at a particular line of code, which is essential if you need to carefully examine the state of an application at a particular point in its execution.

The Debug | Windows submenu contains a slew of menu items that can determine what is taking place within an application (values of variables, states of threads, call stack of current thread, etc.): Watch, Autos, Locals, Me, Call Stack, Immediate, Threads, Register, Modules, and Memory. The bulk of these features are only useful if the application is presently not halted on at least one thread. When an application is not being debugged the only menu items found under Debug | Windows are Breakpoints (manage breakpoints) and Immediate (pass commands directly to debugger).

## Setting Breakpoints

A breakpoint can be set using the context in several different ways:

- Right-clicking in the source code window to display the context menu, then selecting Insert Breakpoint.
- The *F9* key toggles breakpoints on or off at the present cursor location.
- Left-clicking the mouse in the ... bar at the left-hand side of the source code.
- Selecting New Breakpoint from the Debug menu is different from the previous options, as you have to specify the location of the break point. You also get the opportunity to configure many more parameter associated with the breakpoint; see the next section *Configuring Breakpoints* for further details.

A breakpoint (once created) appears as a dark red dot to the left of the line code it is associated with, and the line of code is highlighted in dark red:

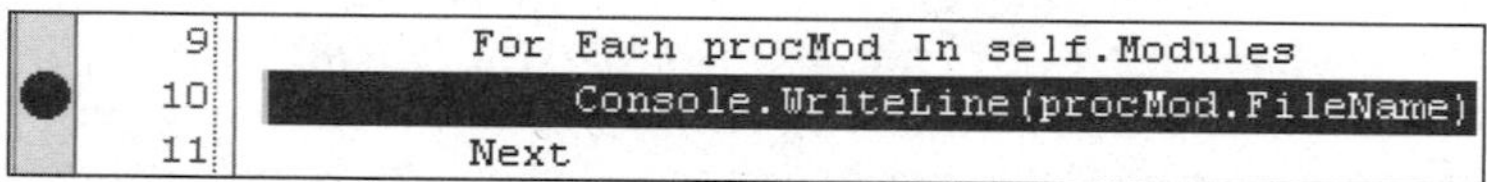

When the execution cursor reaches the location of a breakpoint, execution "breaks" (halts) and the bulk of the Debug | Windows menu items are now available. By breaking or halting, we do not mean that the program terminates; execution is just suspended and can be resumed. The line of code at which execution broke is highlighted in yellow and a yellow arrow is placed over the red dot corresponding to the breakpoint:

```
For Each procMod In self.Modules
    Console.WriteLine(procMod.FileName)
Next
```

## Configuring Breakpoints

When you select the Debug | New Breakpoint menu item or the Breakpoint Properties option available from the context menu displayed when you right-click over a line of code that has a breakpoint set a dialog is displayed.

The New Breakpoint dialog is as follows and the Configure Breakpoint dialog displays very similar options:

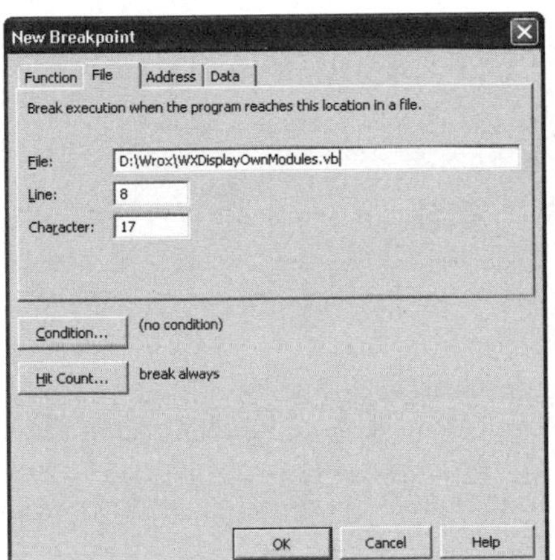


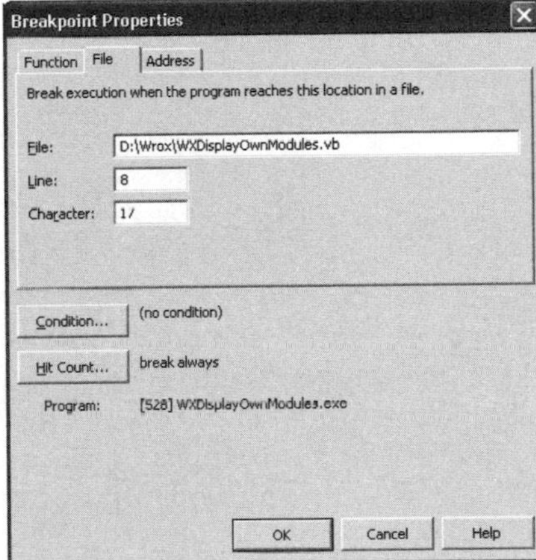


By default, break points are set to brake always at a particular line of a particular file. The tabs of the New Breakpoint dialog reveal that there are more styles of break point than this:

- Function – specifies a breakpoint associated with a particular property or method. When the specified property/method is reached (or a function in C/C++), program execution will be halted.
- File – specifies a breakpoint associated with a particular file, line number, and possibly even character offset within a line. When execution reaches the specified point, the application breaks. This is the style of breakpoint created when using *F9* to toggle a breakpoint on.
- Address – specifies a breakpoint associated with a particular instruction memory location. VB.NET developers do not tend to think of their applications containing code that is located at a specific memory location. Once compiled though, a VB.NET application is just assembly instructions residing at memory locations.
- Data – specifies a breakpoint associated with a particular variable. The breakpoint triggers whenever the variable is modified anywhere in the application.

In the previous New Breakpoint screenshot the File tab is selected and the breakpoint exists in a particular file (`D:\Wrox\WXDisplayOwnModules.vb`), at a given line number (8) and at a specific character offset within the line (17). The breakpoint is triggered unconditionally (there is no condition specified that will cause the breakpoint to trigger) and each time it is hit (since the hit count specified break always).

The character offset adds a bit of intrigue to the idea of a VB.NET breakpoint. As a language, VB.NET typically contains one statement per-line so the character offset appears to be meaningless. Actually, this is not the case as a colon can be used to specify multiple statements on a line, hence the character offset of seventeen corresponds to the assignment `b=1` in the following code snippet:

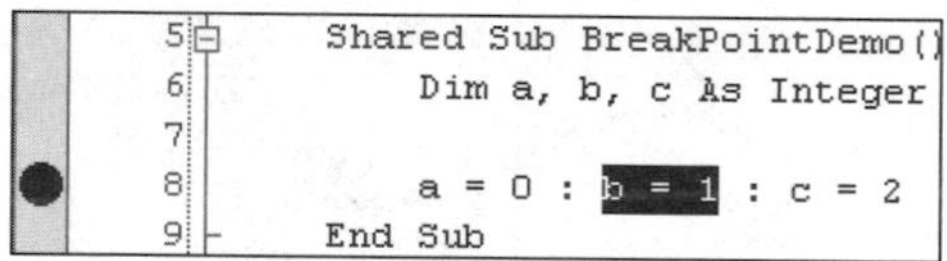


## Breaking at a Specific Function

Consider a case where you are debugging an application and a specific method/property is not behaving correctly. Yes, it is possible to scroll through the source code and set a breakpoint in the method/property. It is vastly simpler to just type in the name of the method or property and create a breakpoint associated with that method or property.

This per-function breakpoint is settable when the Function tab of the New Breakpoint dialog is displayed. An example of this flavor of New Breakpoint dialog is as follows:

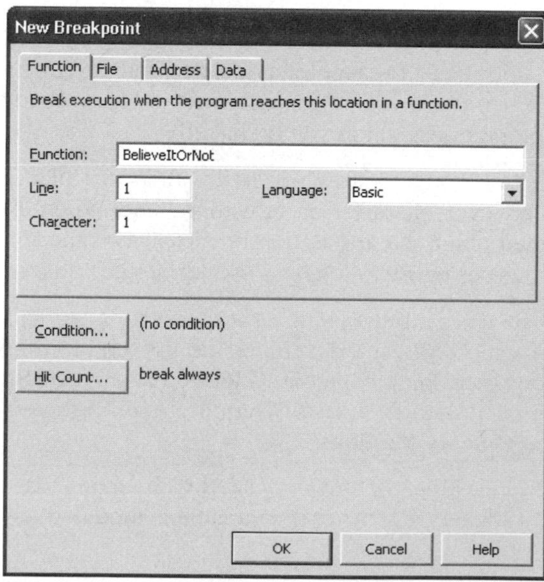

The Function tab of the New Breakpoint dialog contains a language drop-down list. By default, this is set to Basic for VB.NET projects. The ability to change this is available if for some reason the language displayed does not match the function's language.

Within the previous screenshot, this information determines the location of the breakpoint:

- Function – specifies the name of the method at which to break. If there are multiple overloads of a method name, you can select the right one based on the method signature (the parameters associated with that version of the method). For instance, if the `BelieveItOrNot()` method has two overloads

  ```
  Sub BelieveItOrNot(ByVal income As Decimal)
  Sub BelieveItOrNot(ByVal justWonTheLottery As Boolean, _
                     ByVal amNotDreaming As Boolean)
  ```

  When OK is clicked, a Choose Breakpoints child dialog is displayed that allows a specific version of `BelieveItOrNot()` to be selected:

  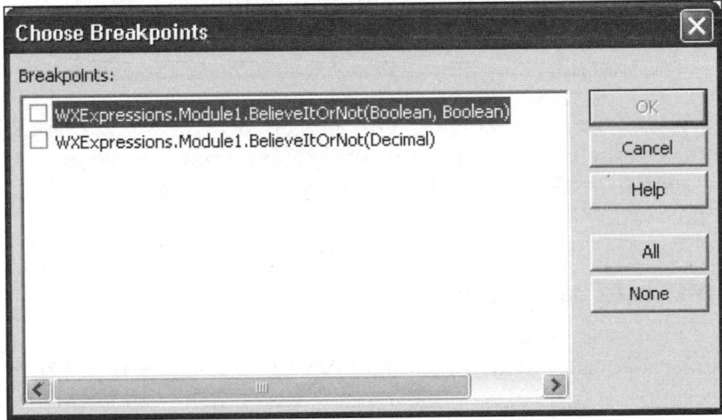
  

  It is possible to select both versions of the `BelieveItOrNot()` method in the Choose Breakpoints dialog thereby setting multiple per-function breakpoints simultaneously.

- Line – by default this is 1 (break at the first line of the function) and this value should usually be changed. After all, if you want to set a break point on a specific line just use a normal file breakpoint.

- Character – this is set by default to 1 (break at the first character in the line specified for the given function) and this value should not be changed.

Function breaks are indicated by a red dot in the source code window, but unlike file break points, there is no highlighting of the actual source code.

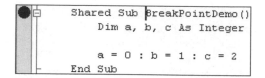

```
Shared Sub BreakPointDemo()
    Dim a, b, c As Integer

    a = 0 : b = 1 : c = 2
End Sub
```

MSDN explains (inaccurately) that you can specify the values for Line and Character under the Function tab giving an alterative value for line number or character position. For the most part MSDN is a fantastic resource but in this one case, it is incorrect. The values for Line and Character must both be 1. The New Breakpoint dialog will accept different values for Line and Character but running the application results in the following message box:

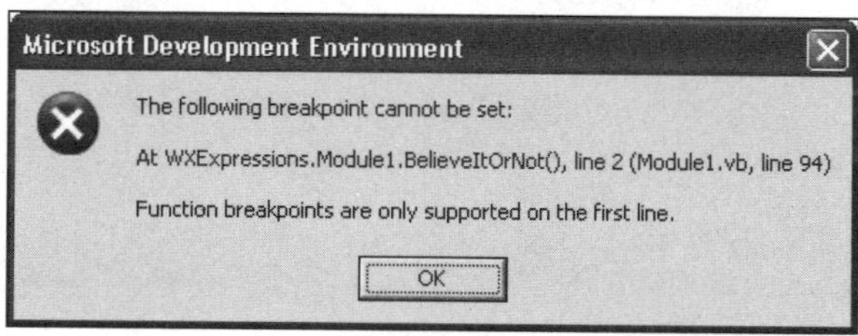


The program will execute even though it contains an incorrect breakpoint but execution will halt at the entry point to the application. For example in a console application, execution would halt inside the `Main()` method if the application contains an invalid breakpoint.

### Breaking on Data Modification

The most innovative style of breakpoint is break on data modification. Such a breakpoint can be associated with a data item (variable) and when that data item changes, the breakpoint halts execution precisely where the modification took place. As grandma used to say, "Prepare to be disappointed". The Data tab of the New Breakpoint dialog contains a drop-down list labeled Language that includes Basic (VB.NET). This seems to indicate that you can set breakpoints associated with a particular data value in VB.NET code. This is not the case as data breakpoints are only available for unmanaged code. Attempting to specify a data breakpoint in VB.NET displays a message box, which informs you that: Basic does not support data breakpoints.

## Fine Tuning New Breakpoints

Regardless of the breakpoint type created (Function, File, Address, or Data) each instance of the New Breakpoint dialog contained a button labeled, Condition..., and a button labeled, Hit Count.

- Condition... – this allows you to specify that execution should only halt at the breakpoint if some conditional (an evaluated statement) is true or a specific variable has been modified.
- Hit Count... – specifying this option means that execution should only break at the breakpoint after the location has been "hit" (reached) during execution some number of times.

## Break on Conditional

Clicking on the Condition... button displays the Breakpoint Condition dialog:

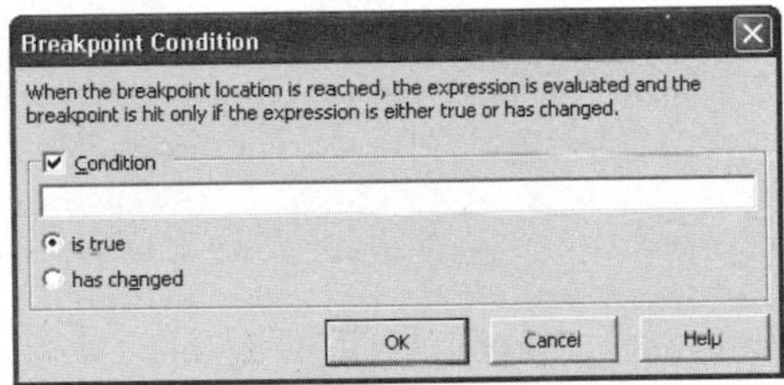


The previous screenshot contains a tantalizing but empty textbox for specifying a conditional expression. When this expression is true (if the is true radio button is selected) or has changed (if the has changed radio button is selected) then execution will break at the breakpoint. Use the language you are currently working in to specify expressions. When coding in VB.NET, the conditionals are VB.NET, when coding in J# specify conditionals in J# and so on.

To demonstrate conditionals, consider the `BelieveItOrNot()` method from the WXExpressions console application:

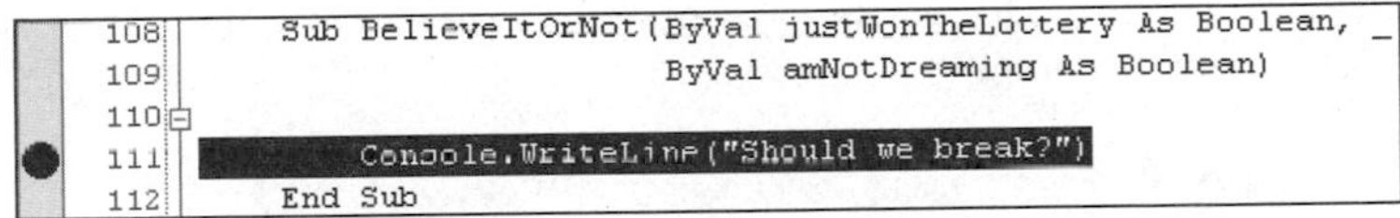


The breakpoint visible in the previous screenshot is associated with a conditional. This conditional is associated with a rare case (where the value of each parameter passed to `BelieveItOrNot()` is `True`). The conditional expression in order to achieve this is as follows:

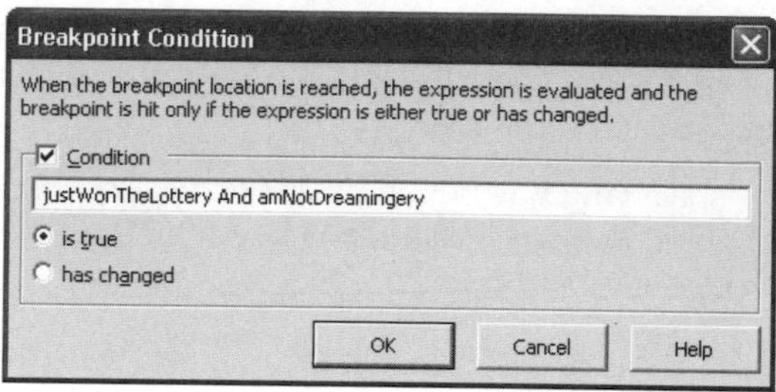


The VB.NET code (the conditional expression) that must evaluate to true in order for the breakpoint to break is quite legible, since it is simply VB.NET. Only your imagination (and the VB.NET syntax) limits the possible uses of this feature. You could specify a breakpoint to fire when a variable (or some combination of variables) is set to an unexpected value, when some end case is true, the last time a loop is executed, etc.

The ability to specify expressions is not solely limited to the Breakpoint Condition dialog. It will be shown later in that chapter, that expressions can also be used when examining data values using the Watch window and QuickWatch dialogs. Clearly not every aspect of every language (including VB.NET) is useable within the conditional textbox; we will look at these limitations in the *VB.NET Expressions* section later in the chapter

## Break on Hit Count

Consider a bug that occurs after a particular line has executed a hundred times or a thousand times. It is not practical to single step a thousand separate times through a range of code. For this reason, it is possible to associate a hit count with a breakpoint. After the region of code associated with the breakpoint has been executed the number of times specified by the hit count, the breakpoint kicks in, and execution halts.

Clicking on the Hit Count... button in the Breakpoint Properties or New Breakpoint dialog displays a Breakpoint Hit Count child dialog:

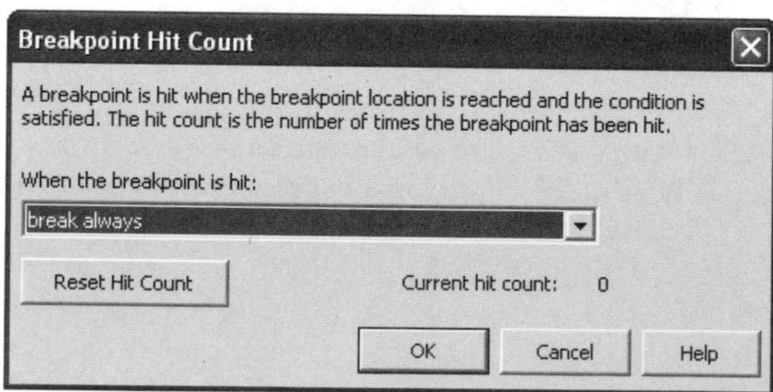


The drop-down list under the label When the breakpoint is hit: contains the following entries:

- break always – break at the location of the breakpoint regardless of the hit count.
- break when the hit count is equal to – break at the location when the code has been executed a specific number of times where this number of times.
- break when the hit count is a multiple of – break at the location when the code has executed n more times. So if n were equal to ten then the code would break at ten, twenty, thirty, etc.
- break when the hit count is greater than or equal to – break at the location time after the hit count has reached a certain value and then break each time after that.

When you select any option except break always, the Break Hit Count dialog contains a textbox for specifying the desired hit count:

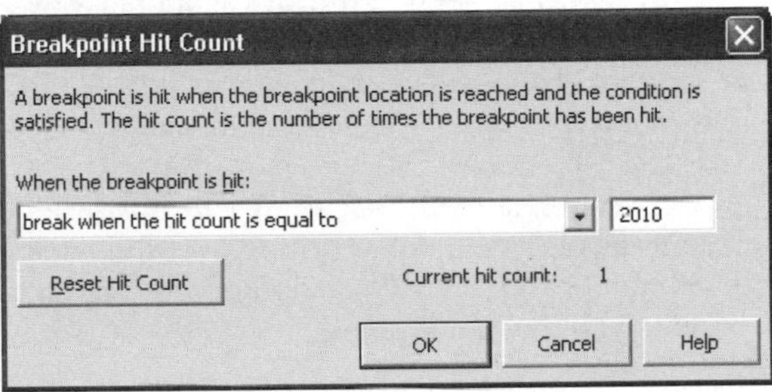


The Current hit count label displays the number of time the code associated with the break point has executed; obviously this will be zero for new break points. The hit count is also set to zero each time you restart the application.

The Reset Hit Count button in the previous screenshot sets the value of Current hit count to zero. For example, if the Current hit count was 2050 then we are past the trigger point (2010) and the application will not halt at this breakpoint again as it is set to break when the hit count is equal to. Clicking the Reset Hit Count button means that the hit count would be set to zero. Under this circumstance, 2010 more hits at the location in the code would result in the breakpoint being triggered again (execution halted).

## Managing Breakpoints

The Debug menu provides a variety of menu items pertinent to breakpoint management. These items are available whether the debugger is active or not:

- New Breakpoint – this displays the New Breakpoint dialog.
- Clear All Breakpoints – this menu item is only available if the present application contains a breakpoint or breakpoints. This menu item will delete all the breakpoints associated with the solution if selected.

- Disable All Breakpoints – this menu item causes all breakpoints to be disabled. Such breakpoints still exist but they will not cause an application to halt execution until they are re-enabled. An empty red circle (rather than the filled circle that represents active breakpoints) indicates that a break point is disabled. Any code that would be highlighted when the breakpoint is active, is contained is outlined with an unfilled red box (such as the following):

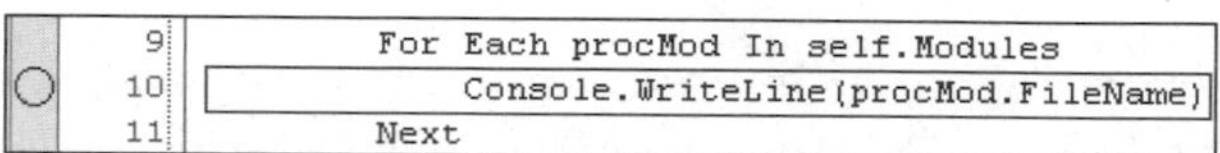

For Each procMod In self.Modules
Console.WriteLine(procMod.FileName)
Next


- To disable individual breakpoints use the Disable Breakpoint option from the context menu available when right-clicking over the line of code that is associated with the breakpoint in question.

- Enable All Breakpoints – this menu item causes all breakpoints to be enabled. The Enable All Breakpoints menu item is only displayed while at least one breakpoint is disabled. Once all breakpoints have been enabled, the Enable All Breakpoints menu item is no longer displayed on the Debug menu.

  To enable individual breakpoints use the Enable Breakpoint option from the context menu available when right-clicking over the line of code that is associated with the breakpoint in question or left-click in the empty red circle associated with the break point

- Debug | Windows | Breakpoints – displays a window containing all breakpoints associated with a solution. This window allows you to view the state of each breakpoint (enabled, disabled), and the conditions under which the breakpoint is triggered.

## Breakpoints Window

The Breakpoints window is useful for managing all breakpoints within a solution. This window is always available whether currently debugging or not. An example of this window is as follows (from the WXExpression project):

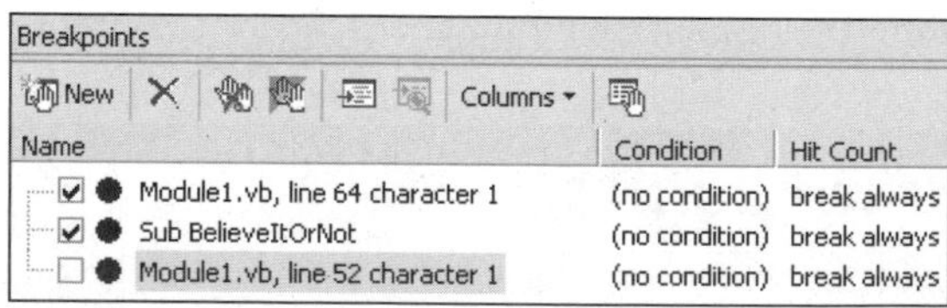

The Conditional and Hit Count columns of the previous window are quite handy because they reveal more than just a red dot in source code, namely the Conditional and Hit Count associated with a given breakpoint. The Breakpoints window allows you to enable and disable individual breakpoints, courtesy of the checkbox to the left of each breakpoint. Toolbar-style icons are provided that can add, delete, clear all breakpoints, disable all breakpoints, go to source code, and go to disassembly code. Using the Columns drop-down list you can add columns showing language, data, and address, and so on to the window. Right-clicking the mouse displays a context menu that allows the properties of a breakpoint to be displayed.

# Viewing Results

The simplest way view data within an application you are debugging is the "mouse hover technique". As the name indicates, hover the mouse pointer over a variable, and hey presto the value associated with that variable appears in a Tooltip (provided of course the variable is in scope):

```
Private _redSox As String
          _redSox = "Never to win a World Series"
```

In the previous screenshot, the mouse cursor is dangling over the `_redSox` data member displaying the value associated with this data member. This is fine for quickly checking one variable, but Visual Studio .NET makes a lot more information available if you know how to find it.

## *Displaying Detailed Debugging Information*

When you are debugging an application, the Debug menu's Windows submenu displays the following menu items:

- Watch – four different Watch windows (Watch 1 through Watch 4) are available to display the value of variables or computed expressions. You can use different windows to categorize the variable you are watching (put variables from one section of code in Watch 1 and from another section of code in Watch 2). So the variables in scope for a particular section of code can all be viewed together. Grouping by similar scope is a practical way to make use of the four Watch windows.
- Locals – this window lists the Name, Value, and Type of all variables defined in the local scope.
- Autos – this window displays variables visible close to the current line.
- Me – shows the data members and properties associated with the current object.

- Memory – four different Memory windows (Memory 1 through Memory 4) are available for displaying values stored in memory. By specifying a memory address and the range, locations before and after the address are viewable.

We'll look at all these options in detail except for Memory; as this isn't that relevant for debugging managed applications, we'll leave that window until Appendix B, *Debugging Unmanaged Code.*

## Locals

The Locals window (Debug | Windows| Locals) displays all variables local to the current context such as the following including the parameters passed to a method:

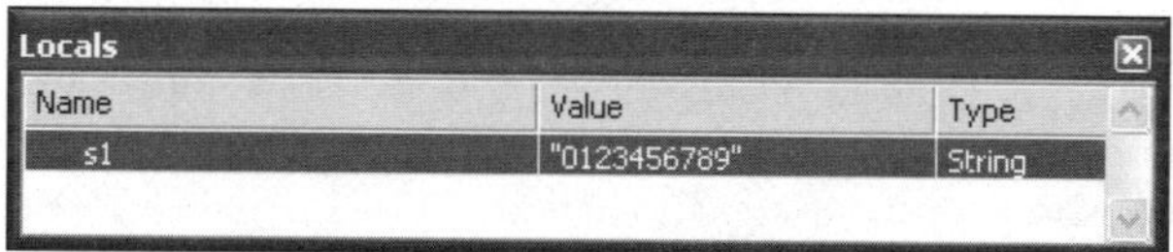


The Local window is quite WYSIWYG and not highly configurable. Right-clicking on the Local window displays a context menu that switches the display between hexadecimal and decimal form.

For complex data types and objects, a plus symbol displayed on the left:

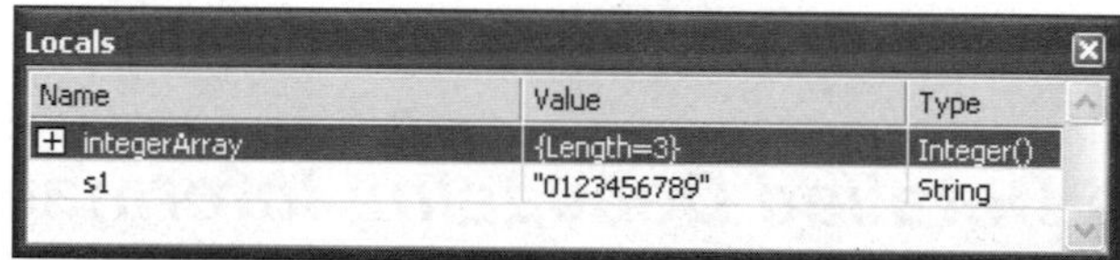


This allows you to expand the view and access the data members that it contains:

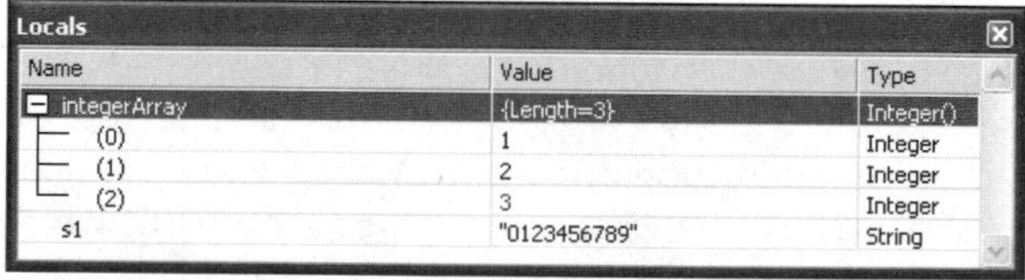


When stepping through an application the value of any variable that has changed since the last step is displayed in red. By double-clicking in the value column, the value of a data member can be selected and altered. This is useful when you've spotted an error but want to continue debugging the rest of the code. You can also test the effects a planned change might have with out actually changing the code.

## Autos

The Autos window is a focused subset of the Local windows. It displays, only the variables visible plus or minus two commands from the currently executing line of code. The Autos window like the Locals window can display integer data in decimal or hexadecimal format.

These windows can become very cluttered, especially with Windows Form applications where there are many complex data types in scope at any one time. To pick out just the values you are interested in view them in a watch window.

## Me and This Window

The heading to this section mentions Me and This for a reason. In VB.NET the value for the current class or structure instance is accessed using the `Me` keyword. In C# and C++ the `this` keyword is used. Visual Studio .NET has a miniscule bug related to Me and This. In a VB.NET application that is being debugged with Visual Studio .NET, the Debug | Windows | Me menu item is sometimes not visible after an application has been started. Instead Debug | Windows | This is visible. Whether Me or This, the values displayed in the This window (a.k.a. the Me window) corresponds to the data members and properties of `Me`.

For the Windows Forms application WXAppDomainDemo, the Me windows appears as follows when Debug | Step Over is hit just once to initiate program execution:

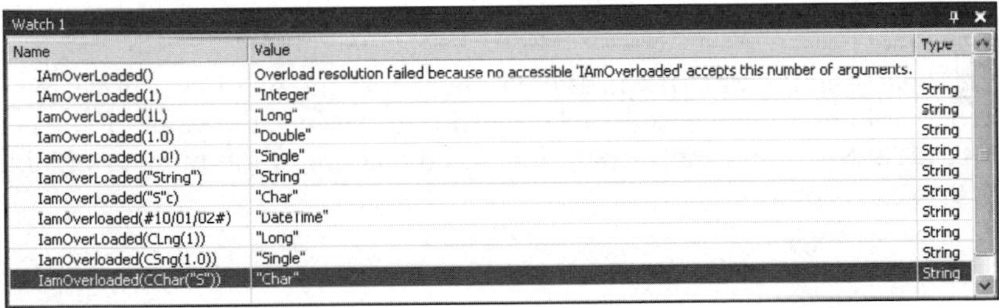


In the previous screenshot, the columns Name, Value, and Type are self-documenting. The base class of Me is always the first data member under the name column.

A Windows Forms application was used to demonstrate the Me window because the class from which execution originates when *F10* is pressed is derived from the `Form` class. Anything derived from a `Form` class has a nearly unmanageable amount of information in the Me window. The moral to this tale is, "Simpler data types than classes derived from `Form` are best displayed in the Me window."

## Watch

The development environment controls the Locals, Autos, and Me/This windows. Of all the windows that can view variables and debugger expressions, Watch is the most granular (you pick what is displayed). The benefit of this is that any variable (say variable, `x`) or expression (say, `Math.Power(i2, 2)`) displayed is selected by the developer. The downside is that when `x` (the variable) or `i2` (the variable in the expression) goes out of scope, the Watch window cannot determine the value to display. With Locals, Autos, and Me/This you see only valid entities. Data types can be added to the Watch window by typing their name in a free row at the bottom, dragging and dropping from another window (such as Locals) and using the Add Watch menu item of the source editor window's context menu

You can have up to 4 Watch windows (Watch 1 through Watch 4), each of which can contain multiple variables. These variables can be fully qualified as is the case in the following screenshot where the contents of `Dim retVal As DataSet` is examined in detail.

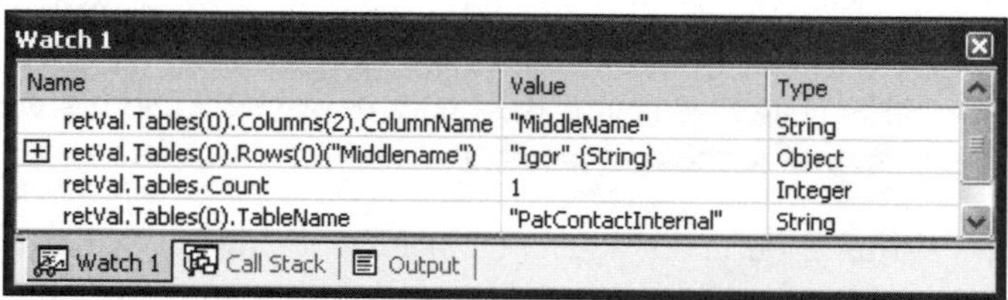


The previous instance of Watch 1 shows that the name of the zero-th table in the `DataSet` is `"PatContactInternal"`. This value or any non-read-only, non-constant value is modifiable in the `Watch` window. Further more the windows shows the name of the second column in the zero-th table (`"Middle Name"`), the value of the column named `"Middle Name"` for the zero-th row and the count of the number of tables (`retVal.Tables.Count`).

In order to further demonstrate the Watch window, consider the rather mundane variable:

```
Dim coinage As Decimal = 12.34
```

The Watch window displays `coinage` as having a value of 12.34D; `String.Format` can spice up the display of this humble variable. Using `{0:C}` within `String.Format` and different `CultureInfo` instances (from the `System.Globalization` namespace) we can display the value of `currency` for different languages and cultures: English-Great Britain (`"en-GB"`), German-Germany (`"de-DE"`), Japan-Japanese (`"ja-JP"`):

Watch 1

| Name | Value | Type |
|---|---|---|
| String.Format("{0:c}", coinage) | "$12.34" | String |
| String.Format(new CultureInfo("De-de"), "{0:c}", coinage) | "12,34 €" | String |
| String.Format(new CultureInfo("En-gb"), "{0:c}", coinage) | "£12.34" | String |
| String.Format(new CultureInfo("Ja-jp"), "{0:c}", coinage) | "¥12" | String |
| coinage | 12.34D | Decimal |

Right-clicking on the Watch window displays a context menu that switches integer data types between hexadecimal and decimal display. This change is global to the Watch window in that it changes the display behavior of all integer data types. If only one needed to be displayed in hexadecimal form the `String.Format("0x{0:X}", varName)` expression could be used. `String.Format` is not required in order to use the Watch windows but by using it, the Watch window becomes far more useful.

## QuickWatch

Underneath the Debug menu is the QuickWatch (*Ctrl + Alt + Q*) menu item. Selecting this displays a dialog that allows you to evaluate a variable or expression. The basic idea is that this dialog acts as a scratch pad or calculator that does not clutter up the Watch window.

The QuickWatch is modal therefore it is not possible to access any other functionality of Visual Studio .NET until the QuickWatch modal dialog is closed. The QuickWatch dialog appears as follows (for variable, `_i1`, from project WXExpressions):

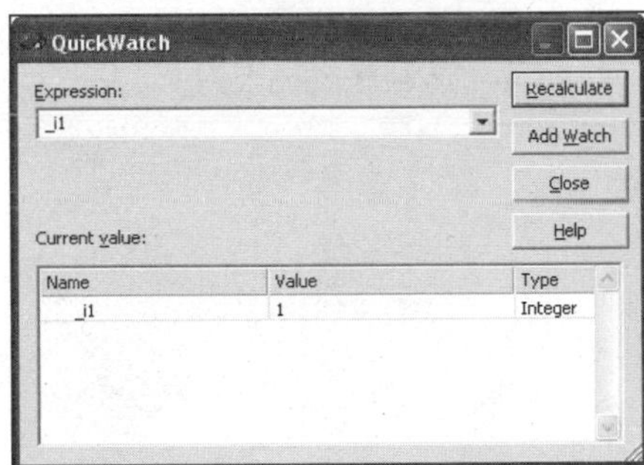


The value specified in QuickWatch dialog's Expression listbox is displayed under the Current value list (`_i1` has a value of `1`).

As expressions go the value of variable `_i1` is rather mundane. Under the Expression label, a drop-down list of previously used expressions is available and some of these are a bit more flamboyant than merely viewing `_i1`:

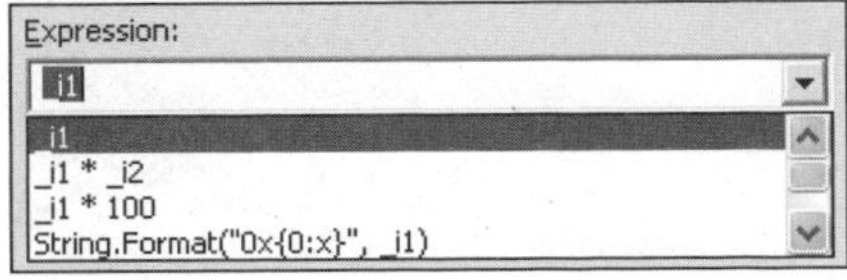

It should be clear from the previous screenshot that QuickWatch (and Watch, Me, etc.) are capable of more than just displaying a single variable, namely displaying expressions using those variables.

The Recalculate button will re-compute the value of the expression. Clicking on the Add Watch button will add the expression to the Watch window. Clicking Add Watch gives the expression more permanence than QuickWatch since the expression goes away when the QuickWatch dialog is closed while the Watch window can be displayed continuously. Additionally, the values in the Watch window are saved in the solution's `*.suo` file.

# VB.NET Expressions

As mentioned previously Watch, QuickWatch, and Breakpoint Condition can make use of expressions written in VB.NET. This functionality is provided courtesy of Visual Studio .NET's built-in VB.NET expression evaluator.

## *Variables, Functions, and Properties*

The expression evaluator can make use of any variable, function, or property within the current point of execution's local scope. The exception to this rule is that the expression evaluator cannot use local constants. In order to demonstrate the power and flexibility of Visual Studio .NET's expression evaluator, consider the following code snippet from the WXExpressions console application:

```
Const _i1 As Integer = 1
ReadOnly _i2 As Integer = 1
Private _i3 As Integer = 1

Function GetValue() As Integer
  Return 1
End Function

ReadOnly Property GetData() As Integer
  Get
    Return 1
  End Get
End Property

Sub IdentifiersAndTypes()
  Const i4 As Integer = 1
  Dim i5 As Integer = 1
End Sub
```

The previous code's variables (`_i1`, `_i2`, `_i3`, `i5`), function (`GetValue()`), and property (`GetData`) can be used to compute a value displayed by the Watch window:

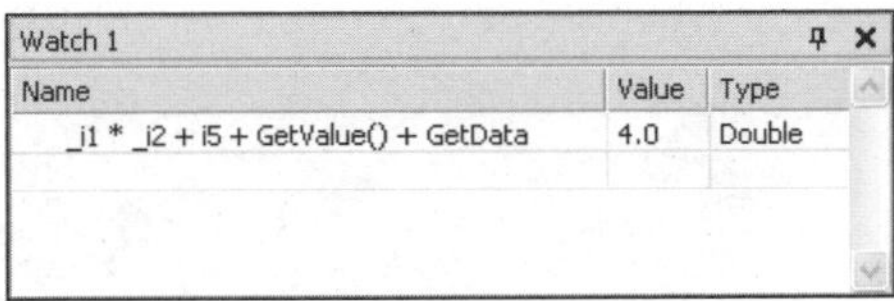


The only entity not used in the previous expression was `i4`. This makes sense since `i4` is a local constant and hence it is not available in expressions. Using `i4` in an expression would display an error message in the Watch window's Value column, Name i4 not declared.

> **Variables can be used in the expression evaluated but cannot be declared in such expressions.**

## Function and Property Side Effects

When the expression is evaluated the function and or property is evaluated in the context of the program presently being debugged. To understand this, consider the following `Danger()` function from the WXExpressions console application:

```
Function Danger() As Integer
  TransferFunds(100)
  Return Receipt()
End Function
```

Placing the `Danger()` method in a QuickWatch, Breakpoint or Watch expression will cause each method inside `Danger()` to be executed. Each time the application is single stepped the value of `Danger()` will be updated; hence `Danger()` will be executed again and again. The `Danger()` method can potentially be called countless times even if the application itself does not explicitly call `Danger()`.

## Overloaded Methods and Casts

The expression evaluator is perceptive enough to recognize overloaded methods. If our class defined the following overloaded methods:

```
Function IAmOverloaded(ByVal ByValx As Integer) As String
  Return Integer
End Function
Function IAmOverloaded(ByVal ByValx As Long) As Integer
  Return Long
End Function
Function IAmOverloaded(ByVal ByValx As Double) As Integer
  Return Long
End Function
Function IAmOverloaded(ByVal ByValx As Single) As Integer
  Return 4
```

```
End Function
Function IAmOverloaded(ByVal ByValx As String) As Integer
  Return 5
End Function
Function IAmOverloaded(ByVal ByValx As Char) As Integer
  Return 6
End Function
Function IAmOverloaded(ByVal ByValx As DateTime) As Integer
  Return 7
End Function
```

We could explicitly choose between the different overloads for the values specified in the expression by directly identifying the data types involved:

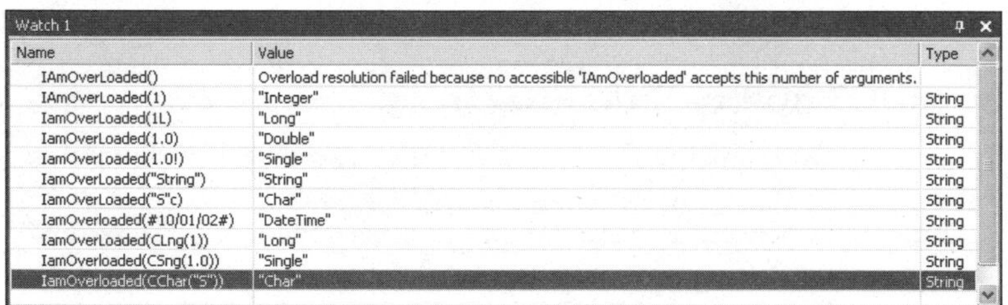


You could achieve the same precision using casting operators such as `CByte`, `CChar`, `CDate`, `CDec`, `CDbl`, `CInt`, `CLng`, etc.

**You cannot identify the `CType` cast in an expression evaluated by the debugger.**

## Structures and Classes

Both structures and classes can be specified as the expression evaluated, such as the `_pt` data member of type `System.Drawing.Point`:

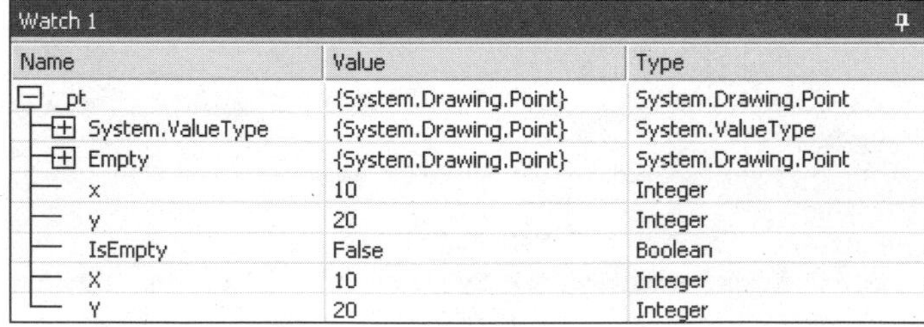

Displaying the contents of the `Point` structure just to see the `X` property takes up quite a few lines within the Watch window. It is possible to left-click the mouse on the `X` property then dragged and drop it within the Watch window:

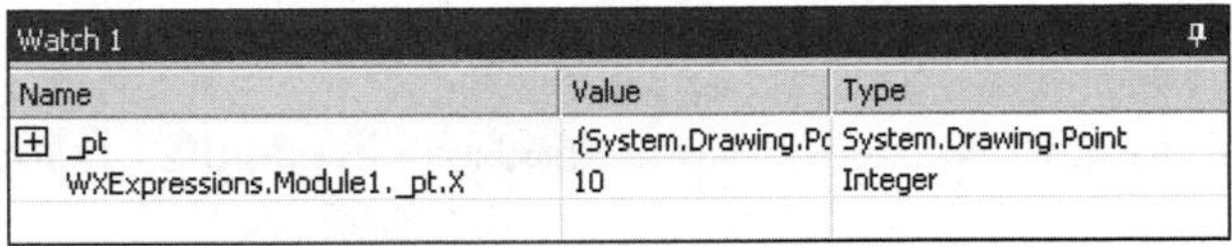

Watch 1

| Name | Value | Type |
|---|---|---|
| ⊞ _pt | {System.Drawing.Pc | System.Drawing.Point |
| WXExpressions.Module1._pt.X | 10 | Integer |

It would have been quite quick to have manually typed `_pt.X` in the Watch window so drag-and-drop was not a colossal time saver in this context. For a vastly more complicated data type (such as a class with multi-level derivation ancestry), the drag-and-drop approach can really save a lot of unnecessary typing.

Classes can also be displayed using the expression evaluator. Just as with the Me/This window, the expression evaluator is smart enough to display the most derived level of the class. To understand this, consider the `_tw` data member found in the WXExpressions project:

```
Private _tw As TextWriter = New StreamWriter("c:\ILikePhoGa.log")
```

The data member of is type `System.IO.TextWriter` but the most derived type is actually `System.IO.StreamWriter` since the inheritance hierarchy for `StreamWriter` is as follows:

```
System.Object
  System.MarshalByRefObject
    System.IO.TextWriter
      System.IO.StreamWriter
```

When `_tw` (type, `TextWriter`) is displayed, it is shown in the Watch windows as follows:

Watch 1

| Name | Value | Type |
|---|---|---|
| ⊟ _tw | {System.IO.Stream\ | System.IO.TextWriter |
| ⊟ [System.IO.StreamWriter] | {System.IO.Stream\ | System.IO.StreamWriter |
| ⊞ System.IO.TextWriter | {System.IO.Stream\ | System.IO.TextWriter |
| DefaultBufferSize | 1024 | Integer |
| DefaultFileStreamBufferSize | 4096 | Integer |
| MinBufferSize | 128 | Integer |

The top-level properties and data members are from `StreamWriter` while the second level of properties and data members are from `TextWriter`; this continues up the inheritance hierarchy, ultimately reaching `System.Object`.

## Attribute and Operator Limitations

There are some limitations to what you can call from the expression evaluator; for instance, it is not possible to call a method within the expression evaluator that is associated with the `WebMethodAttribute` class (`System.Web.Services` namespace). This class identifies a remote method since the method resides on a web service rather than locally. Executing such methods is beyond the capabilities of the expression evaluator.

Another limitation of the expression evaluator applies to the `TypeOf` operator. It is possible to use the `TypeOf` operator in conjunction with the `Is` keyword in order to return `True` or `False` with respect to the type associated with an instance:

| Name | Value | Type |
|---|---|---|
| TypeOf scoreGoalThatWinsWorldCup Is MyFate | True | Boolean |
| TypeOf williamShakespeare Is DependentOnMeForWritingIdeas | True | Boolean |

Unfortunately if the `TypeOf` operator is used in an expression without the `Is` operator, then an error results.

## Invalid Keywords

The expression evaluator is powerful but there are limitations. The debugger expression evaluator does not support the following VB.NET keywords: `AddressOf`, `Case`, `Catch`, `End`, `Error`, `Exit`, `Finally`, `Goto`, `On Error`, `Return`, `Resume`, `Select`, `Stop`, `SyncLock`, `Throw`, `Try`, and `With`. Attempting use them results in an expression that cannot be evaluated.

## Managing Large Data Members

Large data items are difficult to view in Visual Studios .NET's data viewing windows, such as Watch. One way to mitigate this problem is to use `String.SubString()`. To demonstrate this consider a variable, `Constitution`, of type `String` that contains the entire text of the US constitution. The `String` class's `SubString()` method can be used to make this large data member visible in manageable chunks (start at offset `4779` and display `51` characters) such as the following:

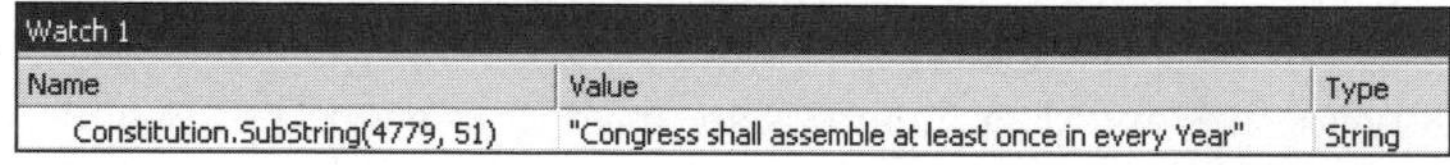

Watch 1

| Name | Value | Type |
|---|---|---|
| Constitution.SubString(4779, 51) | "Congress shall assemble at least once in every Year" | String |

# The Call Stack

As methods (or properties) are called, an entry (assembly name, class, and method name) is made on the call stack – the method is pushed on the stack. Any methods/properties that this method calls are pushed on to the stack after it. When a call returns from a method/property, the corresponding entry is removed from the call stack – popped from the stack. Each thread maintains its own call stack and provided the thread is halted, the stack can be viewed in the Call Stack window (Debug | Windows | Call Stack).

From a debugging standpoint, the call stack is like an archeological record. In archeologically, each layer dug represents a period of time that we can study individually. The call stack provides precisely this ability for code. The top of the stack is what is currently happening. The next level down (the method/property that called the current method/property) contains local data members and parameters that are not visible in the current scope of execution. Examining these data members and parameters can provide debugging insight into what is currently happening and why. Each layer of the stack provides similar insight. Global variables are variables associated with a common instance (`Me`) and are the same regardless of stack level.

The individual entries displayed in the Call Stack window contain the name of the method/property called and the language the function is implemented in. A partial view of the call stack associated with the `WXShowCallStack` solution is as follows:

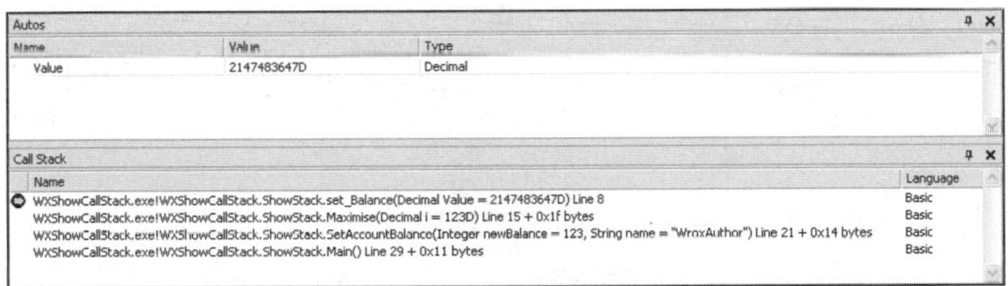


The top entry in the call stack windows contains a red dot to the left inside which is a yellow arrow. This means that the application is stopped at a breakpoint inside the `Balance` property (a red dot on screen) and the current point of execution is at this location (a yellow arrow on screen). The values visible in the Locals window (for example) when the stack frame entry is set to the top of the call stack correspond to the variables initialized thus far within `Balance`.

Within the previous screenshot, the `SetAccountBalance()` method (third entry in call stack) calls the `Maximise()` method (second entry in the call stack). Double-clicking on the third entry in the call stack window moves the visible scope to the data accessible:

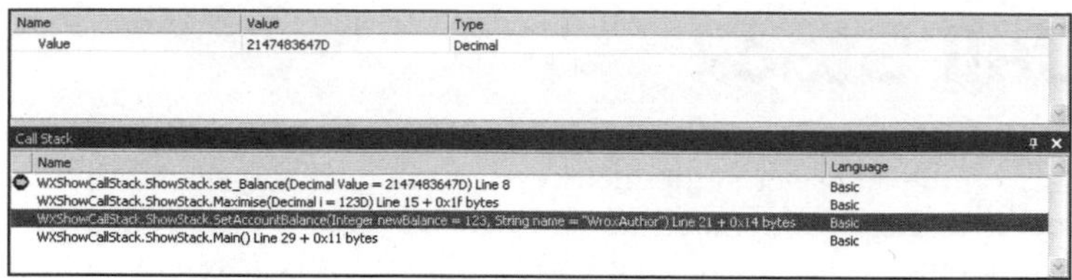


After this double-click, the Call Stack window places a green arrow next to the current level of the stack (the `SetAccountBalance()` method); the Switch to Frame menu item in the call stack's context menu has the same effect.

Within the source code associated with the `SetAccountBalance()` method, the line of code that is currently referred to is highlighted in green. If the Locals window (or any of the other data windows) is examined after this double-click, then the variables displayed and parameters correspond to the `SetAcccountBalance()` method (the current level viewed within the call stack). Examining the value passed to the `SetAcccountBalance()` and the value passed to the `Balance` property it should be clear that something odd has happened along the way,

In the previous screenshot of the Call Stack window, an observant reader might have noticed that no module names were visible; hiding the module's name enables us to see the full name of the methods within the screenshot. Using the Call Stack window's context menu, we can select just the entries we are interested in:

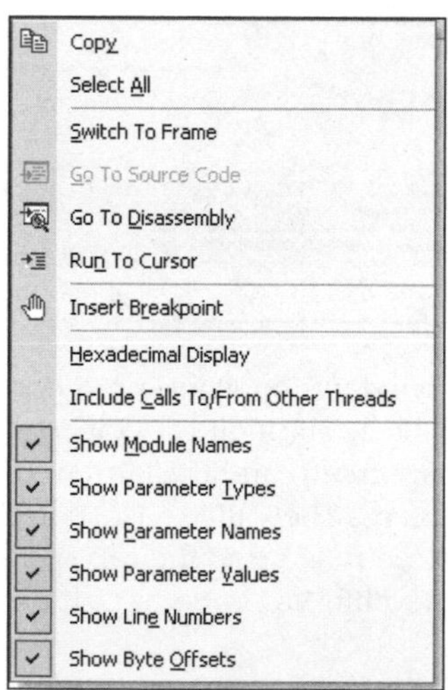


The various checked entries in the context menu (Show Module Names, Show Parameter Types, Show Parameter Names, etc.) correspond to the values displayed for each entry in the call stack.

Remember each thread is associated with a separate call stack. In a multithreaded application, the window displayed by Debug | Windows | Threads enables you to move execution between threads to view different call stacks. The call stack displayed in the Call Stack window corresponds to the currently executing thread. Multithreaded development (and the nuances of Debug | Windows | Threads) is reviewed in Chapter 3.

# Modules

Modules in this context means files that adhere to the Common Execution Format (COEF). This includes managed and unmanaged executables and dynamically linked libraries (executable DLLs or DLLs that only contain data/resources). Assemblies are a type of module that contains managed code and therefore run within the Common Language Runtime (CLR).

Modules (in particular their qualified path) are important to debugging because they indicate precisely what code is executing. Using the Modules window, it would for example be possible to ascertain you are using the DLL `c:\WrongVersion\useful.dll` instead of `c:\RightVersion\useful.dll`.

When debugging a VB.NET project, the Modules submenu item potentially does not do what its name seems to indicate. This menu item displays all the modules associated with the assembly presently being debugged rather than the modules associated with the process presently being debugged. Remember a process is a Windows concept but an assembly currently executing (being debugged) might be oblivious to its supporting Window infrastructure. These modules may contain managed or unmanaged code depending on the debugging situation.

Demonstrating the Modules submenu is the following screenshot taken of the Modules window while the `WXExpresions.exe` application is being debugged

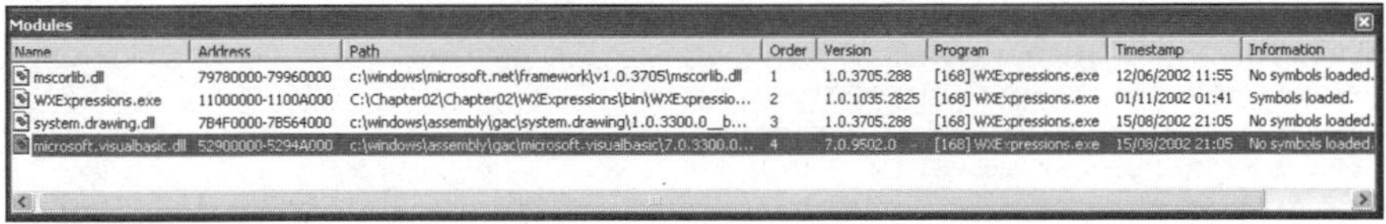

Modules

| Name | Address | Path | Order | Version | Program | Timestamp | Information |
|---|---|---|---|---|---|---|---|
| mscorlib.dll | 79780000-79960000 | c:\windows\microsoft.net\framework\v1.0.3705\mscorlib.dll | 1 | 1.0.3705.288 | [168] WXExpressions.exe | 12/06/2002 11:55 | No symbols loaded. |
| WXExpressions.exe | 11000000-1100A000 | C:\Chapter02\Chapter02\WXExpressions\bin\WXExpressio... | 2 | 1.0.1035.2825 | [168] WXExpressions.exe | 01/11/2002 01:41 | Symbols loaded. |
| system.drawing.dll | 7B4F0000-7B564000 | c:\windows\assembly\gac\system.drawing\1.0.3300.0__b... | 3 | 1.0.3705.288 | [168] WXExpressions.exe | 15/08/2002 21:05 | No symbols loaded. |
| microsoft.visualbasic.dll | 52900000-5294A000 | c:\windows\assembly\gac\microsoft.visualbasic\7.0.3300.0... | 4 | 7.0.9502.0 | [168] WXExpressions.exe | 15/08/2002 21:05 | No symbols loaded. |

Notice in the Modules window that the WXExpresions uses assemblies that have both the DLL and EXE extension. It is possible for a Windows process to load and execute multiple assemblies with EXE extensions.

Just because the previous example only showed modules of type assembly, does not mean that the Modules window does not show unmanaged modules. The true usefulness of the Modules window comes not in whether or not it shows managed or unmanaged modules. It comes from the various columns displayed within the Modules window, because these let developers be sure they are debugging with the specific modules they expect (for example an application running for a Chinese/Singaporean user should not be loading assemblies that specify French/Canadian as their culture). Under .NET we could tell the difference between these DLLs because of their path (`fr-CA` for French/Canadian and `zh-SG` for Chinese/Singaporean). The columns displayed for the Modules window are as follows:

- Name – name of the module displayed.
- Address – address where the module was loaded within the process address space.

  In the event that an application terminates catastrophically, the address displayed when it crashes corresponds to the address where the crash took place. This address in turn corresponds to a module since each module is loaded over a range of addresses as displayed in the Modules window.
- Path – location from which the module was loaded, which might not actually be the location on disk where the module is located. The previous screenshot shows modules loaded from `C:\Windows\Microsoft.NET\Framework\v1.0.3705` and modules being contained in `C:\Windows\assembly\GAC`. This directory corresponds to the Global Assembly Cache (a global repository for assemblies shared by multiple applications).

| Path |
|---|
| C:\WINDOWS\assembly\GAC\System.Drawing\1.0.3300.0__b03f5f7f11d50a3a\System.Drawing.dll |
| C:\WINDOWS\assembly\GAC\System.Windows.Forms\1.0.3300.0__b77a5c561934e089\System.Windows.Forms.dll |
| C:\WINDOWS\assembly\GAC\System\1.0.3300.0__b77a5c561934e089\System.dll |
| C:\WINDOWS\Microsoft.NET\Framework\v1.0.3705\diasymreader.dll |
| C:\WINDOWS\Microsoft.NET\Framework\v1.0.3705\fusion.dll |
| C:\WINDOWS\Microsoft.NET\Framework\v1.0.3705\mscorjit.dll |
| C:\WINDOWS\Microsoft.NET\Framework\v1.0.3705\mscorlib.dll |
| C:\WINDOWS\Microsoft.NET\Framework\v1.0.3705\mscorsn.dll |
| C:\WINDOWS\Microsoft.NET\Framework\v1.0.3705\mscorwks.dll |

- Order – order in which the modules were loaded for a given application. For managed application `mscorlib.dll` is always loaded first, hence it has an order of 1.
- Version – version number associated with the module. It is possible for an application to be running and for it to access multiple versions of the same module at the same time (side-by-side versioning). Each version of the assembly corresponds to a separate module with the same file name. Under this scenario, the file name is a key qualified fully by the version number.

- Program – the process that loaded the module, including the application name and corresponding Program ID. Visual Studio .NET can debug multiple processes so the modules used by each separate program will be displayed in the Modules window.
- Timestamp – timestamp corresponding to the module's build date.
- Information – indicates whether or not debug information (in the form of a PDB file) was loaded in conjunction with the assembly. Debug information is not available with applications built without debug information, including the system assemblies `mscorlib.dll` and`System.drawing.dll`

The Timestamp column may seem like a useless bit of trivia when in fact it is a key piece of information that is useful for debugging. Microsoft for example puts the timestamp to good use. If you are running Windows XP, under the Windows, System32 directory a large number of DLLs are time stamped as follows: 08/23/2001 05:00 AM. This timestamp is not when the DLL was installed but instead reflects when Microsoft cut the gold CD for deployment (August 23, 2001) and that the product is Windows NT 5.0 (05:00 AM), which developed into Windows 2000 and Windows XP.

*While working for a large hardware company on tablet PCs, I was forced to work with a build environment developed by the team's usability engineer (a GUI engineer strong on theory, weak in reality). The build environment frankly did not always work correctly. The* Modules *window was a lifesaver because it often showed that part of the application not installed correctly. For example, once the* Path *column showed bulk of the DLLs that were being debugged were in the system's Trash folder.*

## Modules Context Menu

It is possible to right-click on the Modules window and display a context menu:

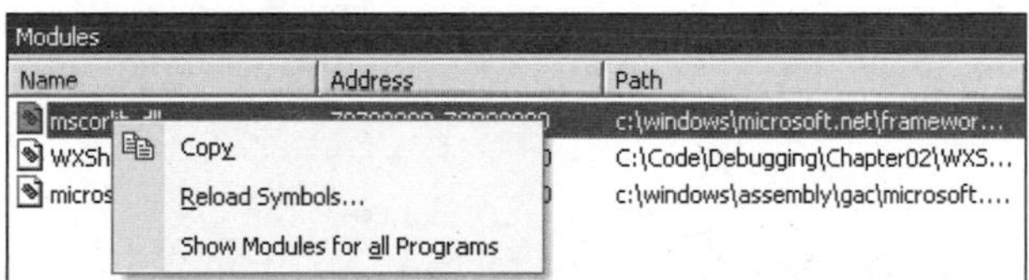


The Copy menu item displayed in the context menu simply copies the row of information to the clipboard in text form. This information can be useful because it is explicit with respect to the identity of the module.

Debugging information for managed assemblies is contained in program database files, which are only usually created with debug builds of an application. Hence, this information is not available for framework assemblies. If the `*.pdb` file for an assembly is available but not in the default location expected by the assembly, it can be loaded manually using Reload Symbols. For more information of program database files, see Chapter 5.

The Show Modules for all Programs menu item is only available on the context menu if the instance of Visual Studio .NET currently running is debugging multiple processes. Under this circumstance, the Show Modules for all Programs menu item displays the modules for every process being debugged rather than just one at a time.

### DLL Hell and the Global Assembly Cache (GAC)

The little anecdote about Recycle Bin DLLs was indicative of the syndrome Microsoft calls "DLL Hell". To enable COM DLL's to be located quickly by an application they were registered by there class IDs in the windows registry. This effectively means that only one version of a COM DLL can be used on any one machine. Unfortunately, COM DLLs had fast but brittle binary interfaces; even minor changes could have unexpected effects. If an application installed an updated version of a DLL this could easily cause applications that requires the old version to fail.

.NET puts an end to all this complexity by simplifying how applications are deployed (hence reducing bugs). Modules are loaded based on their fully qualified name, which includes the version number, allowing multiple versions of the same DLL to reside in the same machine in blissful harmony.

## *Modules Not Where you Expect*

The assemblies displayed in the Modules window included several assemblies that are stored in the GAC. The idea behind that GAC is to provide a standard place for .NET and third-party assemblies to reside. All assemblies in the GAC must meet certain requirements such as having a valid strong name, making it impossible for two assemblies to be confused with each other, even if they have the same filename, version number, and so on.

From those assemblies previously displayed the `system.dll`, `system.drawing.dll`, `system.windows.forms.dll`, and `microsoft.visualbasic.dll` are contained in the global assembly cache. Developers can also add their own assemblies to this cache using a utility that ships with .NET, `gacutil.exe`.

Using Windows explorer it appears that the contents of the GAC are found under the Windows install directory's `Assembly` subdirectory. An example of this is shown in the following Windows explorer screenshot:

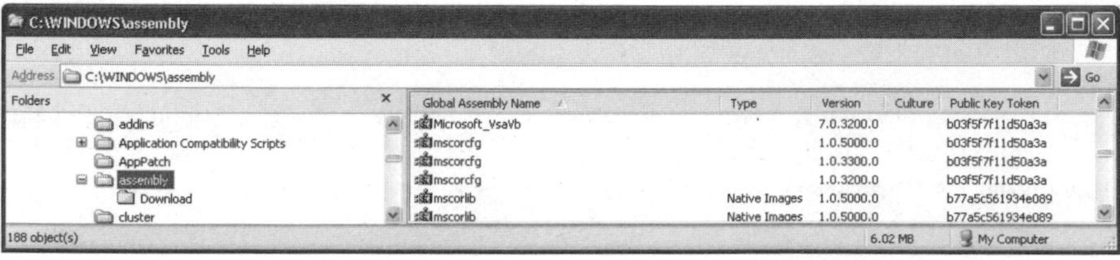

There are marked inconsistencies between the contents of the `C:\Windows\Assemblydirectory` and the Modules window. For example, there is no `mscorlib.dll` found under `C:\Windows\assembly`, instead this DLL (stored in the GAC) is physically found under `C:\windows\microsoft.net\framework\v1.0.3705\mscorlib.dll`.

This confusion is thanks to Windows Explorer because a shell extension is used to display the contents of `C:\Windows\Assembly`. When working with modules and locations Windows Explorer does not show the actual location. The paths in the Modules window are actually the accurate ones.

Should more exploration be required use the `/L` option of `GacUtil.exe`. The `/L` option lists the contents of the global assembly cache. This information could come in handy when debugging the install process. When an application is installed, certain assemblies may be placed in local directories while others are placed in the GAC. `GacUtil.exe /L` is a way to clarify what went where or what already resides where.

# Summary

The Debug menu supports a vast number of debugger features. Not only can variables be displayed (Autos, Locals, and Me/This) but complex expressions can also be evaluated and the results of these expressions can be displayed. Remember that an expression can have side effects specifying a method in an expression can have serious implications on the applications execution. If the method purges all employees from the company database, the Watch window or QuickWatch dialog could provided an exciting means by which to achieve rapid unemployment.

Most developers are content to simply associate a breakpoint with a specific line in the code. Breakpoints can actually be set based on line number, data modification, and function location. Furthermore, breakpoints can be associated with a modifying condition, making them much more powerful than they might seem at first.

Now we have covered the basics, in the next chapter we will go on to look at the debugging issues related to threads, exceptions, and processes.

VB.NET

# Debugging

Handbook

3

# 3

# Exceptions, Threads and Processes

The final suite of features supported by Visual Studio .NET tackle some of the most complex elements of debugging. Here we look at configuring Visual Studio .NET to handle different categories of exceptions, manage debugging threads, and interact with processes.

- **Exceptions** – as a debugger, Visual Studio .NET can be set up to ignore exceptions or to break execution when an exception is thrown. As Hamlet might say, "To break or not to break execution" is a question that depends on the debugging scenario; we will examine both approaches, with some sample scenarios.
- **Multi-Threading** – in some respects debugging a multi-threaded application is just like debugging two (or more) single threaded applications at the same time inside one instance of Visual Studio .NET. The complexity is in how to navigate the multiple threads within the debugger.
- **Processes** – attaching directly to a running process allows you to debug an application that you don't have to source code for and even legacy unmanaged applications written using VC++6, VB6, and so on. We will also examine the pros and cons of debugging while a solution is loaded or launching the debugger from Task Manager or Visual Studio .NET.

# Debugging Exceptions

Before VB.NET and the infrastructure of the .NET Framework, Visual Basic error handling was a bit chaotic. Each variety of VB (VB 6, VB Script, and VBA) handled errors differently. Furthermore, different languages handled errors in completely different ways (C++, JScript, VB, etc.). With the advent of .NET came cross-language unification of error handling. VB.NET, C#, J#, managed C++, JScript.NET, etc. can all handle errors the same way, via exceptions. The support Visual Studio .NET offers comes in the form of the Debug menu's Exceptions menu item.

## Exceptions Review

An exception can be thrown programmatically by an application, or when specific code encounters an error. Divide a number by zero and the .NET Framework generates an exception of type `System.DivideByZeroException`; run an application where a required DLL is missing and you get a `System.DLLNotFoundException`. Each of the aforementioned exceptions derives from a common base class, the `Exception` class (more on this class later).

The term that best describes how an exception moves through an application is "thrown" since the mechanism for handling exceptions is to catch them (throw/catch get it?). It is possible for an application to gracefully handle a thrown exception by catching it. This is achieved by declaring a protected region in the code (using the `Try` keyword and terminated by `End Try`) and by using the `Catch` keyword to specify which exceptions are to be handled.

If an exception is thrown within a `Try` region, the exception type raised is compared in order to each `Catch` clause and the point of execution moves to the matching `Catch` clause, executing any associated code. When an exception is caught, it is considered to have been **handled,** as it is not passed on and hence you do not need to worry about it further.

If there is no matching `Catch` block, the exception continues up the stack searching for another `Try/Catch` region. If there is no corresponding `Catch`, the **unhandled** exception causes most application types to terminate rather abruptly. This means that garbage collection does not perform final object cleanup because the unhandled exception causes the application to cease execution ungracefully. This does not mean that the operating system leaks memory or other resources, but it does mean that an application may not have performed every step it is intended to perform.

The previous warning does not apply to all application types. For example, ASP.NET applications run DLLs inside IIS (Internet Information Services) they do not crash because all exceptions generated are handled by the server.

To understand how thrown exceptions match to catch blocks, consider the following code snippet:

```
Try
  Dim fStream As FileStream = File.Open("BogusFile.txt", _
                                         FileMode.Open)
Catch ex As FileNotFoundException
  Console.WriteLine("So sorry, file not found")
End Try
```

Executing `File.Open()` throws a `FileNotFoundException` if the file, `Bogus.txt`, does not exist. Since the `Catch` clause specifies precisely this exception type, it catches the exception and the code within is executed.

It would have been possible to specify a `Catch` clause such as the following and still handle the exception:

```
Catch ex As Exception
    Console.WriteLine("So sorry, error encountered")
End Try
```

The `Catch` clause above is associated with the `Exception` class, which is the base class of all exception types. Therefore, this clause catches all exceptions including our `FileNotFoundException` class. The disadvantage of catching all exceptions is that, as demonstrated by the above error message, you cannot be specific about what caused the error.

## Multiple Catch Clauses

It is possible for a `Try` region to be associated with multiple `Catch` clauses. Under this circumstance the .NET runtime attempts to match each `Catch` clause in order against the type of exception raised. If the first `Catch` clause is a match, then the exception is handled there. If the first clause is not a match then the .NET runtime proceeds to the second clause to see if it handles the exception. Demonstrating this is the following snippet of code that catches a `FileNotFoundException` exception type (the first exception type caught) followed by an `Exception` exception type (a "catch all" for any other exception thrown):

```
Try
  Dim fStream As FileStream = File.Open("BogusFile.txt", _
                                         FileMode.Open)
Catch exFNFE As FileNotFoundException
  Console.WriteLine("So sorry, file not found")
Catch ex As Exception
  Console.WriteLine("Some other exception found: " & ex.ToString())
End Try
```

As was previously discussed, the `File.Open()` method when invoked throws an exception of type `FileNotFoundException`. Since the aforementioned exception type is the first one specified in the list of exception clauses, it handles the exception raised.

As a rule, place the `Catch` clauses of the most derived exception types (such as `FileNotFoundException`) before `Catch` clauses associated with exception base classes. The `Exception` class itself is the base class of all exceptions and should therefore by the last exception type caught.

## Managing Exceptions in Visual Studio .NET

The Visual Studio .NET Exceptions menu item is available under the Debug menu both while debugging a project and before a debugger is launched. The point of the Exceptions menu item is to manage the exceptions that take place while an application is running under the Visual Studio .NET debugger. As we've just seen, exceptions fall into two main categories:

- Exceptions handled by the application being debugged – if the source code contains a `Try/Catch` region that catches the exception or catches a suitable base class of the exception, it is considered to be a handled exception.
- Unhandled Exception – if the application's source code does not contain a `Try/Catch` region capable of handling the exception, the exception is unhandled.

Custom Exceptions – it is possible to define your own application-specific exceptions.

For each category of exception, the Exceptions window (Debug | Exceptions) lets you chose whether the exception causes the debugger to break at the point where the exception is raised or lets the source code proceed normally (either for a handled or unhandled exception as the case might be). This behavior of breaking at an exception or proceeding normally only applies to applications being debugged under Visual Studio .NET. The Exceptions window's controlling of an application's behavior in no way applies to applications running outside the confines of the Visual Studio .NET debugger. The Exception window that supports managing exception behavior is as follows:

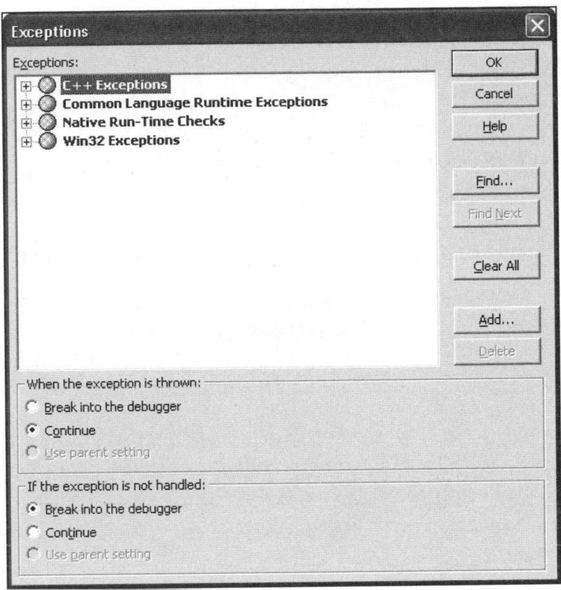


It is possible it set behavior at two points in the exception lifecycle: when it is thrown (this applies to all exceptions), or if it is not handled (this obviously applies to only unhandled exceptions). The region at the bottom of the Exceptions windows is where each category (handled and not handled) of exception is administered. Under the When the exception is thrown label is a series of radio buttons that manage how the debugger behaves in that case:

- Break into the debugger – causes the debugger to break at the precise point that threw the exception even if the source code provides a `Try/Catch` for handling the specific exception.
- Continue – this is the default setting and means that the Visual Studio .NET debugger will not intervene and therefore the exception handling proceeds without debugger intervention.
- Use parent setting – causes the exception to use the behavior associated with the next level up in the exception hierarchy. For the previously displayed Exceptions window, the exceptions displayed are root exception categories (C++ Exceptions, Common Language Runtime Exceptions, etc.) and hence have no parents.

The unhandled exceptions in the Exceptions window are coordinated using the radio buttons displayed under the If the exception is not handled label. The default behavior for an unhandled exception is for the debugger to break at the precise location in the code where the exception took place. It is possible instead to continue execution. Remember that an unhandled exception may cause a program to terminate. It is also possible to defer an unhandled exception's behavior to be that of the exception's parent.

## Exception Hierarchy

How an exception behaves under the debugger typically defaults to the same behavior as that exception's parent. The term parent refers to categories of exceptions as specified by the Exceptions window. The root parent of each .NET exception is the Common Language Runtime Exceptions category. Actually, the Exceptions window does not only show .NET exceptions, it also shows:

- Win32 Exceptions – these are encountered only in unmanaged applications
- Native Run-Time Checks – this is a category of exception associated with the integrity checks run on managed applications
- C++ Exceptions – a variety of exceptions for unmanaged VC++ .NET code

Beneath the Exception window's Common Language Runtime Exceptions category is a list of all namespaces within the .NET object hierarchy that contain exceptions. Beneath this level in the tree is a list of each exception type within a namespace. From an exception management standpoint, it is therefore possible to manage Common Language Runtime Exceptions at the:

- Category Level – dictate exception behavior for all Common Language Runtime exceptions
- Namespace Level – dictate exception behavior for all exception types within a particular namespace
- Exception Type Level – dictate exception behavior for a specific exception type or specific exception types

This list of namespaces found under the Common Language Runtime Exceptions category is as follows and affords Visual Studio .NET a means by which to manage exceptions under the broad categorization of all exceptions within a specific namespace:

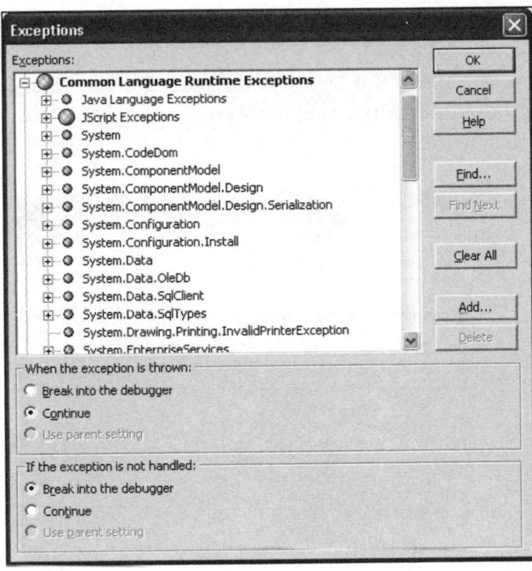


Clicking on the plus character next to the System namespace displays all the exceptions contained within the System namespace. One namespace displayed within the Exceptions window only contains a lone exception. The System.Drawing.Printing namespace's only exception is InvalidPrinterException. For this reason the specific exception is displayed underneath the Common Language Runtime Exceptions category rather than the namespace itself.

It is possible to manage an exception's behavior within Visual Studio .NET at the exception type level rather than under the broadly defined Exceptions window categories or at namespace level. For example the `System.IO.FileNotFoundException` exception could behave one way (break even when the exception is thrown) when an application is being debugged while the exception `System.IO.EndOfStreamException` could be managed a different way entirely (let the application's `Try/Catch` handle the exception without debugger intervention).

To understand why per-exception management is important consider the System namespace categorization. There are approximately fifty different exception types within this namespace. The exception types exposed by the `System` namespace include `AppDomainUnloadedException`, `ApplicationException`, and `ArgumentException` categories. The previous three exceptions are the first three exception types that fall under the System namespace category. Each of the previous three exceptions has no real function relationship. This diversity in functionality begs for exception management at the per-exception level rather than at the per-namespace level. For these three exception types, the System namespace might be too general a categorization and hence not provide the granularity necessary to track down a bug that manifests itself via a particular exception.

# Specific Exception Management

By default, each exception under the Common Language Runtime Exceptions category continues execution when an exception is thrown. Take the `DllNotFoundException` exception of the `System` namespace:

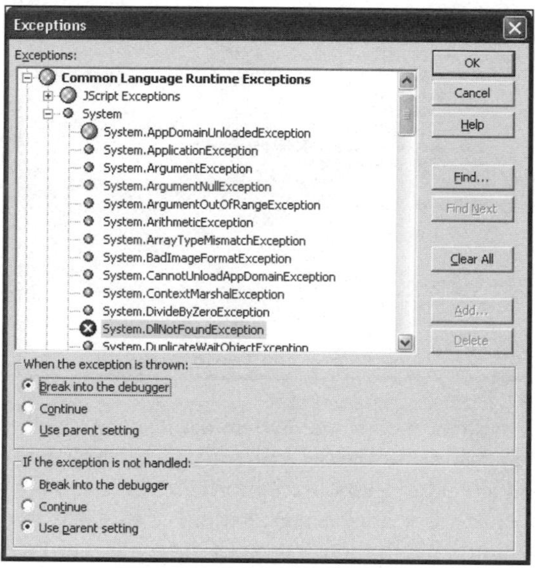


The previous screenshot shows how different types of exceptions within the Common Language Runtime Exceptions | System namespace hierarchy behave. Astute readers may have noticed that the exception level with in the exception hierarchy has one of several different styles of balls in front of it. These balls (big ball, little ball, and red ball containing an X) signify how the exception behaves if it is handled by the application:

- Little ball – the debugger uses the settings associated with the parent categorization when determining how to deal with a handled exception.
- Big Ball – shows that not all settings for that node are inherited from a parent.
- Big Red Ball containing X – specifies that the exception will break into the debugger when the exception in thrown.
- Small Red Ball contain X – This is for exceptions that inherit the behavior of the previous option.

## A Case for Managing Exceptions

After exploring all the intricacies of exception management within Visual Studio .NET it is advantageous to present an example rationalizing why the behavior of exceptions within the debugger should be modified (from the console application WXExceptions):

```
Imports System.IO

Module WXExceptions

  Sub WhereItHappens(fName As String, xmlExtension As Boolean)
    Dim xmlExtension As String = ".xmr"
    Dim normalExtension As String = ".txt"
    If xmlExtension
      File.Open(fName & xmlExtension, FileMode.Open)
    Else
      File.Open(fName & normalExtension, FileMode.Open)
    EndIf

  End Sub

  Sub WhyWeShouldBreak()
    Try
      WhereItHappens("NonExistantFile", True)
    Catch ex As Exception
      Console.Error.WriteLine(ex.GetType())
      Console.Error.WriteLine(ex.Message)
    End Try
  End Sub

  Sub Main()
    WhyWeShouldBreak()
    Console.Read() ' Keep Console window open
  End Sub
End Module
```

In this code snippet an exception thrown within the `WhereItHappens()` method, assuming that `NonExistantFile.xmr` is non existent. The exception is of type `FileNotFoundException`. The default behavior of Visual Studio .NET when debugging this application is to Continue (do not intervene) since the source code handles the exception. This amounts to the exception's `Message` property being written to `Console.Error()`. The exception is caught gracefully in the `WhyWeShouldBreak()` method, which begs the question, why should we break execution in the debugger when the exception is raised, especially given that the exception is handled?

When the `FileNotFoundException` is thrown the `WhereItHappens()` method contains variables that may provide clues as to why the exception is thrown (`xmlExtension` and its crony `normalExtension`). Practically speaking, the data members and variables local to the location where an exception is raised are likely related to the reason why the exception was raised. In the above example you would quickly spot that `fileExtension` is set "`.xmr`" when presumably "`.xml`" is a more likely value.

In order to cause debugger execution to break for `FileNotFoundException` exceptions as in the previous code snippet, take the following steps:

- From the Exceptions windows expand the exception hierarchy until the FileNotFoundException class is shown (Common Language Runtime Exceptions | System.IO). The hierarchy expanded is as follows:

```
Common Language Runtime Exceptions
  System.IO
    FileNotFoundException
```

- From the When the exception is thrown group box in the Exceptions window, select the Break into the debugger radio button.

Now when the WXExceptions application is run within Visual Studio .NET, the debugger now reacts; you might say, Visual Studio .NET now handles the exception. This comes in the form of the following dialog:

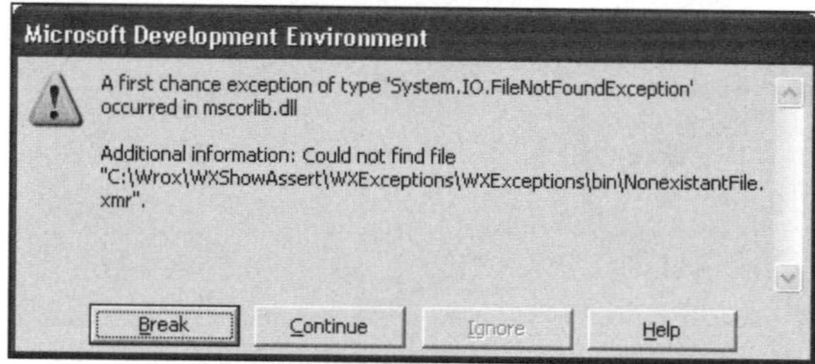


Hitting the Continue button ignores the exception and lets the application handle the exception normally. The Break button causes the application to break at the point that threw the exception allowing you to view the variables local to the `WhereItHappens()` method.

## Unmanaged Exceptions

Exceptions are not a feature inherent to only .NET applications. Legacy C++ applications also dealt with exceptions and since Visual Studio .NET supports unmanaged development, VB.NET developers should be cognizant of what styles of exceptions arise from unmanaged applications. There is a reasonable probability that a VB.NET application calling an unmanaged application may encounter an exception that began life as an unmanaged exception. For example if a VB.NET application calls a legacy COM DLL the COM DLL could (if written poorly) generate an exception because it attempted to divide by zero.

### Win32 Exceptions

The Win32 Exceptions category within the Exceptions window is as follows:

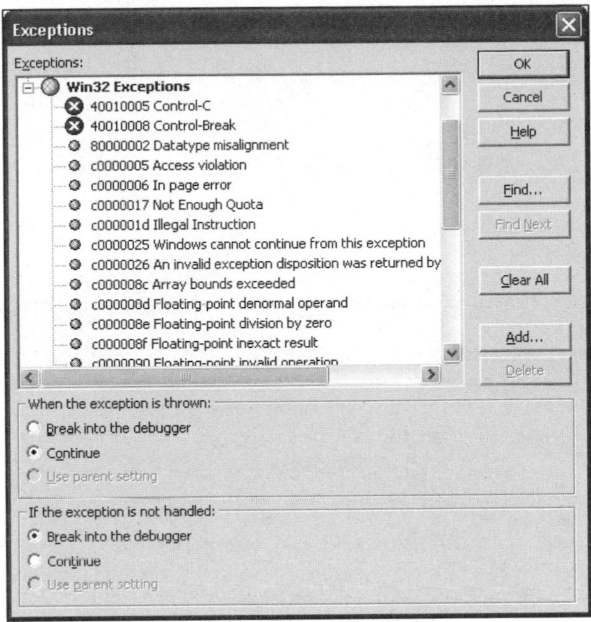


The exceptions handled under the Win32 Exceptions category apply to native (unmanaged) applications and only native applications. The .NET Framework handles such exceptions under the circumstance and converts them into managed exceptions. For example, a Win32 native application might encounter 0xC0000094 Integer division by zero exception while a managed application would encounter the managed variant from the `System` namespace, namely the `System.OverflowException` exception.

Win32 exceptions are raised when a native application encounters a problem that causes a system exception (invalid memory address accessed, illegal instruction, etc.). Only unmanaged C++ applications directly handle this category of exceptions using the `__try/__except` construct with respect to the WXAssemblyLanguage C++, console application.

A VB.NET executable can encounter (indirectly) a Win32-style of exception. This circumstance takes place when a VB.NET application (such as the WXExceptionsV1 console application) calls an unmanaged C++ application (such as the COM server WXRaiseUnamanged) and said COM server raises a Win32 exception. The methods exposed by COM objects should return errors via the method's return value so a raised exception is not indicative of technically proper behavior. The `WXWin32Exception` C++ method raises a Win32 exception as follows by dividing an integer variable by zero (`j / k` where `k=0`):

```
STDMETHODIMP CWXTakeExceptionToSomething::WXWin32Exception(void)
{
    int i, j = 5, k = 0;
```

```
        i = j / k;

        return S_OK;
    }
```

An example of VB.NET code that calls the `WXWin32Exception` method is as follows:

```
    Try
        Dim unmanagedFun As _
            WXRaiseUnmanaged.IWXTakeExceptionToSomething = _
                New WXRaiseUnmanaged.CWXTakeExceptionToSomethingClass()

        unmanagedFun.WXWin32Exception()
    Catch ex4 As Exception
        Console.WriteLine("Type: {0}, Message: {1}", _
                          ex4.GetType(), _
                          ex4.Message)
    End Try
```

The VB.NET code above can call the C++ COM server because a reference was added to the VB.NET project (right-click on References folder, then Add Reference, select COM tab, and choose the WXRaiseUnmanaged COM server). The interoperability DLL that sits between the unmanaged COM server and the managed VB.NET assembly converts the Win32 exception raised into a .NET exception of type, `System.DivideByZeroException`. This exception exposes a `Message` property containing the following text: Attempted to divide by zero.

If a managed application had performed a divide by zero, the Common Language Runtime would have raised a `System.OverflowException` exception. The `System` namespace's `DivideByZeroException` only shows up when a managed application calls unmanaged code and the unmanaged code performs a divide by zero.

## C++ Exceptions

Different types of C++ objects generate different types of exceptions. .NET developers (VB.NET or otherwise) need not be concerned with C++ exceptions unless they are working in a mixed environment (managed VB.NET and unmanaged C++). Unmanaged C++ developers can use the C++ Exceptions category of exception to handle a variety of propriety C++ exception subordinate categories including: `std:exception` (standard C++ exception), `_com_error` (one style of COM error), or `CException` (Microsoft Foundation Class exception).

It is possible for a VB.NET application to encounter a C++ exception. Consider a case where a VB.NET executable (such as the WXExceptionsV1 console application) calls a C++ COM object (such as the `WXRaiseUnmanaged` COM DLL) and the COM object inadvertently raises a C++ exception. We say inadvertently because COM objects are not supposed to throw exceptions. The `WXCPlusPlusException` C++ method raises a C++ exception as follows by specifying `throw 123`:

```
STDMETHODIMP CWXTakeExceptionToSomething::WXCPlusPlusException(void)
{
    throw 123; // this is just a C++ exception
    return S_OK;
}
```

Within a VB.NET application, the `WXCPlusPlusException` C++ method can be called as follows:

```
Try
    Dim unmanagedFun As _
        WXRaiseUnmanaged.IWXTakeExceptionToSomething = _
            New WXRaiseUnmanaged.CWXTakeExceptionToSomethingClass()

    unmanagedFun.WXCPlusPlusException()
Catch ex3 As Exception
    Console.WriteLine("Type: {0}, Message: {1}", _
                      ex3.GetType(), _
                      ex3.Message)
End Try
```

The previous bit of code catches a managed exception via VB.NET's `Try/Catch` construct. The interoperability bridge that resides between the C++ COM Server and the VB.NET managed application translates the C++ exception into an exception of type `System.Runtime.InteropServices.SEHException`. The `Message` property associated with the `ex3` exception is the rather cryptic, External component has thrown an exception. For those curious as to what the `SEHException` exception refers to, Structure Exception Handling (SEH) is the name given to underlying exception handling implemented by Win32.

## Native Run-Time Checks

The Native Run-Time Checks are exceptions associated with natively developed Visual C++ 7.0 code. This useful feature is new to Visual Studio .NET. The reason for Native Run-Time Checks is because natively developed C++ code can get corrupted within the application and the application had no way to identify or report the problem. For example in an unmanaged C++ application, an application could overwrite crucial data or even overwrite the code associated with its program.

The Native Run-Time Checks category of exception allows unmanaged C++ applications to detect (via exceptions getting thrown) stack pointer corruption, casts causing data loss, stack memory corruption, or un-initialized variables. None of the aforementioned exceptions apply to the development of managed code, but they could be encountered in a mixed (managed and unmanaged code) development environment.

# Advanced Exception Management

Visual Studio .NET's Exceptions window contains a column of buttons that facilitate some advanced exception management tricks. The Find and Find Next button allow the exception hierarchy to be searched for exceptions matching a string. For example if you click on the Find button and enter `FileNot` the exception hierarchy will open up to:

```
Commmon Language Runtime Exceptions
  System.IO
    FileNotFoundException
```

The Find and Find Next buttons save an MSDN lookup when you are not sure the namespace a particular exception is found in.

## Managing User-defined Exceptions

The ability to dictate if the debugger breaks at or ignores a genre of exceptions is rather useful debugging functionality. This functionality is also available to user-defined exceptions such as the following exception found in the WXExceptions console application:

```
Class DentalRecordNotFoundException
  Inherits Exception
  Public Sub New(ByVal s As String)
      MyBase.New("No Dental Records were found" & s)
  End Sub
End Class
```

The Exceptions window contains an Add button. The type of exception added (C++ exception, Common Language Runtime, etc.) depends on the category highlighted in the Exceptions window at the time the Add button is clicked.

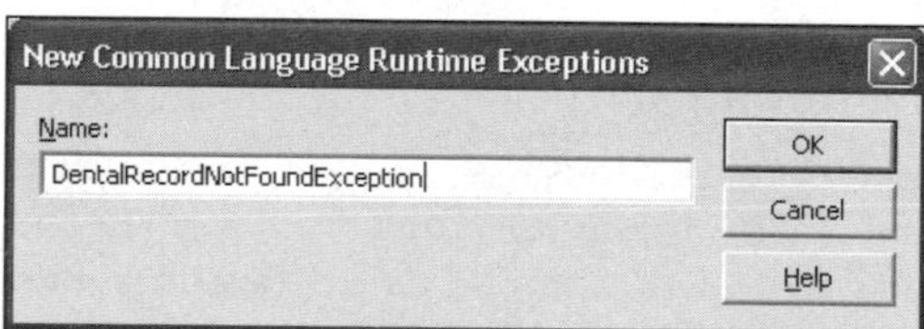


Clicking on OK in the previous screenshot adds the `DentalRecordNotFoundException` class to the list of exceptions displayed in the Exceptions window (under the Common Language Runtime Exceptions category). This means that henceforth you can mange the `DentalRecordNotFoundException` in the same manner as every other exception (break when thrown, continue even if not handled, etc.).

The dialog displayed when Add is clicked does not validate the name entered, so if an incorrectly spelled name is entered the exception will do nothing when managed by Visual Studio .NET. There is no warning given and no compilation error is generated. The names of exceptions are not case-sensitive so `ThisIsAnException` is equivalent to `THISISANEXCEPTION`.

The Clear All button on the Exceptions window clears all user-defined exceptions. There is also a Delete button on the Exceptions window to individually delete user-defined exceptions.

> **The class name `DentalRecordNotFoundException` deliberately contained the suffix, `Exception`. Each class derived from the `Exception` base class in the .NET Framework contains the `Exception` suffix. So, it seems sensible to also use the suffix `Exception`, in all user-defined exception classes. Remember, standardization can help reduce bugs because developers more readily recognize the class's purpose.**

## The Exception Class

Thus far, all the talk has been about how to manage exceptions (classes derived from the `Exception` class) and no mention has been made of the `Exception` class itself. In the Microsoft programming world, exceptions first appeared in the early 1990s as part of C++. The problem with C++ exceptions is that once they are thrown there is no way to find out which line of code threw the exception. Simply knowing "file not found" does not do a great deal of good from a debugging standpoint if there are ten thousand locations at which files are opened and can hence be "not found".

The `Exception` base class used by all managed exceptions remedies the aforementioned shortcoming with the following properties:

- `Source` – this property of type `String` gets and sets the location that threw the exception. When `Source` is not explicitly set, it defaults to the name of the assembly that threw the exception.
- `StackTrace` – this property of type `String` returns the stack trace corresponding to the where the exception was raised. This stack trace can show which point within the .NET Framework threw a particular exception.

In order to demonstrate how the `StackTrace` property exposes aspects internal to the .NET Framework or the internals of non-debug assemblies consider the following stack trace generated when from our earlier WXExceptions example:

```
at System.IO.__Error.WinIOError(Int32 errorCode, String str)
at System.IO.FileStream..ctor(String path, FileMode mode, FileAccess access, FileShare share,
Int32 bufferSize, Boolean useAsync, String msgPath, Boolean bFromProxy)
at System.IO.FileStream..ctor(String path, FileMode mode, FileAccess access, FileShare share)
at System.IO.File.Open(String path, FileMode mode, FileAccess access, FileShare share)
at System.IO.File.Open(String path, FileMode mode)
```

```
at WXExceptions.WXExceptions.WhereItHappens(String fName, Boolean extension) in
C:\Wrox\WXShowAssert\WXExceptions\WXExceptions\WXExceptions.vb:line 9
at WXExceptions.WXExceptions.WhyWeShouldBreak() in
C:\Wrox\WXShowAssert\WXExceptions\WXExceptions\WXExceptions.vb:line 17
```

This stack trace shows the methods called within our application but it also shows the methods within the `System.IO` namespace courtesy of the metadata associated with an assembly. Stored within an assembly's metadata is a description of every method and every parameter. The information (displayed in the stack trace) clearly aids in debugging.

For the final two methods in the stack trace, the file name and line number are also provided. This is because the assembly in which they reside contains debug information. The true power of `StackTrace` comes in code that contains debug information. For example, it is quite clear which method called what in the WXExceptions application (WXExceptions.vb:line 17 called WXExceptions.vb:line 9, etc). This information is quite a boon when it comes to reverse engineering the location that threw an exception and subsequently why, especially in more complex applications.

## InnerException

The `Exception` class contains the `InnerException` property. This property is of type `Exception` and the property corresponds to the exception that caused the current exception. To understand this, consider an application used by computer novices. The underlying database could generate an extremely technical error that is important to debugging the application. This technical database error would just cause extreme FUD (Fear, Uncertainty, and Doubt) in the novice users. The solution is to have an application that generates a complex error, such the class `WXComplexDBException`, from the WXException project:

```
Class WXComplexDBException
    Inherits Exception

    Public Sub New()
        MyBase.New("Invalid status group setting or " & _
                   "Incorrect Active Directy configuration " & _
                   "or improper workgroup data sharing")
    End Sub
End Class


Public Class WXReadFromDB
    Public Sub WXGetSomeData()
        Throw New WXComplexDBException()
    End Sub
End Class
```

Catch the complicated exception (that will become the inner exception):

```
Try
Catch innerException As WXComplexDBException
End Try
```

Create a gentle exception appropriate for a novice user. When creating the gentle exception make sure to pass the complex exception as a parameter to the gentle exception's constructor:

```
Public Sub WXInsureWeAreGentle()
    Try
        WXGetSomeData()
    Catch innerException As WXComplexDBException
        Dim gentleException As New Exception( _
                "Please contact your database administator", _
                innerException)
    End Try
End Sub
```

When the gentle error is ultimately caught, display its message to the end user (say to `Console.WriteLine`) and display the complicated message where an administrator can retrieve it (`Console.Error.WriteLine`):

```
Public Sub WXGentleToEndUser()
    Try
        WXInsureWeAreGentle()
    Catch ex As Exception
        Console.WriteLine(ex.Message)
        If Not ex.InnerException Is Nothing Then
            Console.Error.WriteLine(ex.InnerException.Message)
        End If
    End Try
End Sub
```

The `InnerException` property is not only usable to differentiate between complex and gentle exceptions. The `InnerException` property just adds more information to an exception (the `InnerException` exception) without losing any of its original information. For example, the code snippet below adds information regarding the precise program state to the first exception raised as follows:

```
Public Sub WXAsDetailedAsPossible()
    Dim startTime As DateTime = DateTime.Now

    Try
        ' Assume exception raised here
    Catch innerException As WXComplexDBException
        ' First parameter is the type of report generated
        ' Second parameter is what time we started generating the
        '  report
```

```
            ' Third parameter is exception that stopped report generation
            Dim detailedException As _
                New WXSpecificException( _
                        "Stock Options Granted Report", _
                        startTime, _
                        innerException)
            Throw detailedException
        End Try

    End Sub
```

Inner exceptions chain (`ex.Innerexception.InnerException.InnerException`) so it is possible to have two, three, or more levels of nesting. Then again, that might be overkill.

Good debugging requires clear error messages and by saving as much information as possible with respect to the error. This snippet demonstrates both of these debugging principles.

### Practical Debugging and InnerException

To fully understand the `InnerException` property of the `Exception` class, consider a three-tier application (data tier, business logic tier, and presentation tier). Consider a case where the data tier throws an exception of type, `SqlException` generated by the managed ADO.NET provider for SQL Server. In the following example the `SqlException` exception is raised when `conn.Open()` is invoked since the underlying SQL database (`MockCatalog`) does not exist on the local host:

```
    Sub MockDBTier()
        Dim conn As New System.Data.SqlClient.SqlConnection( _
                "Initial Catalog=MockCatalog;Data Source=localhost;")

        conn.Open() ' causes an exception to be raised
        ' access SQL Server here
        conn.Close()
    End Sub
```

The business tier calls the data tier via `MockDBTier` handles, the `SQLException`, saving it off as an inner exception and then throws an exception, understandable to the presentation tier (such as the `WXNoAuctionCatalogAvailableException` exception which indicates the online auction infrastructure needed by the client is not available):

```
    Sub MockBusinessTier()
        Try
            MockDBTier()
        Catch exDB As System.Data.SqlClient.SqlException
            Throw New WXNoAuctionCatalogAvailableException ( _
                        "No auction catalog available", exDB)
        End Try
    End Sub
```

At the presentation tier the `WXNoAuctionCatalogAvailableException` exception could be saved off as an inner exception and an exception containing a message understandable to the client could be raised:

```
Sub MockPresentationTier()
    Try
        MockDBTier()
    Catch exBusObj As WXNoAuctionCatalogAvailableException
        Throw New WXNoItemException ( _
             "Error accessing 'Tickle Me Rattlesnake' doll", _
             exBusObj)
    End Try
End Sub
```

In the previous code snippet, `WXNoItemException` contains an inner exception of type `WXNoAuctionCatalogAvailableException`. The exception of type `WXNoAuctionCatalogAvailableException` already had its `InnerException` property set to an instance of type `SQLException`. The `WXNoItemException` exception contains the `SQLException` exception as its inner, inner exception:

**Figure 1**

What is most important is that the end user receives a message they fully comprehend, namely that the quite popular 'Tickle Me Rattlesnake' doll is not available for purchase. This message is provided by the `Exception` base class's `Message` property. The developer debugging the problems has a veritable arsenal of information all provided via the chained inner exceptions.

A developer reverse engineering the problem knows the location:

- In the data tier where the original error took place and what the specific error is:

```
Try
Catch ex As WXNoItemException
  Dim whereDBErrorTookPlace As String

  whereDBErrorTookPlace = _
    ex.InnerException.InnerException.StackTrace
End Try
```

- In the business logic tier where the data tier error was caught and a new/different error was raised:

```
Try
Catch ex As WXNoItemException
  Dim whereBusinessErrorTookPlace As String

  whereBusinessErrorTookPlace = ex.InnerException.StackTrace
End Try
```

- In the presentation tier where the business logic tier error was caught and a new/different error was raised:

```
Try
Catch ex As WXNoItemException
  Dim wherePresentationErrorTookPlace As String

  wherePresentationErrorTookPlace = ex.StackTrace
End Try
```

The `ShowAllTiers()` method demonstrates an application traversing each level of inner exception thereby completely reverse engineering the problem that took place:

```
Sub ShowAllTiers()
  Try
    MockPresentationTier()
  Catch exDataTier As Exception
    Dim exTraverse As Exception = exDataTier
    Dim level As Integer = 0

    Do
      Console.WriteLine("Exception Level {0}: {1}", _
                        level, _
                        exTraverse.StackTrace)
      exTraverse = exTraverse.InnerException
      level += 1
    Loop While Not exTraverse Is Nothing
  End Try
End Sub
```

The beauty of the `InnerException` property (as demonstrated by the previous code snippet) is that there is no loss of exception information when moving between tiers and therefore each granule of debugging information is available to the debugger even after reaching the presentation tier.

# Debugging Threads

Using Visual Studio .NET's Threads window it is possible to determine the threads associated with an application and manage the threads (start, suspend, resume, and select as thread actively debugged). The mechanism used to display the Threads windows is Visual Studio .NET's Debug menu, Windows menu item, Threads sub-menu item. An example of the Threads window in action is as follows:

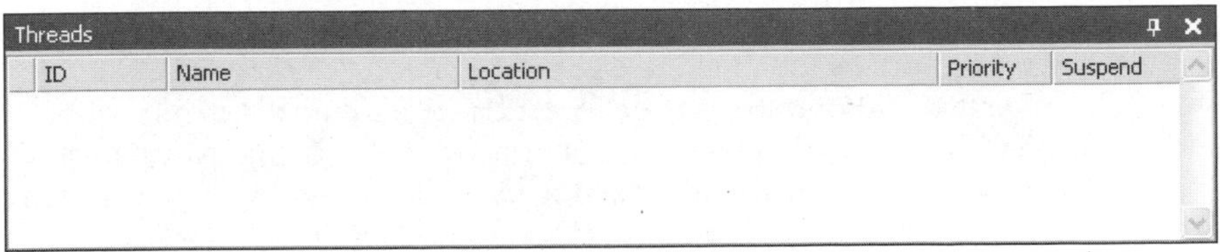


We'll examine the WXThread application in the next section. For the present, the only important point is that it spawns multiple threads.

In the previous Threads window screenshot, where are the threads associated with the application just described? There is a caveat with respect to using the Threads window. This caveat is that at least one thread must be stopped in order for the Threads windows display information with regards to an application's threads and for Visual Studio .NET to allow the management of threads. Stopping is a matter of a breakpoint or initially single stepping or Debug | Break All. An example of the Threads windows visible when the application is stopped in the `WXThreadSwitch` class's `WXThreadRunner()` method is as follows:

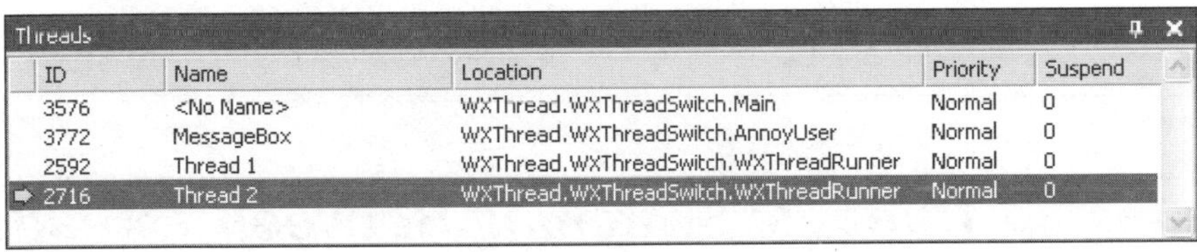
Threads

| ID | Name | Location | Priority | Suspend |
|---|---|---|---|---|
| 3576 | <No Name> | WXThread.WXThreadSwitch.Main | Normal | 0 |
| 3772 | MessageBox | WXThread.WXThreadSwitch.AnnoyUser | Normal | 0 |
| 2592 | Thread 1 | WXThread.WXThreadSwitch.WXThreadRunner | Normal | 0 |
| 2716 | Thread 2 | WXThread.WXThreadSwitch.WXThreadRunner | Normal | 0 |

The arrow (yellow on screen) to the left of thread 2716 indicates the currently active thread. To understand the currently active thread, consider the Call Stack window. The call stack displayed in the Call Stack windows corresponds to the currently active thread just as the location data members displayed in the Locals windows correspond to the currently active thread.

The information displayed in the Threads window pertaining to each thread is as follows:

- ID – this is a unique integer value representing a specific thread instance on a particular machine.
- Name – a name can be associated with a thread using the `Thread` class's `Name` property. This name can be handy when determining what a thread's purpose is, which can clearly aid in debugging a multi-threaded application. As a matter of principle, threads created explicitly by an application should give themselves descriptive names ("Background logging", "Network I/O Handlers", "File Download", or "Monitoring Bank Account").
- Location – the name of the assembly, class, and method that correspond to a thread's entry point.

- Priority – scheduling priority of the thread. The value corresponds to the range of priorities found in the `System.Thread.ThreadPriority` enumeration (`AboveNormal`, `BelowNormal`, `Highest`, `Lowest`, and `Normal`). On a single processor only one thread is being executed at any one time; the system scheduler simulates multitasking by rapidly switching between threads. A higher priority thread get more processor time (if it needs it) than a lower priority thread.
- Suspend – when the value of Suspend is zero, the thread is running (not suspended). The value of the Suspend column corresponds to a count. This count reflects the number of times Win32's `SuspendThread` function has been executed. Each time Win32's `ResumeThread` is called, the Suspend count is decremented until it reaches zero (the case where a thread resumes execution).

The Threads window is interactive, with a right-click on a thread yielding a context menu. The context menu does afford certain mundane niceties such as a Copy menu item. This menu item copies the information associated with all selected threads (ID, Name, Location, etc.) to the clipboard, which is handy for taking a snapshot of the threads running. Moving such snapshots into an editor such as Notepad provides a handy history of threading behavior within an application. Other menu items (Switch To Thread, Freeze, Thaw) provide direct management of running threads.

## Managing Threads: Switching Between Threads

In a multithreaded application with a variety of threads executing simultaneously debugging can be a challenge. On a single CPU machine, only a lone thread at a time truly executes. On a multi-CPU machine, more than one thread can actually execute at the same time. The later case is more likely to demonstrate any issues with locking contention for resources (deadlocks, resources not locked, and performance slowdowns).

To demonstrate the behavior of a multithreaded application and using Visual Studio .NET to switch between threads, consider the following code snippet from WXThread:

```
Imports System.Threading
Imports System.Diagnostics
Imports Microsoft.VisualBasic

Class WXThreadSwitch

  Shared Sub Main()
    Dim th, th2 As Thread
    Dim Count As Integer
    th = New Thread(AddressOf AnnoyUser)
    th.Name = "MessageBox"
    th.Start()
```

```
      For count = 1 to 2
        th2 = New Thread(AddressOf WXThreadRunner)
        th2.Name = "Trace"
        th2.Start()
      Next
      Console.In.ReadLine()
      Return
    End Sub
```

The code snippet above is preambled by `Imports System.Threading` so it can readily use the `Thread` class. The basic idea of the previous code is to spawn three threads each executing the `WXThreadRunner()` method and respectively named: `"Thread 1"`, `"Thread 2"`, and `"Thread 3"`. At this point, the `Main` method waits until the user enters text that will cause the application to terminate since the path of execution leaves the `Main` method.

The `WXThreadRunner()` and `AnnoyUser()` methods are as follows:

```
  Shared Sub WXThreadRunner()
    Dim cycleCount As Integer

    For cycleCount = 1 To Integer.MaxValue
      Debug.WriteLine(Thread.CurrentThread.Name)
      Thread.Sleep(10)
    Next
  End Sub

    Shared Sub AnnoyUser()
      Dim cycleCount As Integer
      For cycleCount = 1 To Integer.MaxValue
        MsgBox("The current count is " & cycleCount)
        Thread.Sleep(10)
      Next
    End Sub
  End Class
```

The `WXThreadRunner` method simply writes the thread's name to the debugger's Output window (`Debug.WriteLine(Thread.CurrentThread.Name)`) and subsequently the thread sleeps for ten milliseconds (`Thread.Sleep(10)`). The reason the threads sleep for ten milliseconds is because if they did not surrender execution, they would suck up all of the CPU time on the machine and Windows would become unresponsive. The `Debug.WriteLine()` method that by default writes to the Output windows is found in the `System.Diagnostics` namespace, which is covered further in Chapter 4. The `AnnoyUser()` method simply displays a message box displaying the current count.

To demonstrate switching between threads, a breakpoint is placed in the previous code at the `Debug.WriteLine()` method before the `WXThread` application is run. Single stepping (Debug | Single Step) through the application reveals the following output being written to the Output window:

```
Thread 1
Thread 2
Thread 2
Thread 1
```

Each time the application is single stepped only a single thread executes. With each single step the application can change threads since other threads must be afforded a chance to run. Visual Studio .NET is automatically changing the currently active thread (the one specified by the yellow arrow in the Threads window).

From the Threads window's context menu, the Switch To Thread menu item provides a certain amount of control of this process. Clicking on the menu item it is possible to switch which thread is the currently active thread. Single stepping at this stage of the game initially starts in the currently active thread but Visual Studio .NET may (likely) change to another active thread. An alternative approach to switch the active thread that does not involve the context menu is to simply double-click on a thread within the Threads window. This makes the double-clicked-on thread the currently active thread.

Using either form of Switch To Thread is helpful for a few instructions but inevitably Visual Studio .NET will shift execution by specifying a new and different currently active thread. If only there was a way to disable (not terminate) a thread thus reducing the number of threads that could be considered as the currently active thread (less jumping between threads or none if all but one thread is 'frozen' with respect to execution).

## Managing Threads: Freezing and Thawing

The way to keep threads from becoming the currently active thread is to freeze them via the Threads window context menu's Freeze menu item. Highlight a thread or threads, bring up the context menu, click on Freeze, and the selected thread or threads are frozen. Within the Threads window, a frozen thread is so indicated by two vertical, blue bars placed to the left of the thread's row in the window. The Suspend column associated with the thread is also incremented by one. A currently running thread (although not necessarily the active thread) has a Suspend count value of zero so when such a thread is frozen its suspend value becomes one.

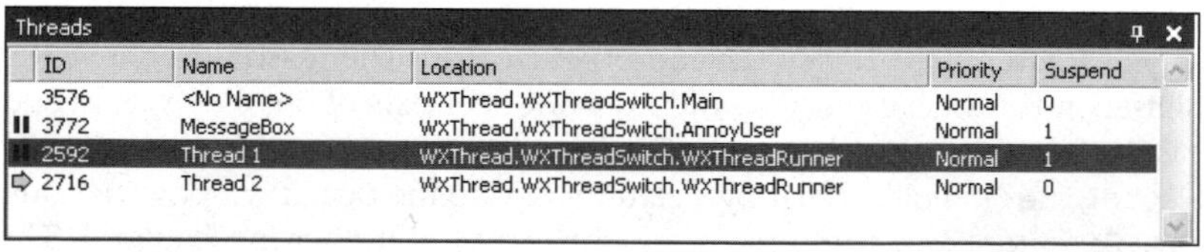

Threads

| ID | Name | Location | Priority | Suspend |
|---|---|---|---|---|
| 3576 | <No Name> | WXThread.WXThreadSwitch.Main | Normal | 0 |
| 3772 | MessageBox | WXThread.WXThreadSwitch.AnnoyUser | Normal | 1 |
| 2592 | Thread 1 | WXThread.WXThreadSwitch.WXThreadRunner | Normal | 1 |
| 2716 | Thread 2 | WXThread.WXThreadSwitch.WXThreadRunner | Normal | 0 |

In the screenshot above the main thread (ID=3576) and one other (ID=2716) are active, while the two other threads (ID=3772, 2592) are suspended. For frozen threads, the context menu no longer contains a Freeze entry; instead, it contains a Thaw menu item that will decrement the frozen thread's Suspend count by one. A thread with a Suspend count of one will have this value changed to zero and thus this defrosted thread is now a viable thread to run as part of the debugging process.

It goes without saying that freezing is a great way to debug extremely complex multi-threaded applications. Imagine an application developed for a small brokerage that runs a mutual fund (a couple of billion in assets). The software in question place orders, downloads real-time stock market data, and generates events based on that data. While debugging the order entry system, it makes sense to freeze (via Thread window Freeze) the live data feed and subsequently the alerts it generates. It would be helpful to name the threads (via the `Thread.Name` property) say, Order Entry, Data Feed, and Alert Meister.

## *Threading and the .NET Infrastructure*

When working with threads it is important to understand the architecture of .NET. For example in an application with a main thread and a spawned thread, there very likely could have been three threads displayed in the Threads window. Someone new to .NET might find the third thread to be disconcerting; don't worry it is most likely garbage collection running in a separate thread. Well-informed .NET developers know this third thread exists for applications launched in the console runtime host, which runs as a workstation. When .NET is running as a workstation, then garbage collection happens on a separate thread. The idea here is to slightly diminish garbage collection by placing it in a separate thread while at the same time ensuring that the user's windows function unimpeded by garbage collection.

For the Internet Explorer runtime host, garbage collection is also performed in a separate thread. When debugging a Window Forms control hosted in Internet Explorer, there could likely be an extra, managed, thread handling garbage collection. The ASP.NET runtime host however, runs as a server and therefore, (in order to optimize performance) garbage collection runs in the same threads as the application's code. Debugging an ASP.NET application we will not see an extra thread for garbage collection. If the ASP.NET accesses a database such as SQL Server, however, the ADO.NET managed provider does spawn threads as part of its database access.

# Debugging Processes

Debugging processes is a two-step process (no pun intended). First you need to get the process running, then you need to attach the debugger to the process. You can do so either by running a process directly from the debugger or attaching to an already running process. In Visual Studio .NET (as was mentioned previously) it is actually possible to debug multiple processes simultaneously within a single instance of Visual Studio .NET. The ways in which a process is attached to the debugger are varied but include Tools | Debug Processes and Debug | Process in Visual Studio, via the Windows Task Manager, and methods exposed by classes within the `System.Diagnostics` namespace (`Debug.Assert()`, `Trace.Assert()`, `Debugger.Break()`, `Debugger.Launch()` etc.), which are covered in Chapter 5.

Once you are debugging a process (or processes), a bit of process management is periodically in order. This management includes pausing execution, terminating the executing process, and detaching the debugger from the process. The Visual Studio .NET mechanism that supports this is the Debug | Processes menu item.

## The Role of the Solution

Visual Studio .NET is a development environment and a debugger. When a solution is loaded, Visual Studio .NET is a development environment capable of debugging but it is actually possible for Visual Studio .NET to just be a debugger. When an application is run from within a solution (via the Debug menu's Start, Step Over, or Step Into) it is obviously possible to debug and between debugging sessions build/rebuild the application.

When a process is attached to, rather than started from within, the debugger things get a bit more complicated. For example if no solution is loaded within Visual Studio .NET, there is no Build or Debug menu. Developers used to using Solution Explorer or Class View in conjunction with debugging will not be afforded such luxury. This is because when Tools | Debug Processes is initiated there was no solution loaded. It is possible to attach to a process using Tools | Debug Processes while a solution is loaded; in that case more debugging niceties such as Solution Explorer and Class View are available.

### The Program Debug File

It is possible to attach the debugger to a process even if we do not have the source code loaded, but how does the debugger associate the instructions in a compiled assembly with the relevant source code files. After all, an assembly does not contain its source code or any direct references to it.

To see what actually is in contained in a compiled assembly we'll need a binary editor. In Visual Studio .NET select File | Open | File and navigate to a directory containing a compiled .NET executable. Don't select the Open button though; next to it is a small down arrow, which allows access to the Open With option, which exposes a rather nifty suite of alternative editors:

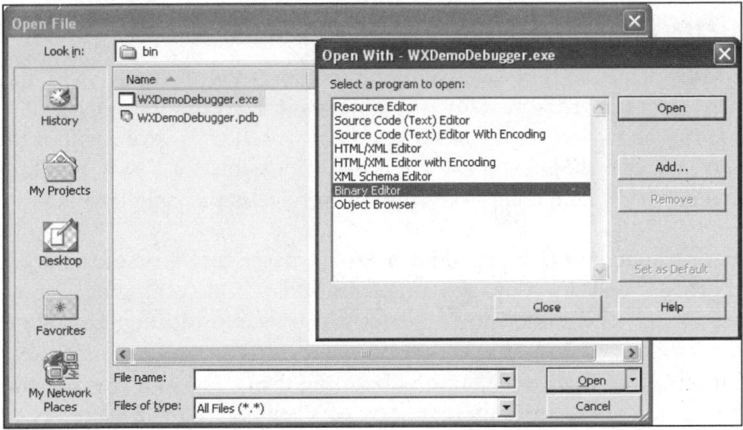


Once you have read through gigabytes of raw database layout in binary (data pages and index pages), you grow to love (and hate) binary editors. Still, such low-level editors are useful for debugging. In this case, the binary editor is displaying the contents of `WXDemoDebugger.exe`. Perusing the file, it should be clear that it contains no source code. If the executable was built as a debug build it will contain a reference to another file generated by Visual Studio .NET (a file with a `*.pdb` extension):

```
00000c30  01 00 00 00 43 3A 5C 56  42 44 65 62 75 67 67 69  ....C:\VBDebuggi
00000c40  6E 67 5C 43 68 61 70 74  65 72 34 5C 57 58 44 65  ng\Chapter5\WXDe
00000c50  6D 6F 44 65 62 75 67 67  65 72 5C 6F 62 6A 5C 44  moDebugger\obj\D
00000c60  65 62 75 67 5C 57 58 44  65 6D 6F 44 65 62 75 67  ebug\WXDemoDebug
00000c70  67 67 65 72 2E 70 64 62  00 00 00 00 00 00 00 00  gger.pdb........
```

The `*.pdb` extension refers to a Program Database File. The program database maps assemblies (executables and dynamically linked libraries) and source code. The `*.pdb` file allows Visual Studio .NET to map `WXDemoDebugger.exe` to its source files. Figure 2 demonstrates how a `*.pdb` serves as a conduit (a debugging database) between assemblies and their source files:

**Figure 2**

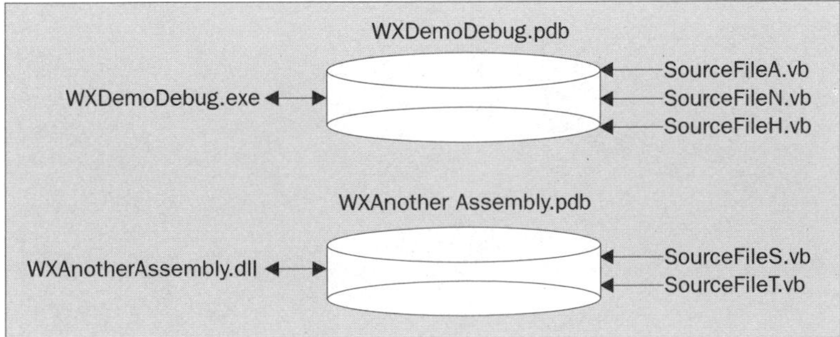

## Attaching to Running Processes

For the purposes of debugging, we may need to attach Visual Studio .NET to a running process. There are many reasons why this is necessary; consider the case of a Windows Service, these run as background tasks and are launched (run) from within the Windows Service Control Manager (SCM). It is not possible for Visual Studio .NET to Debug | Start a service so attaching to a running service is the only option.

In demonstrating attaching to a process via Task Manager, any type of managed or unmanaged process will do. Although a useful approach in debugging Windows services, there is no need to develop a Windows service just to demonstrate it. Instead attaching to a process via Task Manger will be demonstrated using the already discussed WXThread application. Before initiating debugging using Task Manager a critical question should be answered: is there a copy of Visual Studio .NET already running and does this instance of Visual Studio .NET already have the solution associated with the process to be debugged loaded?

Without further ado using Task Manager to debug a process is achieved as follows:

- Run `WXThread.exe` (the compiled version of the application).
- Bring up Task Manager using your favorite approach such as *Ctrl+Alt+Delete* followed by selecting the Task Manager button provided in the dialog displayed..
- With the Windows Task Manager dialog, select the Processes tab.
- Right-click on the process to be debugged and from the context menu displayed selected the Debug menu item as is show in the following screenshot:

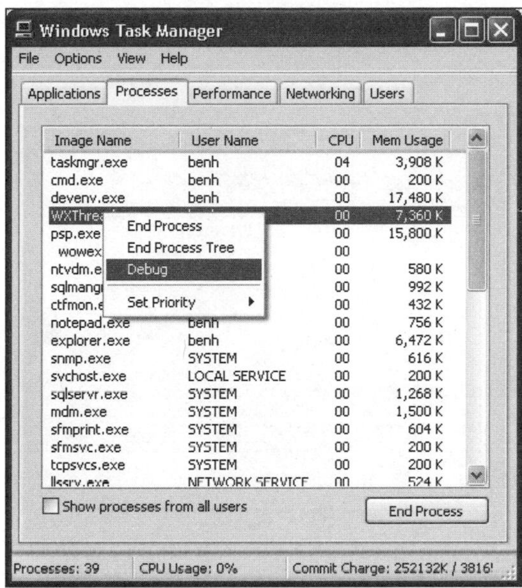


Once the Debug menu item is selected, the following dialog is displayed

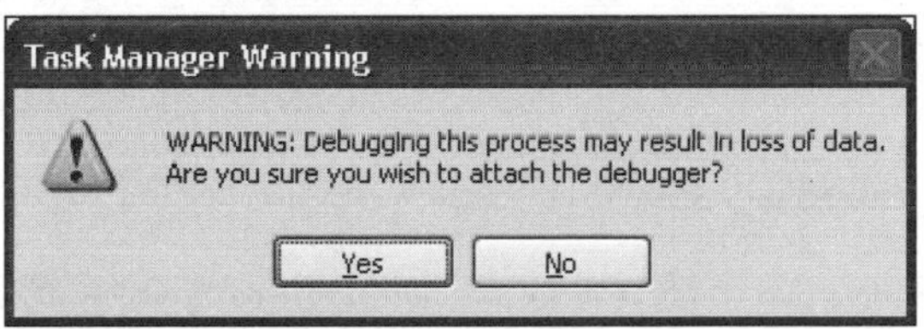


The previous warning has been displayed for years by Microsoft debuggers. To this point, the author has never experienced a "loss of data" but use caution if you are debugging an application performing a critical task (computing the company's Christmas bonuses, running a delicate operation such as chip fabrication, etc.). If you experience a "loss of data", then starting over should be an option because you should not debug in the middle of critical operations anyway.

Click Yes on the previous dialog displays the following Just-In-Time Debugging dialog:

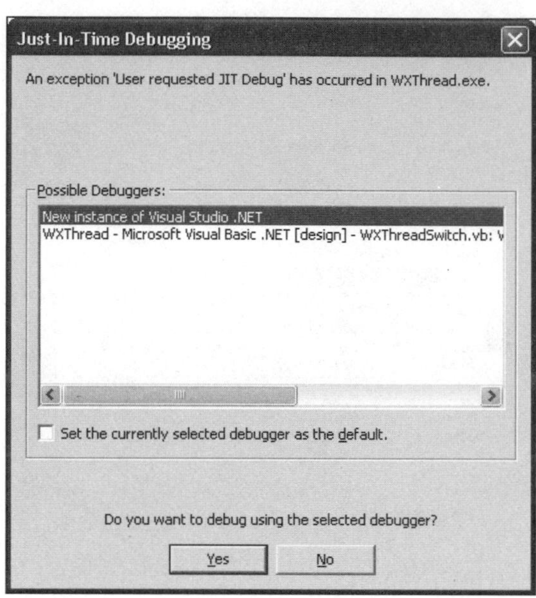


Using this dialog, we can select from the range of debuggers registered with Windows. If you just have Visual Studio .NET installed this will be a new instance in that, you can also attach any currently running instances of Visual Studio.

When you have selected one of the debuggers from the Just-in-Time Debugging dialog, the Attach to Process dialog is displayed:

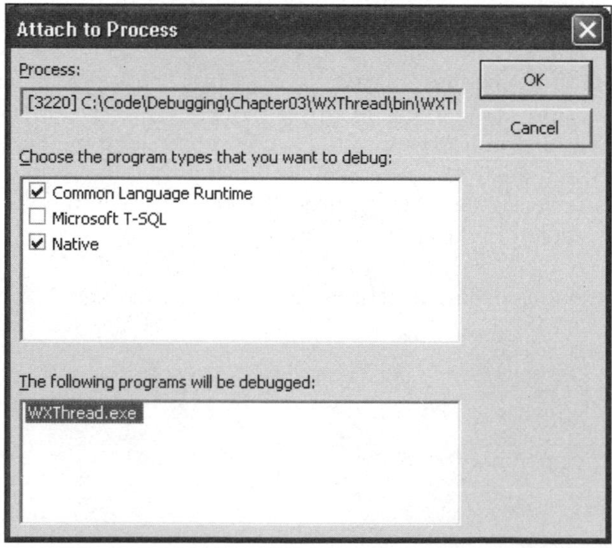

A process may contain more than one sort of application and this dialog allows us to select exactly what we want to debug. The list of available options will depend on, what options are installed and configured for the particular version of Visual Studio .NET. This configuration can be altered on the Debugging | Just-in-Time page of Visual Studio's Options dialog (Tools | Options). The following list maps from the settings in the Attach To Process dialog to the category of application to be debugged:

- C#, VB.NET, and managed C++ applications – debug using Common Language Runtime.
- Unmanaged C++ and Visual Basic 6.0 – debug using Native, this option will only be available if have C++ installed.
- ASP.NET – select Common Language Runtime and Script.
- ASP Script – debug using Script.
- Transact SQL (the language of SQL Server) – debug using T-SQL.

The Attach to Process dialog has already selected Common Language Runtime as the type of program to debug. Since VB.NET is a managed application (hence executing inside the Common Language Runtime) we need to simply select OK in order to launch Visual Studio .NET.

## Process Debugging and Source Code

What exactly happens after you click OK in the Attach to Process dialog depends on how you attached to the process and whether or not the debugging information is available. You could end up:

- Debugging within a build solution
- Debugging with the source code available
- Debugging with no source code

### Attaching a Debugger with the Build Solution

The last choice in the Just-in-Time Debugging dialog (WXThread – Microsoft Visual Basic .NET [design] – WXThread.vb Microsoft Development Environment) attaches `WXDemoDebugger.exe` to a debugger inside the instance Visual Studio .NET that already has the WXThread solution loaded.

Just attaching the debugger does not break the application, to do that select the Break All menu item from the Debug menu. When you've done that, you should see something like this:

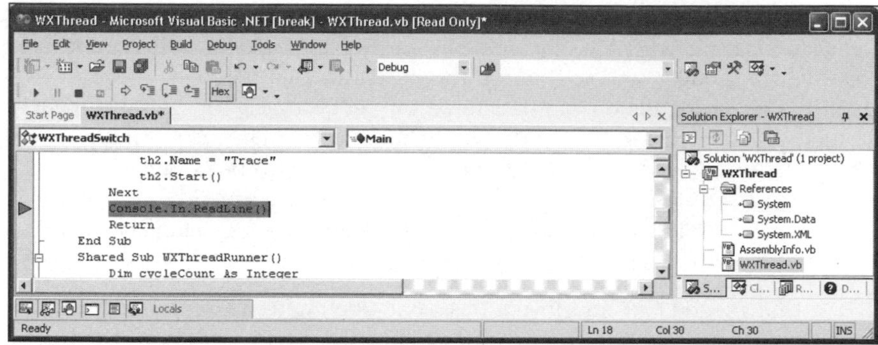

Included in the previous screenshot is the Solution Explorer window. Here the application being debugged gets all the benefits of running in Visual Studio .NET with the solution loaded. Visual Studio .NET contains a Build menu (since the application can be built). All projects, and all files associated with projects are accessible via Solution Explorer. Clearly, the limitation here is that you already need to have an instance of Visual Studio open with the correct solution loaded.

## Attaching a Debugger without the Build Solution

If you don't have the correct solution open, select New Instance of Microsoft Development Environment from the Just-in-Time dialog; the result is a new instance of Visual Studio .NET:

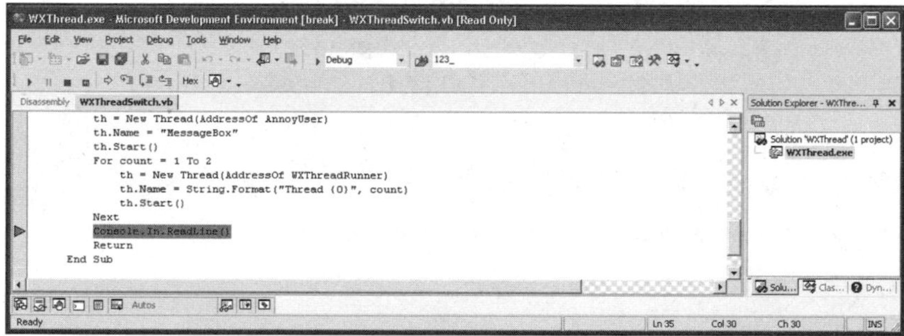

Here the debugger is attached directly to the executable and only the relevant file for the section of code currently being debugged is available. The `*.pdb` file (discussed earlier in the chapter) allows Visual Studio .NET to debug `WXThread.exe` without the benefits of a solution (`*.sln` file) or its projects (`*.vbproj` files). To be technically correct there is a newly created solution file (`*.sln`), but this is not for building the application, it just helps Visual Studio .NET manage the executable and store things like breakpoint settings. Even though this solution file is created, the fundamental relationship is between the executable, the program database (`*.pdb`), and the source code.

The downside of debugging outside a solution and its projects comes when modifying the code, say to fix a bug. There is no way to build a project using only the `*.pdb` file. In fact, the previous screenshot shows that Visual Studio .NET is running without a Build menu.

Regardless of how debugging is performed, the contents of a solutions `*.suo` file is updated by Visual Studio .NET when the application being debugged is closed. Recall from Chapter 1 that `*.suo` stands for Solution User Options file. This file contains such entities as the location of breakpoints. This means that breakpoints can be set and saved. The next time you attach to the process the `*.suo` complete with the previous breakpoints can be accessed.

### Attaching a Debugger without the Source Code

When you launch a debugger, there is one final possibility: that the assembly has no reference to a `.pdb` file (as is usual in a release build) or it can't locate the source files. All is not lost, however; the debugger can (if you want) decompile the assembly, and display the results:

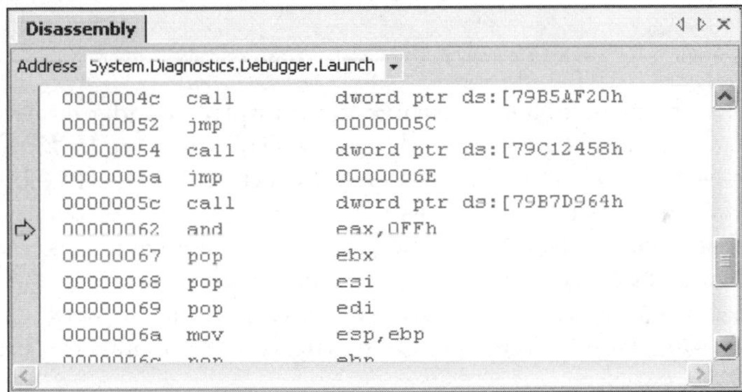


Admittedly, for many people this feature is not that useful but if you can understand assembly language then this view may present you with some useful information. Just as with source code, you can set breakpoints and step through the code.

## *Attaching from within Visual Studio*

To attach to a running process, Visual Studio provides the Process Dialog, which is accessible via the Tools | Debug Processes menu item. When a solution is loaded this dialog is also available using the Debug menu's Processes menu item.

To demonstrate this dialog, consider the case where the WXThread solution is loaded, and an instance of `WXThread.exe` is running on the machine, unattached to any debugger. If we display the Processes dialog, it should look something like this:

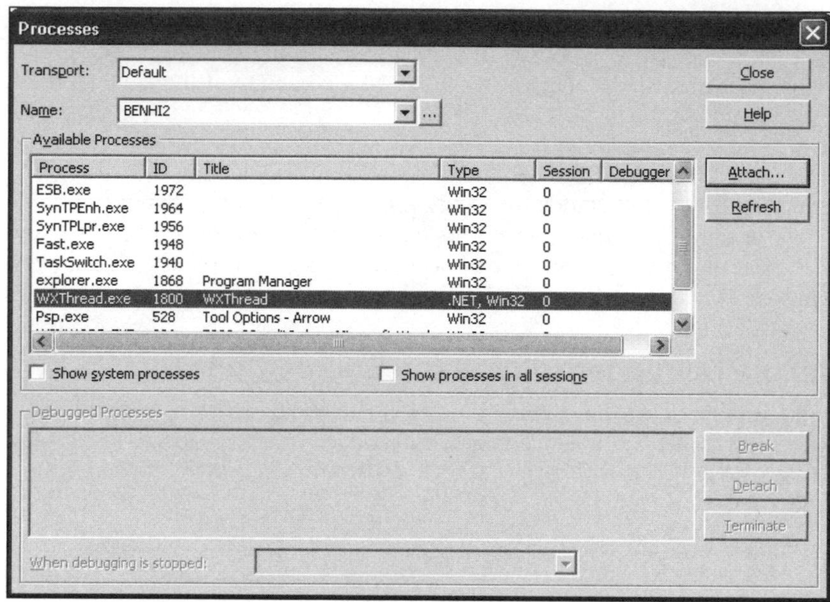


For each process, the name of the executable file is displayed under the Process column heading. This may not correspond to the assembly you are looking for because a managed application can run multiple assembly executables. The ID column contains the system-specific process ID and the Title column contains the text displayed within a Windows title bar, hence some background processes do not have titles. Title can be very useful when trying to determine precisely what process to debug when multiple instances of an executable are running. The Type column relates to what sort of Windows process the executable is running in. The possible options can include Win32, .NET, COM+, etc.

In the screenshot above the Process dialog also has the following features:

- Transport – for VB.NET developers, Default is all that is required. Transport only applies to debugging remote machines and non-Default transports only apply to C/C++ debugging.
- Name – displays the name (machine name BENHI2 is shown above) of the current machine, since the process to debugged is likely local. It is possible to specify another host name in the Name textbox or to browse using the ... browse button and find a host on which to find processes to debug remotely.
- Close – closes the dialog.
- Attach – attaches the current selected process or processes to the debugger. In the previous screenshot only one process was selected (`WXThread.exe`) but it is possible to attach multiple processes simultaneously.

- Refresh – processes are started and processes end. The Refresh button gets the most up to date list of available processes to debug.
- Show system processes – list system-spawned processes in the list of available processes to debug. This is frequently checked when running a service since services are started by the system.
- Show processes in all session – if terminal server is installed then shows processes running in all terminal server sessions.

Notice in the previous screenshot that the Break, Detach, and Terminate buttons were all disabled. These buttons (which allow processes to be managed by Visual Studio .NET) will all be enabled once at least one process is attached to the debugger.

Once the Attach button is clicked, the Attach to Process dialog is displayed (as was the case when debugging via Task Manager):

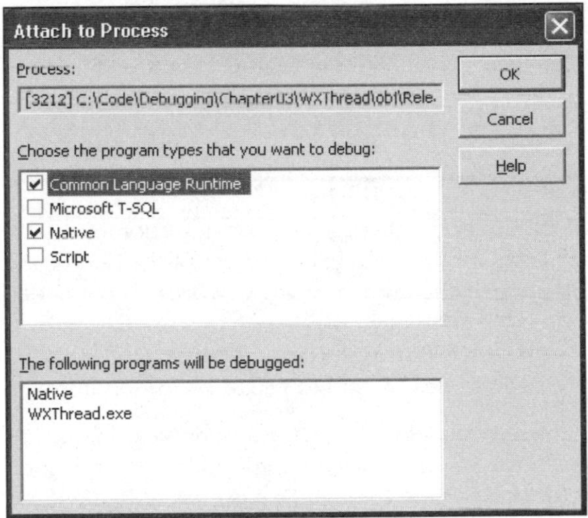


Once again, the Attach to Process dialog affords the developer the choice to debug managed (Common Langue Runtime checkbox), unmanaged (Native checkbox), or both styles of code. Just as before Microsoft T-SQL is an option but a new option is also available, Script. The Script option determines if Visual Studio .NET will debug scripts such as those developed by ASP applications.

*In the chapter on debugging web applications the Script option will be explored in more detail, especially since ASP.NET and ASP pages can coexist in the same project on the same web site and still be debugged by Visual Studio .NET.*

## Managing Processes

The Processes dialog has more buttons enabled (thus allowing the process to be managed) once at a least one process is attached to Visual Studio .NET. An example of this is as follows:

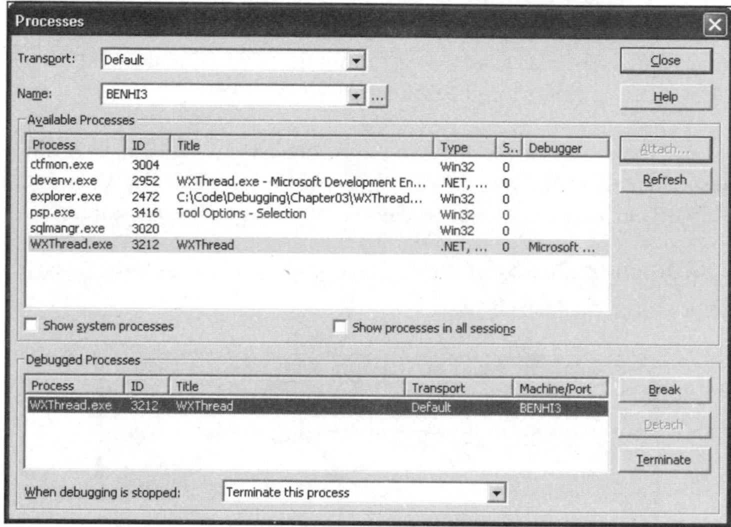

The buttons enabled fall under the Debugged Processes section of the Processes dialog. This section of the dialog allows the ongoing management of the one or more processes being debugged. In the screenshot above, a single process is being debugged.

- Break – causes each thread in the process or processes highlighted under the Debugged Processes section to break execution immediately.
- Detach – cease debugging the process or process highlighted. MSDN claims this is only enabled for managed applications but this not true since it is enabled for unmanaged C++ applications such as Windows services developed with Visual C++ 6.0. In the screenshot above, Detach is disabled because the type of application being debugged is a legacy VB 6 application.
- Terminate – click to terminate the process or processes highlighted. It should be fairly obvious that terminating the process ceases debugging and execution.

Under the Debug menu, there is a Stop Debugging menu item. This menu item pertains to the listbox at the bottom of the Process dialog, labeled When debugging is stopped. This listbox contains the following entries that dictate the behavior of Stop Debugging:

- Terminate this process – when debugging ceases each process being debugged terminates (ceases executing).

- Detach from this process – when debugging ceases the processes being debugged continue to run but run while no longer being debugged by Visual Studio .NET.

### Debugging Multiple Processes

It is possible to debug one or more processes using a single instance of Visual Studio .NET. This technique takes some getting used to because only one solution at a time can be loaded into Visual Studio .NET. It takes a little more work to open up the source files associated with applications whose solution is not loaded. For instance both the client-side and the server-side aspects of a web application can be debugged in the context of the same instance of Visual Studio .NET.

## Determining Which Process to Debug

Attaching to a process using Task Manager or Visual Studio .NET is well and good provided there is only one instance running of a given process. It is possible to have multiple instances of the same executable running. This is especially true with respect to `dllhost.exe` and `svchost.exe` both of which are used to run DLLs as processes. The types of applications run by `dllhost.exe` include ASP.NET applications and certain configurations of service components. With ten versions of a process running, it takes a bit of work to determine which instance is the one that needs debugging.

Within Visual Studio .NET's Processes dialog there is an ID column is associated with each process. This value corresponds to a process's unique ID within the operating system. If the process can communicate this ID to the debugger, then you can select a particular process for debugging.

With the Task Manger dialog, there was no ID column. This is not true for all flavors of Windows but for Windows XP process ID is not displayed by default. Selecting the Task Manger dialog's View | Select Columns menu item displays the following dialog:

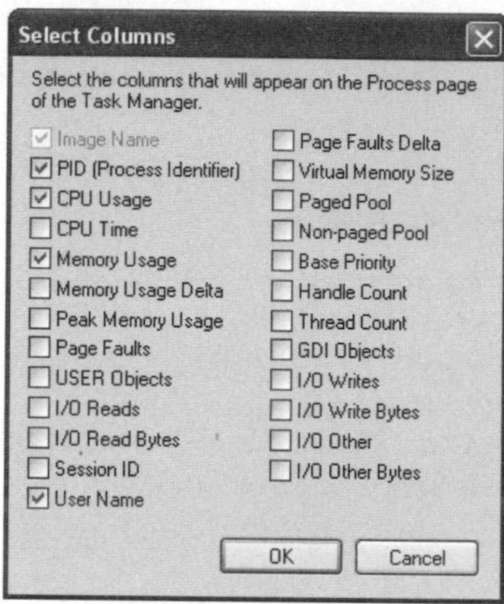


In the Select Columns dialog the PID (Process Identifier) checkbox is available; selecting this will displaying the process ID when the task manager displays processes. The Select Columns dialog contains a plethora of information useful when debugging, especially when tackling performance-related issues. Pages of memory, I/O, system handles, and much more are available using the task manager. Task Manager is not a substitute for Performance Monitor. Task Manager displays information conveniently categorized by process while under Performance Monitor such a categorization has to be set up (which can take a bit of effort).

Now that the process ID is displayed in both Task Manager and the Processes dialog, the application to debug needs to identify its ID. The `System.Diagnostics Process` class provides this information. The steps required for an application to retrieve its own process ID are as follows:

- Invoke the `Process.GetCurrentProcess()` method in order to retrieve a process instance corresponding to the current process. This method is `Shared` so no instance of `Process` is required in order to invoke `GetCurrentProcess()`.
- For the process instance, select the `Id` property (type, `Integer`).

The following code snippet demonstrates this:

```
Dim id As Boolean = Process.GetCurrentProcess.Id()
```

We have already shown how to use `EventLog` to convey information such as process ID. Another common approach used to display the process ID is to use the `MessageBox` class from `System.Windows.Forms`. This approach was often used for services or serviced components (COM+ DLLs run by `dllhost.exe`). The basic approach is to make sure the application references the `System.Windows.Forms.dll` assembly. Once this setup is complete a `MessageBox` such as the following can be displayed using the shared `Show()`:

```
MessageBox.Show("Process ID: " & _
                     Process.GetCurrentProcess.Id.ToString(), _
                 "Debug me please", _
                 MessageBoxButtons.OK, _
                 MessageBoxIcon.Exclamation, _
                 MessageBoxDefaultButton.Button1, _
                 MessageBoxOptions.ServiceNotification)
```

This code snippet appears to have used the most complex variant of all the `Show()` method's overloads. This is true but with purpose. What makes the previous `MessageBox` so handy (besides that it displays the process ID) is the last parameter, `MessageBoxOptions.ServiceNotification`. Applications running in the background on Windows such as services do not usually have permission to interact with the screen. The `MessageBoxOptions` enumeration's `ServiceNotification` value specifies that the `MessageBox` will be displayed even from within a service.

On the plus side, this stops the process's execution thus allowing the debugger to be attached. After the debugger is attached, it is often handy to place a breakpoint after the `MessageBox` (since that is where execution resumes after the `MessageBox` is closed). One the negative side `MessageBox.Show()` stops the process's execution if the `MessageBox` is not closed by an interactive user the application is stuck. Consequently, this technique is not suitable for use in release code – take any message boxes out before you ship the code.

> *Here is salutary tale on why you shouldn't forget to remove those message boxes. A coworker went on vacation to Boston just as we deployed his code. Unfortunately, he had left all the `MessageBox`'s in the release version. I ended up flying to Yadkinville, North Carolina in order to clean up the mess because the customer's service kept stalling due to `MessageBox`'s. He was in Boston enjoying fine food and museums. I was in Yadkinville where the town's only restaurant (a Burger King) had just burned down.*

Using `MessageBoxOptions.ServiceNotification` was an in vogue debugging technique because the `DebugBreak` Win32 function (same functionality as `Debugger.Break()`) did not work inside Windows services or serviced components (at least without some major system tweaking). A break down of the `Debugger`, `Debug`, and `Trace` methods that can actually work with ASP.NET web services, Windows services and serviced components will be presented in Chapter 5.

## Attaching to a Legacy Application

Imagine a case where the Windows service to be debugged is a legacy application written in Visual C++ 6.0. When the per-process context menu provided by Task Manager is displayed, there is no way to choose a legacy version of the debugger (Visual C++ 6.0, Visual Basic 6.0, etc.) even when such an IDE is installed. The just-in-time debugger only launches Visual Studio .NET when the Debug menu item is selected. Visual Studio .NET is the only choice provided for debugging. Visual Studio .NET is the only debugger that can be launched this way even though the application is built with a different IDE installed on the machine (Visual C++ 6.0, Visual Basic 6.0, etc.). Visual Studio .NET is perfectly capable of performing this debugging but is not cable of building the application being debugged.

The reasons Visual Studio .NET is preferred over Visual C++ 6.0 or Visual Basic 6.0, from a debugging point of view, are:

- Visual Studio .NET remembers the break points associated with yet to be loaded DLLs and when such a DLL is loaded, all breakpoints are re-enabled. Such breakpoints would have previously been set with F9 or Debug | New Breakpoint.
- Ability to detach the process being debugged from Visual Studio .NET. Microsoft documentation currently states that only managed applications can be detached. This is unequivocally not true.
- Four Watch windows.
- Four Memory windows (this is a legacy C++ application with a lot of complex buffers).
- You can debug Visual C++ 6.0 applications simultaneously with the portion of the code written in VB 6. Yes, managed code can also be debugged simultaneously with VB 6 and Visual C++ 6.0; this almost seems like a miracle to hard bitten Windows developers!
- The shortcuts for single step, step over, start application, end debugging, etc. are the same for debugging both Visual Basic 6 and Visual C++ 6.0. Using the legacy tools these settings differ (by default) from Visual Basic 6.0's IDE to Visual C++ 6.0's IDE.

# Summary

VB 6 developers certainly experience a bit of culture shock when moving to Visual Studio .NET. Exceptions were not a part of VB 6 but are a part of all .NET-conformant languages. For this reason Visual Studio .NET allows exceptions to be managed (break always, break if not handled, etc.).

Threads are also a new topic to most VB 6 developers; an application may have numerous threads, interacting in complex ways. Freezing threads can reduce this complexity, allowing you to isolate a subset of the threads, such as those required in order to debug a given feature. Do not forget the `Thread` class's `Name` property. The Threads window displays a thread's name; a named thread is easier to debug, as you know what it is for.

By attaching a debugger (Visual Studio .NET) to a running process it is possible to debug applications with out access to the source code, Windows services (which cannot be launched from VS .NET), and legacy applications (C++ 6 and VB 6) that can't be built in visual studio. It is also possible to debug multiple processes in one instance of Visual Studio .NET, which is particularly useful for client-server applications.

VB.NET

# Debugging

Handbook

4

# 4

# Logging and Programmatic Debugger Interaction

In the previous chapters, we concentrated on viewing debugging information in Visual Studio. A vital adjunct to these techniques is the ability to capture information about the state of an application in a more permanent fashion. Logging (as this usually called) is useful for many things but here we will focus on logging information from applications for debugging purposes.

The `Debug` and `Trace` classes are provided to manage the logging within an application. In order to make logging more flexible, multiple trace listeners (essentially proxies for logging destinations) can be registered with the `Trace` and `Debug` classes so that data passed to their various write methods can be logged to multiple destinations. In this chapter, we'll look at .NET's intrinsic trace listeners (default, text file, and event log) and how to use the `TraceListener` base class in order to develop custom trace listeners.

Debugging configuration switches will also be presented. These are used to turn on/off various debugging features depending programmatic state or flags set in an application's configuration file. .NET provides several classes that support this functionality (`TraceSwitch` and `BooleanSwitch`). By extending the `Switch` base class, developers can also create custom switches.

## Windows Event Log

The NT family of operating systems such as Windows NT 4.0, Windows 2000, and Windows XP provide a standard location where applications can log information. This repository is known as the **Event Log**. The information logged to the event log includes log entries generated by the operating system, applications, and security subsystem.

Why is this better than logging to some random file? System administrators know that when Windows applications (or the operating system or the security subsystem) experience an error, they write to the event log. This common logging location comes with nifty features such as an operating system provided GUI (Event Viewer), an ability to be read from remote machines, and an ability to generate events to notify applications when new log entries are available. Before .NET, developing applications that used the event log could be tedious. The `System.Diagnostics` namespace exposes an `EventLog` class, which greatly simplifies the process of logging to the event log, retrieving logged information, and managing logging.

> *If you run code that requires the event log on a Windows 98 or ME machine the .NET runtime simply ignores those calls so your code should still work in most circumstances, although no logging will take place, obviously.*

On Windows 2000 and Windows XP the Event Viewer tool is found under Control Panel | Administrative Tools | Event Viewer:

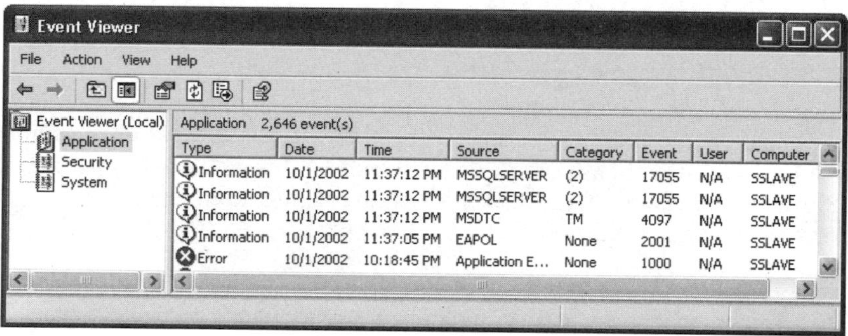


The previous screenshot shows off most crucial features of the event log, most of which correspond to properties of the `EventLog` class:

- `MachineName` – this property corresponds to the host on which the event log resides. In the previous screenshot, the `MachineName` is displayed in the left panel of Event Viewer at the root of the tree view control: Event Viewer (Local). The previous screenshot corresponds to the Local host.
- `Log` – this property corresponds to the name of the log that is accessed by the `EventLog` instance. In the previous screenshot, the `Log` is displayed in the left panel of the application as Application, Security, and System. These are the default system-provided logs. The techniques for programmatically creating additional logs will be discussed latter in the chapter.
- `LogDisplayName` – The name to be shown in event viewer, if different from the `Log` property.

- `Entries` – collection of `EventLogEntry` instances corresponding to a particular `MachineName`, `Log`, and `Source`. Each `EventLogEntry` instance contains properties corresponding to the columns displayed on the right panel of the previous screenshot:

| **`EventLogEntry` Property** | **Event Viewer Column** | **Description** |
|---|---|---|
| `EntryType` | Type | There are five possible types: Information, Warning, and Error are associated with general log entries. Success Audit and Failure Audit are associated with the security log entries generated for events such as a system logons. |
| `TimeGenerated` | Date & Time | The time an entry was generated. |
| `Source` | Source | Each event log entry must be associated with an event source and each event source is registered with an event log. This usually relates to the application creating the log entry but it can be set to any arbitrary string. |
| `EventID` | Event | Together with the event source this uniquely identifies the event type that generate the log entry. |
| `MachineName` | Computer | The name of the computer on which the log entry was generated. |
| `Category` | Category | The text associated with a particular category number. Each event source a can have several associated categories if it is desired to dived up events in a more granular manner. |
| `UserName` | User | The System User name associated with a log entry; this is mainly used by security log entries. |

The `MachineName`, `Log`, and `Source` triplet identifies from what place a log entry originated. An example of this in an entry of the Local (`MachineName`), Application (`Log`), MSSQLSERVER source (`Source`), which corresponds to a local instance of SQL Server. Actually, this is not quite a triplet. Each source can only be associated with a single event log. Specifying the MSSQLSERVER source specifies the Application event log.

Double-clicking on any log entry in the right pane of the Event Viewer application reveals the following Event Properties dialog:

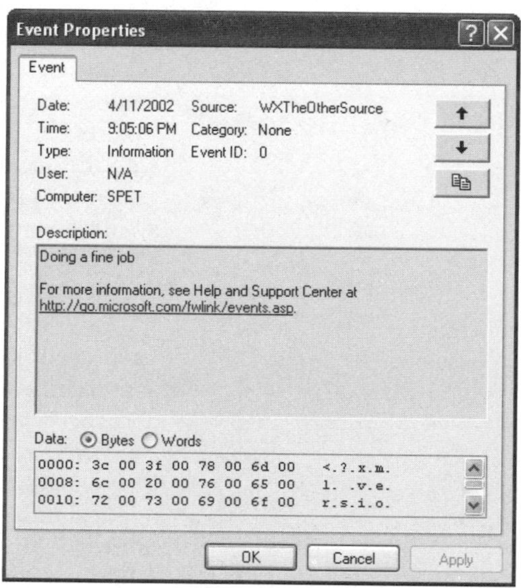


From a programmatic standpoint, the previous screenshot corresponds to an `EventLogEntry` instance. Each item displayed corresponds to a property of the `EventLogEntry` class. Most of the properties displayed have already been mentioned but the following are both introduced for the first time and critical to the interpretation of what is being logged by an `EventLogEntry`:

- `Message` – this property contains the message for the event log entry. In the previous screenshot, it is the text Doing a fine job and a URL displayed under the Description label.
- `Data` – this property is a `Byte` array that contains data associated with the log entry. The textbox underneath the Data label in the previous screenshot contains the log entry's data. Examining the data, you can see that it is displayed as both hexadecimal bytes and text. In this case, the `Data` property is used to contain an object serialized to XML.

The Description pane in conjunction with the `Message` property can be exploited in creative ways. The Description pane is actually a `RichEdit` window that can present URLs in a clickable manner. An ingenious programmer could use the URL to direct the user to a simple help page, or perhaps to post pertinent error information to a web server in the form of URL parameters. Consider the power this provides the application developer: they have available a system-provided UI for displaying event messages, plus that UI (the event viewer) can point to a more-powerful web application. This web application could log the error and could serve to provide even further explanation of the event.

The last tidbit describing the `Data` property is significant. The truly crafty take advantage of a log entry's `Data` property. Of course any data can be placed in this property but consider the possibilities if object instances are assigned to the data property. Serialization can be used to place objects into the `Data` property; recall from the previous chapter that object serialization provides a means by which to dehydrate and re-hydrate an object. The type of serialization shown in the screenshot of the Event Properties dialog was XML serialization. Binary object serialization could also have been used but the advantage of XML is that it is human-readable.

The Event Properties dialog contains a particularly handy button, copy to clipboard (). Clicking on this button copies the currently displayed event to the clipboard. The information is copied in text form and includes such critical information as `EventType`, `Source`, and `Message`. Once the log entry is copied to the clipboard, it can be handily pasted into applications such as Notepad or Word.

## Viewing Event Logs in Server Explorer

It is worth noting that event logs can also be viewed in the Server Explorer pane of Visual Studio, this is probably a more practical way of examining the event logs while developing, and the usefulness of the Source property is particularly apparent:

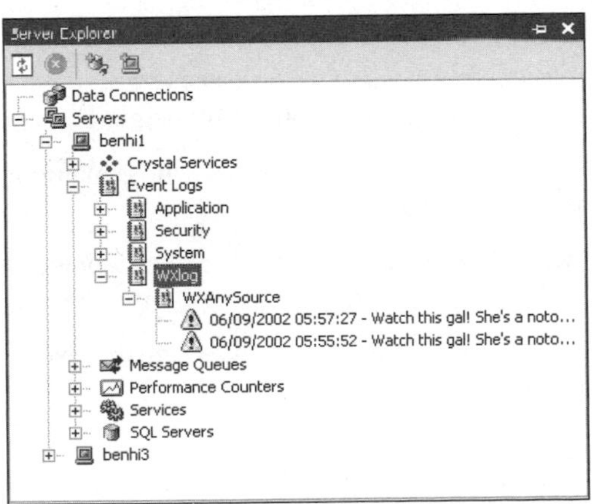

# Event Log Example Application

Applications use the event log to write pertinent error, warning, and informational messages. Here we'll create the WXEventLogWriter Windows forms application, which basically exists just to write entries to the event log; OK this application composed of a single dialog might not win many awards but it is sufficient to demonstrate the programmatic use of the event log:

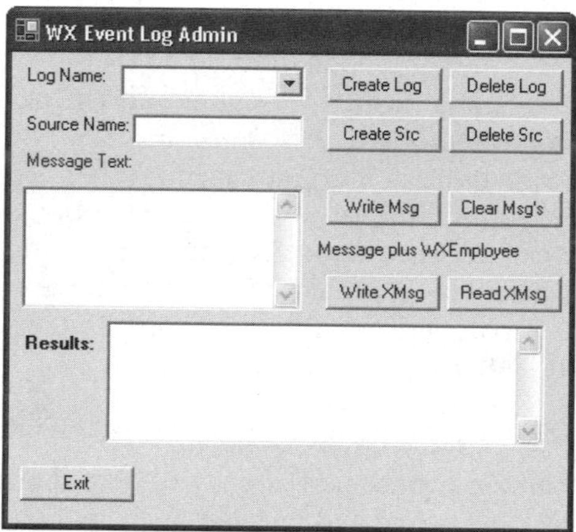


Yes, the previous dialog is a bit crowded, but the functionality should be clear when reviewed in terms of the dialog's buttons:

- Create Log – creates a specific log (a folder) using the name specified in the combo box labeled Log Name. This newly created log will be on the same level as the Security, Application, and System logs provided by the system.
- Delete Log – deletes the log specified in the combo box labeled Log Name; note the system logs can't be deleted.
- Create Src – creates an event log source using the name specified in the textbox labeled Source Name. Examples of event log sources on many systems might include Service Control Manager, IIS, and SQL Server.
- Delete Src – deletes the event log source whose name is specified in the textbox labeled Source Name.
- Write Msg – writes the specified in the textbox labeled Message Text, the Log Name combo box specifies the event log written to.
- Clear Msg's – clears all event log messages for the event log specified in the Log Name combo box.

- Write XMsg – writes a message to the message log where the message writing is specified in the textbox labeled Message Text. The Log Name combo box specifies the event log written to. In addition to the message itself, a `WXEmployee` object (just an example class) will be serialized to XML and written to the event log. The reason to use XML rather then binary serialization is simply a matter of making the data more readable. Recall that by using Event Viewer it was possible to actually read the data field associated with an event log entry.
- Read XMsg – reads a message from the event log specified by Log Name. This message will contain a serialized `WXEmployee` instance that can be de-serialized (made back into an object again) and subsequently used programmatically. The XML read is displayed in the textbox labeled Results.

All output from this application is displayed in the textbox labeled Results. Now we'll look at some of the finer points of the event log using this application.

## Writing Events

An individual log entry is associated with a specific log name and source name. This might lead you to believe that the log name and source name must be created before a log entry can be written. This is the case with the event log-related functions exposed by Windows but under .NET the log and source names do not have to be created before a log entry is written to the event log. An event log entry can be written using a `Shared` version of the `EventLog.WriteEntry()` method or the application can choose to create an instance of `EventLog` and then call a non-`Shared` version of `WriteEntry()`.

An example of creating an `EventLog` (including specifying host, log, and source) and then writing to the event log is show in the method that handles the event when the WXEventLogWriter application's Write Msg button clicked:

```
Private Sub ButtonCreateMessage_Click( _
                                ByVal sender As System.Object, _
                                ByVal e As System.EventArgs) _
                                  Handles ButtonCreateMessage.Click
  Try
    TextBoxResults.Text = ""
    ' Use Environment class to get name of local host (MachineName)
    Dim ev As EventLog = New EventLog(ComboBoxLogs.Text, _
                                      Environment.MachineName, _
                                      TextBoxSourceName.Text)
    ev.WriteEntry(TextBoxMessage.Text)
  Catch ex As Exception
    TextBoxResults.Text = ex.ToString()
  End Try
End Sub
```

In order to understand the previous code, recall that the WXEventLogWriter application contains a `ComboBox`, used to specify the event log (`ComboxBoxLogs`) and `TextBoxes` (the names are self-documenting) for specifying the message to be logged and source name. The hostname parameter to the `EventLog` constructor is specified using the `Environment` class's `MachineName` property. This property corresponds to the local host, which is the name of the machine on which the application is running.

If the log name parameter sent to the `EventLog` constructor contains an empty string (`ComboxBoxLogs.Text`) then the log written to is determined as follows:

- If the event source already exists then the event source will already be associated with a specific event log. Recall that the reason for is because an event source name can only be associated with only a single log. Invoking `WriteEntry()` with the `EventLog.Log` property not set means that the log written to is the same as the log with which the source name is already associated.
- If the event source does not exist and the `EventLog.Log` property is not set then a new event source is created and this event source is associated with the Application log (the default log). The log entry written by `WriteEntry()` would therefore be associated with the Application log in conjunction with the specified source name.

## Possible Errors

When using an instance of type `EventLog` to write a log entry, the following conditions will generate an error:

- If no source name is specified, then `WriteEntry()` will fail because it must be associated with an event source. In order to avoid this error, the source name can be specified via the `Source` property or by using the following form of `EventLog`'s constructor where the third parameter corresponds to the source name:

```
Public Sub New(ByVal logName As String, _
               ByVal machineName As String, _
               ByVal source As String)
```

- If no host name is specified, then `WriteEntry()` will fail. `EventLog` does not default to the local host (current machine). Avoiding this error is a matter of setting the `MachineName` property in advance, specifying the machine name using the previous constructor (the second parameter) or specifying the machine name using the following flavor of the `EventLog` constructor (the second parameter):

```
Public Sub New(ByVal logName As String, _
               ByVal machineName As String)
```

- If the log name specified is different from the log with which that event source is currently associated, then WriteEntry() will fail. As we have said before, an event source is associated with at most one event log.

## Adding Information to a Log Entry

The WriteEntry() method in the previous code snippet simply writes the text that we've typed into the textbox (TextBoxMessage.Text) to the specified event log. The previous example of WriteEntry() is just one of numerous overloads for this method. These overloads allow most properties associated with an event log entry (class, EventLogEntry) to be specified. To understand this, consider the following overload of the WriteEntry() method that contains six parameters:

```
Overloads Public Shared Sub WriteEntry( _
                                ByVal source As String, _
                                ByVal message As String, _
                                ByVal entryType As EventLogEntryType, _
                                ByVal eventID As Integer, _
                                ByVal category As Short, _
                                ByVal rawData() As Byte)
```

Note that the previous incarnation of WriteEntry() is shared and we don't need to instantiate a specific instance of the EventLog to use it. The first parameter corresponds to the event source. Using this method there is no chance to specify a log name that differs from the log name associated with a particular event source.

The rawData parameter provides an especially useful mechanism by which any type of debugging information can be stored. A serialized object is an excellent candidate for inclusion in an event log entry because the object could be recreated at a later date and debugged.

In order to demonstrate using object serialization with the event log, we will use the WXEmployee class. The aforementioned class contains two methods of use when serializing objects to the event log or retrieving such objects from the event log: XMLSerializedToByte() and a two overloads of Create():

```
Public Class WXEmployee

  <XmlElement("LastName")> Public _lastName As String
  <XmlElement("FirstName")> Public _firstName As String

  Public Shared Function Create(ByVal strXML As String) As WXEmployee
    Dim xmlSer As XmlSerializer = _
      New XmlSerializer(GetType(WXEmployee))
    Return CType(xmlSer.Deserialize(New StringReader(strXML)), _
                                WXEmployee)
  End Function
```

```
    Public Shared Function Create(ByVal byteXML As Byte()) As WXEmployee
      Dim unEncode As UnicodeEncoding = New UnicodeEncoding()
      Return Create(New String(unEncode.GetChars(byteXML)))
    End Function
```

One flavor of `WXEmployee.Create()` creates a `WXEmployee` instance given a `byte()` (byte array) representing a previously serialized data instance of this type. Usually classes serialized to XML are de-serialized from strings but the event log's data attribute can only contain binary data. Since it is in binary format, the object is de-serialized (reconstituted) from binary rather than string data.

```
    Public Overrides Function ToString() As String
      Dim xmlSer As XmlSerializer = _
        New XmlSerializer(GetType(WXEmployee))
      Dim strWriter As StringWriter = New StringWriter()
      xmlSer.Serialize(strWriter, Me)
      Return strWriter.ToString()
    End Function

    Public Function XMLSerializedToByte() As Byte()
      Dim unEncode As UnicodeEncoding = New UnicodeEncoding()
      Return unEncode.GetBytes(ToString())
    End Function

  End Class
```

The `XMLSerializedToByte()` method generates an XML serialized version of `WXEmployee` (courtesy of `ToString()`) and then it converts this into an array of bytes using the `GetBytes()` method from the `System.Text.UnicodeEncoding` class.

Using `WXEmployee`, we can write an event log entry that contains a serialized instance of a class (see the final parameter passed to `EventLog.WriteEntry`). This writing is performed when the Write XMsg button is clicked on and the subsequent method is invoked:

```
  Private Sub ButtonWriteMessagePlusEmployee_Click( _
                                 ByVal sender As System.Object, _
                                 ByVal e As System.EventArgs) _
                          Handles ButtonWriteMessagePlusEmployee.Click

    Try
      Dim employee As WXEmployee = New WXEmployee()
      employee._firstName = "Anh"
      employee._lastName = "Nguyen"
```

To simply things we create and populate the instance of `WXEmployee` within this method.

```
      EventLog.WriteEntry(TextBoxSourceName.Text, _
                          TextBoxMessage.Text, _
                          EventLogEntryType.Warning, _
                          7, _
                          0, _
                          employee.XMLSerializedToByte())
    Catch ex As Exception
      TextBoxResults.Text = ex.ToString()
    End Try
  End Sub
```

The `WXEmployee` instance will be extracted from the event log when the topic of reading event log entries is reviewed.

## Managing Event Logs

For a particular machine (host) the system event log contains entities managed by the `EventLog` class. Specifically the `EventLog` class can manage the separate logs within the system event log (the `EventLog.Log` property), can manage event sources within logs (the `EventLog.Source` property), and can manage the individual log entries within a log (the `EventLog.Entries` property).

The `EventLog` methods associated with the management of logs are as follows:

- `Delete()` – deletes a specific log given a parameter corresponding to the log's name (`logName`). Deleting a non existent log results in an error as does attempting to delete a system log (System, Security, or Application). As we have come to expect there is an overload for specifying the host on which the log resides (`hostName`):

```
Shared Sub Delete(ByVal logName As String)

Shared Sub Delete(ByVal logName As String, _
                  ByVal hostName As String)
```

- `Exists()` – as this method's name so subtly alludes to, whether a log exists (`True`) or not (`False`). Hint, hint: use the `Exists` property to make sure that the `Delete` method is only used on event logs that exist. The usual suspects for parameters are the name of the log (`logName`) and optionally the name of the host on which the log resides (`hostName`):

```
Shared Function Exists(ByVal logName As String) As Boolean

Shared Function Exists(ByVal logName As String, _
                       ByVal hostName As String) _
                         As Boolean
```

- `GetEventLogs()` – retrieves a `EventLog` array (`EventLog()`) containing a list of all the logs for a specific host; if no parameter is provided local host is assumed, otherwise the host can be specified as the only parameter to this method:

```
Shared Function GetEventLogs() As EventLog()

Shared Function GetEventLogs(ByVal hostName As String) _
  As EventLog()
```

The WXEventLogWriter application demonstrates each of the log related methods just discussed. For example the aforementioned application uses the `GetEventLogs()` method to populate the contents of a `ComboBox` control when the Windows form is loaded:

```
Private Sub WXEventLogWriter_Load(ByVal sender As Object, _
                                  ByVal e As System.EventArgs) _
                                    Handles MyBase.Load
    Dim evEntry As EventLog = New EventLog()

    For Each evEntry In EventLog.GetEventLogs()
        ComboBoxLogs.Items.Add(evEntry.Log)
    Next

End Sub
```

The implementation of the Create Log button is a bit more involved than you might expect.

There is no direct way to create a new Event Log using the `EventLog` class so we fake it by creating a dummy source name using a GUID (to make it random) and a dummy message so that we can use `WriteEntry()` to force the creation of the log:

```
Private Sub ButtonCreateLog_Click(ByVal sender As System.Object, _
                                  ByVal e As System.EventArgs) _
                                    Handles ButtonCreateLog.Click
  Try
    TextBoxResults.Text = ""
    If ComboBoxLogs.Text.Length = 0 Then
      Throw New Exception("Log name not specified")
    End If
    If EventLog.Exists(ComboBoxLogs.Text) Then
      Throw New Exception("Log already exists")
    Else
      Dim ev As EventLog = New EventLog(ComboBoxLogs.Text)
      ev.Source = Guid.NewGuid().ToString()
      ev.WriteEntry("Dummy message to create log")
      ev.Clear()
      ComboBoxLogs.Items.Add(ComboBoxLogs.Text)
    End If
  Catch ex As Exception
      TextBoxResults.Text = ex.ToString()
  End Try
End Sub
```

We use the `Clear()` method to remove our dummy source name and message and add the name of the log to the log list `ComboBox`.

The as `EventLog` class does contain a `Delete()` method we don't have to jump through all the hoops we needed to when creating one to implement the **Delete Log** button:

```
Private Sub ButtonDeleteLog_Click(ByVal sender As System.Object, _
                                  ByVal e As System.EventArgs) _
                                   Handles ButtonDeleteLog.Click
  Try
    TextBoxResults.Text = ""
    If ComboBoxLogs.Text.Length = 0 Then
      Throw New Exception("Log name not specified")
    End If
    If EventLog.Exists(ComboBoxLogs.Text) Then
      EventLog.Delete(ComboBoxLogs.Text)
      ComboBoxLogs.Items.Remove(ComboBoxLogs.Text)
    Else
      Throw New Exception( _
                   "Deletion failed since log does not exists")
    End If
  Catch ex As Exception
    TextBoxResults.Text = ex.ToString()
  End Try
End Sub
```

## Managing Event Sources

All log entries associated with a given event source will be found within the entries of a particular `EventLog`. This is because of the infamous adage: an event source is associated with one and only one even log on a given machine.

The methods exposed for the `EventLog` class related to managing event sources are as follows:

- `CreateEventSource()` – this method creates a source with the given name (`sourceName`) and associates it with the log name specified (`logName`). If the log of that name does not exist, one is created. If the log already exists, an event source is created and associated with that log. If the `logName` parameter contains an empty string, the source is associated with the Application log by default. It is possible to specify a hostname in order to create an event source on a remote machine.

```
Shared Sub CreateEventSource(ByVal sourceName As String, _
                             ByVal logName As String)

Shared Sub CreateEventSource(ByVal sourceName As String, _
                             ByVal logName As String, _
                             ByVal hostName As String)
```

- `DeleteEventSource()` – deletes an event source by specifying the name of the event source (`sourceName`). No log name is required because each event source is associated with a single log so there the log in which the source resides is already known internally. It is possible to delete an event source on a remote host. This involves setting the hostname parameter to the value of the remote host in which the source to be deleted resides. The `DeleteEventSource()` method does not remove the existing event log entries for the event source deleted. Those remain even though the event source is deleted.

```
Shared Sub DeleteEventSource(ByVal sourceName As String)

Shared Sub DeleteEventSource(ByVal sourceName As String, _
                             ByVal hostName As String)
```

- `SourceExists()` – returns `True` if the specified source name (`sourceName`) corresponds to an existing event source. An error is raised if `DeleteEventSource()` is called on a nonexistent event source, so `SourceExists()` can be used as a check beforehand. With respect to the `SourceExists()` method, the purpose of the `hostName` parameter (second version of `SourceExists` shown below) should be clear by now.

```
Shared Function SourceExists(ByVal sourceName As String) _
                               As Boolean

Shared Function SourceExists(ByVal sourceName As String, _
                             ByVal hostName As String) _
                               As Boolean
```

- `LogNameFromSourceName` – given a source name (`sourceName`) and a host (`hostName`), this returns the log name for the said source. This is possible because each source is associated with a single log:

```
Shared Function LogNameFromSourceName(ByVal sourceName As String, _
                                      ByVal hostName As String) _
                                        As String
```

The WXEventLogWriter Windows Forms application demonstrates each of the previous methods in action. These methods are straightforward and it turns out that Windows Forms code is more complicated then the `EventLog`-specific methods. For example the following code snippet uses the `Text` property of a `TextBox` instance (`TextBoxSourceName` containing the source name) to determine if an event source exists (`EventLog.SourceExists`). If the source does not exist, it is created, which also requires a `String` value corresponding to the log name (`ComboxBoxLogs.Text`):

```
Private Sub ButtonCreateSource_Click( _
                              ByVal sender As System.Object, _
                              ByVal e As System.EventArgs) _
```

```
                                    Handles ButtonCreateSource.Click
    Try
      TextBoxResults.Text = ""
      If EventLog.SourceExists(TextBoxSourceName.Text) Then
        Throw New Exception("Event source already exists")
      Else
        EventLog.CreateEventSource(TextBoxSourceName.Text, _
                                   ComboBoxLogs.Text)
      End If
    Catch ex As Exception
      TextBoxResults.Text = ex.ToString()
    End Try
  End Sub
```

Similarly the delete source, method checks to see if the source exists an calls `DeleteEventSource()` if it doesn't.

```
  Private Sub ButtonDeleteSource_Click( _
                                  ByVal sender As System.Object, _
                                  ByVal e As System.EventArgs) _
                                    Handles ButtonDeleteSource.Click
    Try
      TextBoxResults.Text = ""
      If TextBoxSourceName.Text.Length = 0 Then
        Throw New Exception("No source name specified")
      End If
      If EventLog.SourceExists(TextBoxSourceName.Text) Then
        EventLog.DeleteEventSource(TextBoxSourceName.Text)
      Else
        Throw New Exception( _
                    "Deletion failed since source does not exists")
      End If
    Catch ex As Exception
      TextBoxResults.Text = ex.ToString()
    End Try
  End Sub
```

## Managing Log Entries

Managing individual log entries is the last piece to cover in the topic of event log administration. The following method aids in administering log entries formally:

- `Clear()` – for a specific event log instance, removes all event log entries.

With respect to the `EventLog.Clear()` method is it import to recognize that event logs do not fill up. Instead, when a log reaches a maximum size it begins overwriting previous entries. Care should be taken in using `Clear()` simply because event logs often contain information critical to debugging an application or host-specific configuration issue. The application WXEventLogWriter does contain an example of using the `Clear()` method, so be careful!

Here is the code for the WXEventLogWriter Clear Msg's button:

```
Private Sub ButtonClearMessages_Click( _
                                ByVal sender As System.Object, _
                                ByVal e As System.EventArgs) _
                                  Handles ButtonClearMessages.Click
  Try
    TextBoxResults.Text = ""
    ' Use Environment class to get name of local host (MachineName)
    Dim ev As EventLog = New EventLog(ComboBoxLogs.Text, _
                                      Environment.MachineName, _
                                      TextBoxSourceName.Text)
    ev.Clear()
  Catch ex As Exception
    TextBoxResults.Text = ex.ToString()
  End Try
End Sub
```

It simply creates a new `EventLog` instance and calls its `Clear()` method.

## Security Constraints

Why are methods like `CreateEventSource()` even needed if `WriteEntry()` automatically creates event logs and sources? The answer is security! When an event log or event source is created the keys are added to the Windows registry (more on this later). This requires a set of security permissions that differ from simply writing to an event log. Usually `WriteEntry()` will simply query the Windows registry (under the covers) in order to verify the name of the event log and event source. Developers specifying `WriteEntry()` are not even aware that this is taking place behind the scenes. However, when the event log and/or event source are created by `WriteEntry`, a different set of permissions are needed (create registry permissions instead of just read permissions).

To show how security can affect using the `EventLog`, create an ASP.NET application on Windows XP professional with IIS installed. ASP.NET applications run under the `aspnet_wp` user account. With default settings, the following error will be generated if an ASP.NET application attempts to create an event log or event source:

System.Security.SecurityException: Requested registry access is not allowed.

This error is produced because the default permissions associated with the `aspnet_wp` user account do not include the ability to create entries in the Windows registry.

The behavior of ASP.NET on a certain configuration of Windows XP is not meant to be a comprehensive review of security. Instead, it should serve as a friendly reminder that the .NET environment and the most recent versions of Windows are going to place a lot more focus on security. The side effects of this will include restrictions on how we access certain features exposed by .NET including debugging features. For more information on these security issues see the *Visual Basic .NET Code Security Handbook* (Wrox Press, 2002; ISBN: 1-86100-747-7).

## Reading Event Log Entries

Each event log entry is represented by an instance the `EventLogEntry` class. For a given `EventLog` the event log entries are contained in the `Entries` property (a collection of `EventLogEntry` instances). An `EventLog` instance can be instantiated by specifying the name of an event log and optionally the host. In addition, the `Entries` property can be accessed by specifying event log, host name, and event source; this will just return `EventLogEntry` instances for the specified event source.

```
   Private Sub ButtonReadMessagePlusEmployee_Click( _
                        ByVal sender As System.Object, _
                        ByVal e As System.EventArgs) _
                          Handles ButtonReadMessagePlusEmployee.Click
     Try
       TextBoxResults.Text = ""
       Dim ev As EventLog = New EventLog(ComboBoxLogs.Text, _
                                         Environment.MachineName, _
                                         TextBoxSourceName.Text)
       Dim result As DialogResult
       Dim logEntry As EventLogEntry
```

`ComboBoxLogs` and `TextBoxSourceName` are controls in the `WXDemoEventLogWriter` application used to specify the name of the event log and event source respectively.

The contents of the `EventLog` instance's `Entries` property are traversed using the `Count` and `Item` properties and the `GetEnumerator()` method. In order to exploit `GetEnumerator()` (the method exposed because `EventLogEntry` implements the `IEnumerableinterface`) `For Each` code such as the following can be written.

```
       Dim currentCount As Integer = 1
       Dim maxCount As Integer

       maxCount = ev.Entries.Count

       For Each logEntry In ev.Entries
```

The following code deals with the case where more entries were added to the event log while we were traversing it:

```
         If currentCount > maxCount Then
           maxCount = ev.Entries.Count
         End If
```

Interacting with the `EventLogEntry` instances is a matter of reading the properties exposed by this class (`Message`, `EventID`, `Data`, `Source`, etc.). At an earlier point in this chapter, a `WXEmployee` instance was placed in the data property of an event log entry.

```
        Dim strCaption = String.Format("Employee {0} of {1}", _
                                  currentCount, maxCount)
        Try
          Dim employee As WXEmployee = _
                                  WXEmployee.Create(logEntry.Data)
```

The above code reads the data property and reconstitutes it into a `WXEmployee` instance. If this operation fails (because that log entry does contain a `WXEmployee` data) then an exception is throw, the code catches this, and we just display the type and message of the entry.

```
          TextBoxResults.Text = employee.ToString()
          Dim strEmployee = String.Format("Name: {0} {1}{2}{3}: _
            {4}{2}{2}" & "OK to select next, Cancel to quit", _
            employee._firstName, employee._lastName, _
            Environment.NewLine, logEntry.EntryType.ToString, _
            logEntry.Message)
          result = MessageBox.Show(strEmployee, strCaption, _
                                  MessageBoxButtons.OKCancel)
        Catch ex As InvalidOperationException
          Dim strEmployee = String.Format("{0}: {1}{2}{2}" _
            & "OK to select next, Cancel to quit", _
            logEntry.EntryType.ToString, logEntry.Message, _
            Environment.NewLine)
          TextBoxResults.Text = _
            "This entry does not contain employee data"
          result = MessageBox.Show(strEmployee, strCaption, _
                                  MessageBoxButtons.OKCancel)
        End Try
```

Displaying the event log entries is a trivial exercise in using the `Show()` method of the `MessageBox` class. To show the XML representation of the `employee` instance of `WXEmployee` we call its `ToString()` method.

One .NET facility used in order to display data is the `Environment.NewLine` property, which corresponds to a newline character for whatever environment the code is presently running on. The other benefit associated with this implementation is that the `MessageBox` displayed exposes the OK and Cancel buttons. These two buttons allow users to see the next entry in the event log (OK) or to quit traversal (Cancel):

```
        If (result = DialogResult.Cancel) Then
          TextBoxResults.Text = ""
          Exit For
        End If
      Catch ex As InvalidOperationException
        result = MessageBox.Show("This entry contains no data", _
                            strCaption, MessageBoxButtons.OKCancel)
      End Try
```

```
            currentCount += 1
        Next
      Catch ex As Exception
        TextBoxResults.Text = ex.ToString()
      End Try
    End Sub
```

Obviously we have left out the Windows designer-generated code that is needed to complete this application; the full code can be found in `WXEventLogWriter.vb`, which is part of the book's code download.

If you run this application you should see something like this:

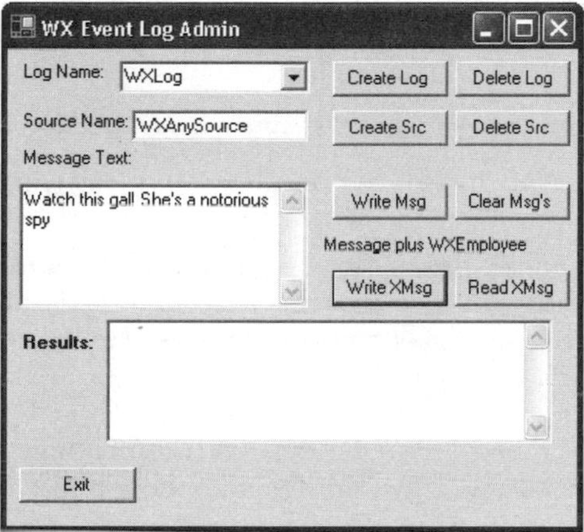


Here we have created an event log called "WXLog" and a source called "WXAnySource"; then we can write messages to and read messages from that Log.

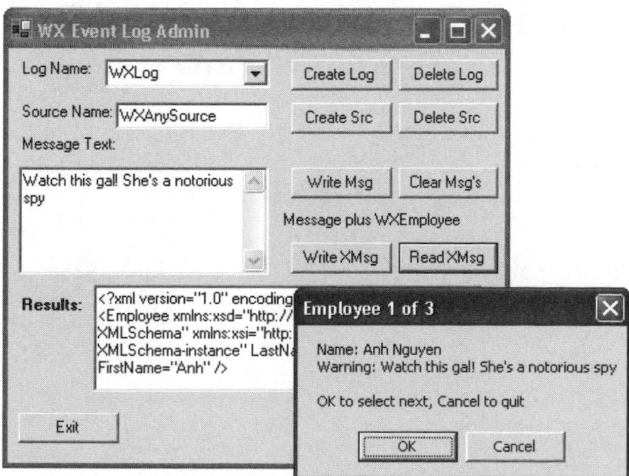

## Receiving Notification of New Log Entries

In many cases it might be desirable to actively monitor informational messages, errors, and warnings written to the Windows event log. If the EnableRaisingEvents property (type Boolean) of the EventLog class is set to True, whenever an entry matching the specific event log instance (Log plus an optional MachineName, and optional Source) is written, an event (EntryWritten) will be triggered:

```
Public Event EntryWritten As EntryWrittenEventHandler
```

The signature for the method that must be implemented to receive EntryWritten notifications is dictated by the delegate associated with this event (the EntryWrittenEventHandler delegate). The handling method's signature must match the following delegate (parameter for parameter):

```
Public Delegate Sub EntryWrittenEventHandler( _
                                    ByVal sender As Object, _
                                    ByVal e As EntryWrittenEventArgs)
```

In this declaration, the sender parameter corresponds to the EventLog instance that raised the EntryWritten event. The e parameter (of type, EventWrittenEventArgs) exposes the Event property that is of type EventLogEntry corresponding to the entry written to the system event log.

As the EventLog class is derived from the System.ComponentModel this namespace's Component class is is available as an option in the Toolbox window provided by Visual Studio .NET when developing a Windows Forms application.

Most controls are visual in nature (Button, TextBox, ComboBox, etc.), but there are also behind-the-scenes controls that include FileSystemWatcher, PerformanceCounter, and of course EventLog. Using the Toolbox's Components category an EventLog control can be associated with the Windows Forms application by simply dragging an EventLog control from the Toolbox and dropping on the form itself.

Here we'll develop a simple winforms application WXEventLog that can receive notification of entries added to the WXLog event log. The form simply consists of a ListBox, three Buttons, and an EventLog control.

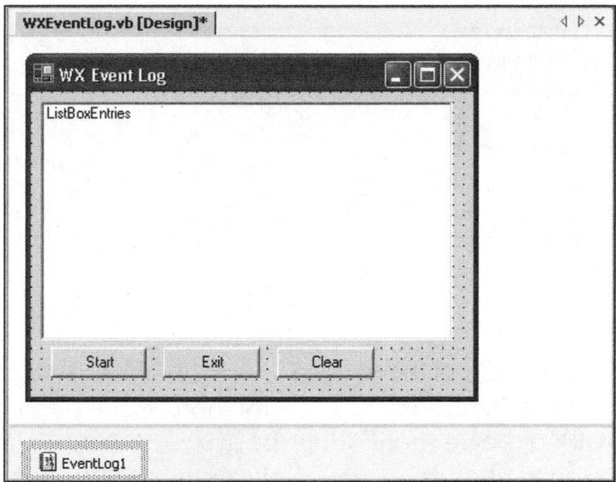


In order to specify the properties associated with EventLog1 (our instance of `EventLog`) simple select `EventLog1` (click on it) and display the properties dialog (View | Properties menu). An example of this is as follows:

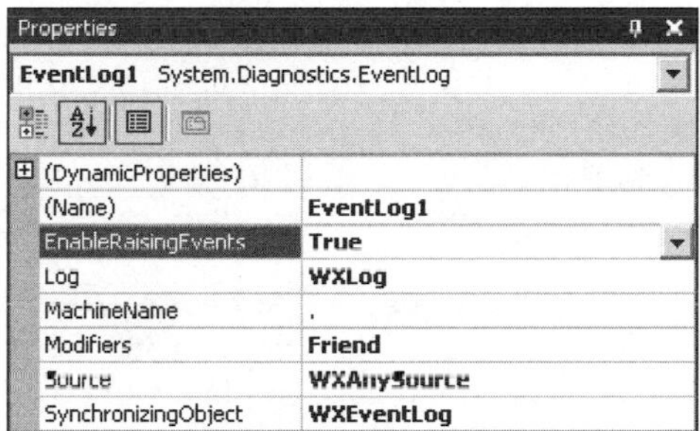


To suit our purposes, the properties in the previous screenshot will be configured as follows:

- `EnableRaisingEvents` – Set to `True`
- `Log` – set to "`WXLog`"
- `Source` – set to "`WXAnySource`"

These settings enable `EventLog1` to invoke the `EventWritten` event (`EnableRasingEvent=True`) when an event log entry is written to the `WXLog` log and the `WXAnySource` event source. What remains is to associate a method with the `EventWritten` event to handle this invocation.

The code generated by the previous screenshot is found in the application's `InitializeComponent()` method. The code from this method is created by Visual Studio .NET's Windows.Forms designer and is as follows (some of the garnishments added by the designer have been removed for clarity):

```
' Create Button instances, ListBox instance here
EventLog1 = New System.Diagnostics.EventLog()
EventLog1.BeginInit()

EventLog1.Log = "WXLog"
EventLog1.Source = "WXAnySource"
EventLog1.SynchronizingObject = Me
' Initialize Button instances, ListBox instance here

EventLog1.EndInit()
```

In this code snippet the creation of `EventLog1` using `New` and assigning `Log` and `Source` is self-explanatory. The `BeginInit()` method is called to ensure that the `EventLog` instance will not begin monitoring the system event log and firing `EventWritten` events until after the entire application is setup. Remember that other controls (`Button` instances and a `ListBox`) will work with `EventLog1` in order to display the events received from the event log notifications. Once these other controls are fully configured, the `EventLog` instance's `EndInit()` is called.

The `SynchronizingObject` property specifies that the events received from the `EventLog` instance should be handled by the same thread in which this instance was created. Why did threads suddenly appear? By default, a thread from the system-provided thread pool is used when an `EntryWritten` event is generated. In a Windows Forms application, passing in any old thread from the system thread poll can cause thread affinity problems, which could generate an exception.

The `SynchronizingObject` property is set to `Me` because the `Forms` class is derived from the `Control` class and the `Control` class implements the `ISynchronizeInvoke` interface. The `ISynchronizeInvoke` interface implemented by the Windows Form ensures that the handling of an `EntryWritten` event is completed before another `EntryWritten` is permitted to fire.

> *While we are on the subject of threads, it is also worth noting that if you are writing to the event log from a multi-threaded application you must obtain an exclusive lock on the* `EventLog` *object. This is to ensure that you don't generate a race condition when two threads are simultaneously accessing the* `EventLog` *object. A full description of the complexities of thread-safe programming can be found in the* Visual Basic .NET Threading handbook, *(Wrox Press, 2002; ISBN 1-86100-713-2).*

This task of creating the method to associate with the `EventWritten` event is handled by double-clicking on the `EventLog1` instance displayed when the application is shown in design mode. This double-click causes the Windows Forms designer to generate the appropriate method the source for the application:

```
    Private Sub EventLog1_EntryWritten( _
      ByVal sender As Object, _
      ByVal e As System.Diagnostics.EntryWrittenEventArge) _
        Handles EventLog1.EntryWritten
    End Sub
```

With the basic shell of the method in place, the event monitoring application can be implemented. The following controls were added to our form in order to facilitate the display of event log entries:

`ButtonStartStop` – this `Button` when clicked enables the handling of `EntryWritten` events. When it is clicked again they are disabled. The method for handling this is as follows:

```
  Private Sub ButtonStartStop_Click(ByVal sender As System.Object, _
                                    ByVal e As System.EventArgs) _
                                      Handles ButtonStartStop.Click

    If String.Compare(ButtonStartStop.Text, "Start") = 0 Then
      EventLog1.EnableRaisingEvents = True
        ButtonStartStop.Text = "Stop"
    Else ' we are Stop
      EventLog1.EnableRaisingEvents = False
      ButtonStartStop.Text = "Start"
    End If
  End Sub
```

`ListBoxEntries` – this `ListBox` contains each event log entry read when an `EventWritten` event is invoked.

Given a `Button` to start/stop activation and a `ListBox` in which to place log entries, the `EventLog1_EntryWritten()` method can be implemented as follows:

```
  EventArgsPrivate Sub EventLog1_EntryWritten( _
    ByVal sender As Object, _
    ByVal e As System.Diagnostics.EntryWrittenEventArgs) _
      Handles EventLog1.EntryWritten
```

We could just use the `EventLog1` data member but using `sender` means the method could handle `EventWritten` events for multiple `EventLog` instances:

```
    Dim evLog As EventLog = sender
    Dim logEntry As EventLogEntry = e.Entry

    If 0 = String.Compare(logEntry.Message, _
                          "Stop spying on me") Then
      EventLog1.EnableRaisingEvents = False
```

Since we were handling events, the button said "Stop" indicating "push to stop handling". We are disabling the event handling so the button should be set to "Start" and can now be clicked to re-enable event handling

```
      ButtonStartStop.Text = "Start"
    Else
      ListBoxEntries.Items.Add(String.Format("{0} {1}: ""{2}""", _
      logEntry.TimeGenerated, logEntry.Source, logEntry.Message))
    End If
  End Sub
```

The previous code snippet checks the log entry's `Message` property for the key phrase, "Stop spying on me". This is a command from the application generating the log entries. The command means, cease and desist from monitoring. In programming terms, this means setting the `EnableRaisingEvents` property to `False` (stop monitoring the event log).

If the `Message` property is not a cease-and-desist command, then a log entry is added to the `ListBoxEntries ListBox` so it can be displayed on the form. Fear not, in the source code for this application there is also a Clear button that clears the `ListBoxEntries`. This lets the user purge the `ListBox` periodically; otherwise; the contents of the `ListBox` would grow in an unbounded fashion.

If you run the WXEventLog and WXEventLogWriter applications together, we can see how it all works. It is important to run WXEventLogWriter first so we know that the WXLog event log has been created.

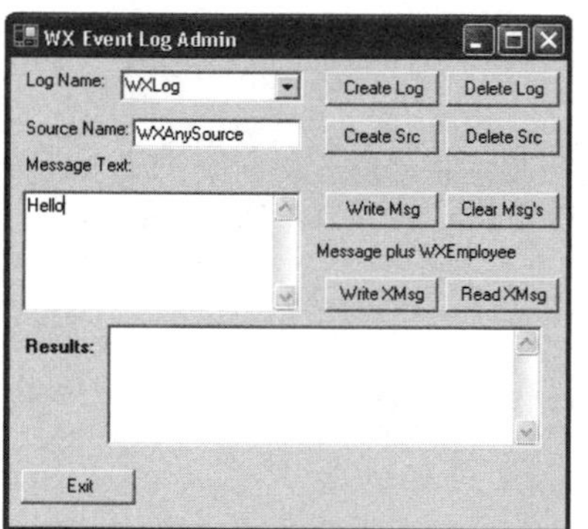


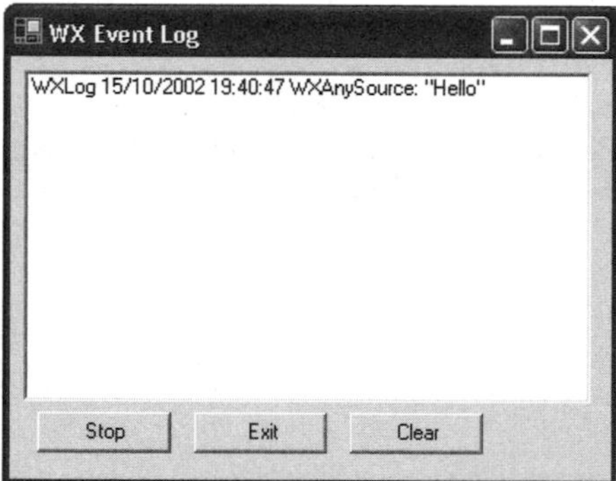


The figure above show writing an event using WXEventLogWriter and the event generated being shown in WXEventLog. Now try what happens.

# Event Log Infrastructure and Windows

The .NET Framework is presently built on top of the Win32 API. This API offers system services, including (along with many others) the manipulation of the event log. When working directly with the Win 32 API, a developer had to register an event log source before it could be used. .NET handles these registration steps with such straightforward methods as `WriteEntry()`. The steps previously performed by a Win32 application to set up an event log are worth noting because it demonstrates the amount of complexity .NET hides from the developer:

- Create a message file. This file contains strings each referenced by an index. Each string was a message to be placed in the event log corresponding to a particular event source. This allowed the messages associated with the event log to be localized (so that one message file could be installed for a French machine, another for an Italian machine, etc.). This file was typically created with the Message compiler (`MC.exe`) Win32 utility.
- Create a key in the Windows registry corresponding to the custom event log (if a custom event log is to be used). In the following registry path, "NNN" refers to the name of the custom event log. In the examples, shown thus far WXLog was used as a custom event log.

```
HKEY_LOCAL_MACHINE\System\CurrentControlSet\Services\
  EventLog\NNN
```

- Create an entry under an event log corresponding to the event source to be registered. The following for example places an event source name MMM (such as `WXAnySource`) under the `Application` log:

```
HKEY_LOCAL_MACHINE\System\CurrentControlSet\Services\
  EventLog\Application\MMM
```

- Add a `EventMessageFile` string value underneath the event source. The value associated with this entry contains the full path corresponding to the event source's message file.

The following screenshot shows the perks provided by the `EventLog` class, namely that it created the `WXLog` event log and the `WXAnySource` and `WXTheOtherSource` event sources:

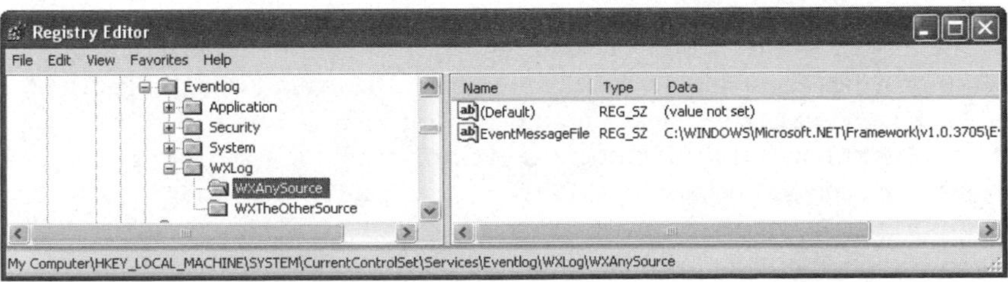

The value of the `EventMessageFile` key from the previous screenshot in its entirety is as follows:
`C:\WINDOWS\Microsoft.NET\Framework\v1.0.3705\EventLogMessages.dll`

Since the message file is compiled and referenced in the registry, how do strings from .NET applications make it into the event log?.

.NET uses one message file (`EventLogMessages.dll`) for every event log source. The sole purpose of this message file is to provide a way to write a string to the event log. This file contains just message, `"%0"`. The only functionality provided by this lone message is that its contents can be specified using a single parameter (the zero-th parameter).

When `EventLog.WriteEntry()` is invoked a string is specified as this function's sole parameter. This lone parameter to `WriteEntry()` is actually a replacement string used to replace the `%0` of the lone resource string entry in the `EventLogMessages.dll` resource file.

The `EventLogEntry` class can be used to read entries written by .NET applications (entries that are a string substituted for `%0`) and entries written by legacy applications. Legacy applications might contain multiple parameter values to be substituted. This is permissible for legacy applications because their messages can contain numerous parameter substitutions (`%0`, `%1`, `%2`, etc.). The `EventLogEntry` class actually can read the replacement strings provided by legacy applications logging to the event log. These replacement strings are read via the `EventLogEntry.ReplacementString` property.

If the string was logged using `EventLog.WriteEntry()` then the `ReplacementString` array will contain a single entry that will be identical to the `EventLogEntry.Message` property (the message contained in the event log). If the event log entry was logged by a Legacy application not using `EventLog` to perform logging, then there may be zero replacement strings or many replacement strings. The `WXEventLog.vb` file contains a piece of code that shows how .NET handles event log messages:

```
Dim replacement As String

For Each replacement In logEntry.ReplacementStrings
  Debug.WriteLine("Replacement: " & replacement)
Next
```

## Backing up Event Logs

There is one feature of the Windows event log API that is not exposed directly by .NET. This feature provides the ability to backup a copy of the event log to a file. The Win32 function `BackupEventLog()` backs up an event log to a file and the `OpenBackupEventLog()` function opens a backup event log for reading. These legacy functions can be accessed using the `DllImportAttribute` class found in the `System.Runtime.InteropServices` namespace. Using the aforementioned Win32 functions in conjunction with .NET supported interoperability .NET developers can gain access to the event log backup feature.

# The Debug and Trace Classes

The oldest trick in the debugging handbook is to print information to the screen. However a screen is not always available (ASP.NET applications, Windows Services, etc.) and it is not always a good idea to print to the screen anyway. The `System.Diagnostics` namespace includes the `Trace` and `Debug` classes that offer a more flexible alternative.

The `Trace` and `Debug` classes provided support for logging by allowing a single log write method (`Write()` or `WriteLine()`) to reach multiple destinations (screen, file, etc.). Additionally these classes expose methods (`Assert()` and `Fail()`) that allow a `MessageBox` to be displayed that provides a developer with the opportunity to do one of the following:

- Start debugging the application
- Ignore the `Assert()/Fail()` and just run the application normally
- Terminate the execution of the application

While these classes do exposed identical methods there is an important difference, `Trace` is (typically) enabled for both release and debug builds, while `Debug` is (typically) enabled only in debug builds.

The write methods exposed by `Trace` and `Debug` (all of which are shared) are certainly not quantum physics:

- `Write()` – writes text to the logging destinations associated with `Trace` or `Debug` (depending on whether `Trace.Write()` or `Debug.Write()` is invoked). You can either pass in a `String` or an object with a `ToString()` method. For this and the other write methods, a category `String` can also be specified:

  ```
  Dim category 1 As String = "Some Category"
  Trace.Write("Some Message" , category1)
  ```

  This is then prefixed before the main entry and produces the following log entry:

  Some Category: Some Message

  Confusingly this is totally unrelated to the category property that is part of EventLog entry.
- `WriteLine()` – writes text with a line terminator to logging destinations associated with `Trace` or `Debug`.

- WriteIf(), WriteLineIf()– writes text (WriteIf()) or writes text with line terminator (WriteLineIf()) only if a certain condition is true, such as the following, which logs when the weather in England is not cloudy (a circumstance rarely logged):

```
Debug.WriteLineIf(weather <> EnglishWeather.Cloudy, _
                  "I can get a tan!")
```

The Trace and Debug classes are each separately associated with a collection of listeners (classes implementing the TraceListener base class). A listener is a destination for logging information that comes in a variety of flavors. Both the Trace and Debug classes contain a Listeners property that corresponds to the collection of listeners. As the name collection implies, individual listeners can be managed by this collection. For example, Debug.Listeners.Add() can add a listener to Debug's Listeners collection while Debug.Listeners.Remove() will remove one. The System.Diagnostics namespace provides various types of listener:

- DefaultTraceListener – By default, Trace and Debug are associated with the DefautlTraceListener. The name of this trace listener (Name property) is not surprisingly "Default". The destination of this listener is Debugger.Log() and the underlying Window's method, OutputDebugString(), which sends a message. If no debugger is attached this trace listener will be ignored (calling it will not generate an exception).

- TextWriterTraceListener – the logged text can be written to any class derived from TextWriter such as the System.IO.StreamWriter class. The Out and Error properties of the Console class are both of type TextWriter so therefore Console.Out() and Console.Error() are viable candidates to serve as a TextWriterTraceListener:

```
Dim justAFile As TextWriterTraceListener = _
  New TextWriterTraceListener(New StreamWriter( _
                                  "C:\JustALogFile.log"))

Trace.Listeners.Add(justAFile)
Debug.Listeners.Add(New TextWriterTraceListener(Console.Out))
```

- EventLogTraceListener – log text is written to the event log and associated with a particular event source such as the following where the AnySourceName event source is logged to:

```
Trace.Listeners.Add(New EventLogTraceListener("AnySourceName"))
```

- Custom Listener – applications can create their own class derived from the TraceListener base class. For example a WXLogItToSQLServer class could be developed that wrote the text received from Trace and/or Debug to a table residing in a SQL Server database.

An example of an environment where `Trace` and `Debug` are associated with a variety of listeners (including sharing listeners) is as follows:

**Figure 1**

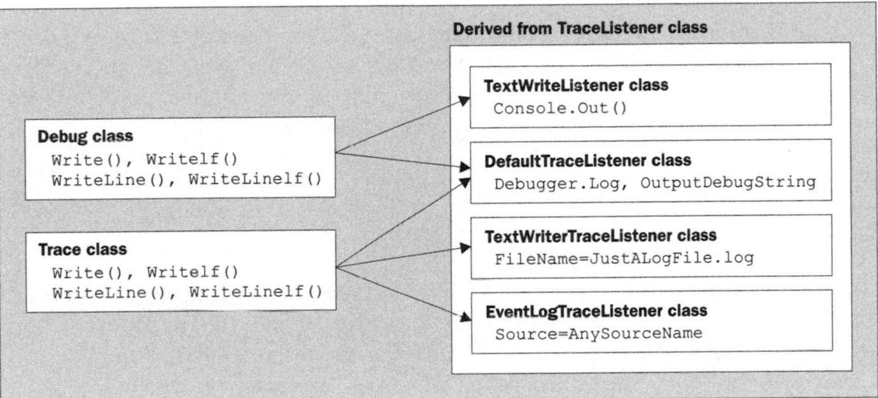


In the previous diagram, each flavor of the `write()` method called for the `Debug` class passes text to the console window (`Console.Out()`) and to the output channel monitored by a debugger. The `Trace` class's write methods pass their text to the output channel monitored by a debugger, a file (`JustALogFile.log`), and the event log (event source: `AnySourceName`).

Once configuration is complete (trace listeners associated with the `Debug` class or `Trace` class or both) then the application can blissfully log without actually needing to know the specific logging destinations:

```
Debug.WriteLine("Evaluate the performance of this code " + _
                "customers are complaining about it")
Trace.WriteLine("Starting process: " + DateTime.Now.ToString())
```

The previous code snippet shows both `Trace` and `Debug` performing a `WriteLine()` operation. The text associated with the `Trace.WriteLine()` is the kind of thing that would be safe to put in a log that is viewed by customers. The text associated with the `Debug.WriteLine()` is rather unprofessional and any quality software shop would not want such text viewed by customers. Recalling that the `Debug` class only associated with debug builds, it should be obvious that this will not be a problem.

## Debug/Trace Setup

The basic steps required to enjoy the fruits of the `Trace` and `Debug` classes are:

1. Define the `TRACE` flag in order to enable the methods of the `Trace` class to generate logging text and define the `DEBUG` flag in order to enable the methods of the `Debug` class to generate logging text. If the appropriate flag (`TRACE` or `DEBUG`) is not defined then the methods associated with the corresponding class are ignored.
2. Create trace listeners (custom trace listener, `TextWriterTraceListener`, or `EventLogTraceListener`) and associate them with the `Trace` class, `Debug` class, or both classes. It is possible to also remove the default trace listener (the one whose logging goes to `Debugger.Log()`) or to create no trace listeners and simply rely on the default trace listener.
3. Call the methods associated with the `Trace` and `Debug` classes (`Assert()`, `Fail()`, `Write()`, `WriteLine()`, etc.).

As just pointed out, the first step in working with `Trace` and `Debug` is to define `TRACE` and `DEBUG`. Arnold-Schwarzenegger-style developers can take the macho route and define `TRACE` and `DEBUG` using command-line version of the VB.NET compiler (`vbc.exe` with /d:TRACE=True and/or /d:DEBUG=True). It is also possible to define said options programmatically (in source code):

```
#Const DEBUG=1 ' enable Debug.xxx methods
#Const TRACE=1 ' enable Trace.xxx methods
```

A simpler approach to setting `DEBUG` and `TRACE` is to use a Visual Studio .NET project's property page. To see the defaults or to modify them select View | Properties, which displays the Property Pages dialog for the project currently selected:

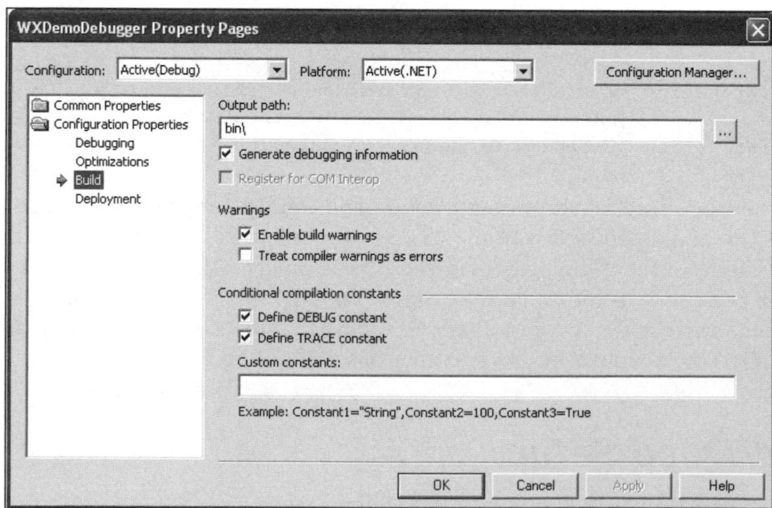

In the Property Pages dialog screenshot notice that Configuration Parameters | Build is selected. The active configuration is Debug, which means that TRACE and DEBUG are selected. If the active configuration is set to Release then only TRACE is selected.

With `TRACE` and `DEBUG` both set to `True` (or not), the trace listeners can now be set up.

> *Each flavor of trace listener is derived from the* `TraceListener` *base class, which means they all inherit the* `Name` *property that gets and sets the name an application associates with a trace listener. This property can be displayed, or used as the key to determine which trace listener to remove when it is no longer needed by an application.*

Let's look at the constructors associated with each kind of trace listener. The `TextWriterTraceListener` class is constructed using the following:

- `Sub New()` – creates a "yet to be setup" event listener, which needs to have its `Writer` property (type `TextWriter`) assigned. Note that if you want to use a file or a stream as the destination you must create the listener with the correct constructor as it is not possible to assign them latter as you can for a `TextWriter`.
- `Sub New(Stream)`, `Sub New(Stream, String)` – creates a trace listener associated with a instance of an class derived from the `Stream` base class (`FileStream`, `MemoryStream`, `CryptoStream`, etc.) and can specify a name to associate with the trace listener (the `String` parameter). An example of creating a stream (corresponding to the file `c:\PutLogInfoHere.log`) and associating it with a trace listener is as follows:

```
Dim myTraceListener As New TextWriterTraceListener( _
  New FileStream("c:\PutLogInfoHere.log", FileMode.Create))
```

- `Sub New(String)`, `Sub New(String, String)` – creates a trace listener associated with an file name (the first parameter instance of type `String`); you can also specify a name to associate with the trace listener (the second `String` parameter).
- `Sub New(TextWriter)`, `Sub New(TextWriter, String)` – creates a trace listener associated with a instance of a class derived from the `TextWriter` base class (`StreamWriter`, `StringWriter`, etc.) and can also specify a name to associate with the trace listener (the `String` parameter).

The `EventLogTraceListener` class is constructed using the following:

- `Sub New()` – creates a "yet to be setup" event listener, which needs to have its `EventLog` property assigned (a property not surprisingly of type, `EventLog`).

- Sub New(EventLog) – creates a trace listener associated with the EventLog specified. Recall that the EventLog allows the event source, hostname of the event log and the log name to be specified. The following snippet shows an EventLogTraceListener being associated with an EventLog fully qualified by log name, hostname, and event source name:

```
Dim myEventLogTracListener As EventLogTraceListener = _
  New EventLogTraceListener(New EventLog("AnyLogName", _
                                  "AnyHostName", "AnyEventSource"))
```

  No name needs to be specified for an EventLogTraceListener instance, the trace listener's name defaults to the name of the event log the trace listener writes to.

- Sub New(String) – associates trace listener with event log writing to the event source specified by the lone parameter (type, String). Using this constructor the hostname and log name do not need to be specified for the event log. The host defaults to the local host and since each event source is associated with a single event log, there is no need to specify the name of the event log.

# Formatting Log Output

There is a bit more to managing Debug and Trace output than a slew of write methods and the Listeners property. For example, the Debug and Trace classes can take advantage of the IndentLevel and IndentSize properties exposed by each trace listener:

- IndentLevel – an Integer property that sets how the log text is indented for all trace listeners associated with Debug or Trace. The amount indented on writing to each TraceListener is IndentLevel * IndentSize.

- IndentSize – Integer property that gets and sets number of spaces indented per-IndentLevel for all trace listeners associated with Debug or Trace.

The indent-level property can be altered for each write request using the following methods:

- Indent() – the method increments the value of the IndentLevel property by one

- Unindent() – the method decrements the value of the IndentLevel property by one

Using these methods, indenting can be used to make logged information more readable; for instance, you might log the start-up and shut-down sequences for an application:

```
Initialization Sequence Start: 12/07/02 18:05:50
  Load Configuration Files
      Load Main Config File
          Success
      Load User Config File
          Success
    Open Database Connections
        Open Database Connection 1
            Success
        Open Database Connection 2
            *** Warning Connection Initialization Failed
Initialization Sequence End: 12/07/02 18:05:52
Shutdown Sequence Start:
    ...
```

## Closing Trace Listeners

The Debug and Trace classes implement the Flush() method, which lives up to its name and flushes the buffers for each trace listener, writing out their contents. Also exposed by the Debug and Trace classes is the Close() method. This method closes each trace listener for either Debug or Trace and ensures that all buffers are flushed before the trace listeners are closed. Care should be used when calling this because Trace and Debug can share trace listeners. To understand where things can be askew consider the following rather tranquil looking snippet of code:

```
Dim sharedListener As TextWriterTraceListener = _
  New TextWriterTraceListener("WXCommonLog.log")

Trace.Listeners.Add(sharedListener)
Debug.Listeners.Add(sharedListener)

' main body of code would be implemented here

Trace.Close()
Debug.WriteLine("About to open Database X")
```

The final line of code (Debug.WriteLine()) is highlighted because it causes an exception to be raised as follows:

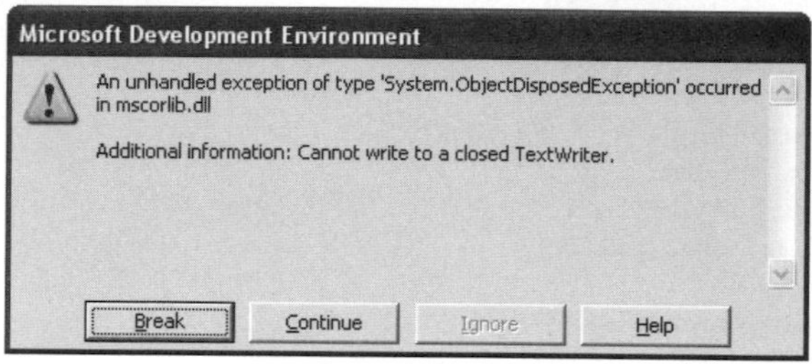


The exception explains what happens fairly clearly. When `Debug` performs a `WriteLine()` an attempt is made to write to the file `WXCommonLog.Log`. This file has already been closed because `Trace.Close()` was called.

Things are different for the default trace listener though, (the trace listener that writes to `Debug.Log` and `OutputDebugString`); it is possible to call the `Close()` method in `Trace` without sabotaging `Debug`. It is also possible to invoke `Debug.Close()` without sabotaging a `Trace` class's write. This is because separate trace listeners are created for `Trace` and `Debug`. Actually, this is a valuable lesson – where possible create two instances for a trace listener rather than sharing one between `Trace` and `Debug` (unless you like generating exceptions in your code).

## Developing a Custom TraceListener

By deriving from the `TraceListener` class we can create a custom trace listener. The `TraceListener` class is abstract, which means it contains a method or methods that a derived class must implement. The specific methods the custom trace listener (the derived class) must implement are:

```
Public Overloads Mustoverride Sub Write(ByVal message As String)
Public Overloads Mustoverride Sub WriteLine(ByVal message As String)
```

There are other overloads of these methods but we only need to implement the string version for each of them. The other `TraceListner` methods can be overrided if needed:

```
Public Overridable Sub Close()
Public Overridable Sub Flush()
Public Overridable Overloads Sub Fail(ByVal message As String)
Public Overridable Overloads Sub Fail(ByVal message As String, _
                                      ByVal detailMessage As String )
Protected Overridable Sub WriteIndent()
```

The WXDBTraceListener.vb source file contains a complete implementation of a custom listener that writes to a SQL Server database. Why a database? Certain applications do all their processing via database, others via e-mail, and others via the registry or Active Directory. When working in a mostly database world, it only makes sense to log to the location where the rest of the application is writing.

The WXDBTraceListener class contains a data member for the connection to the SQL Server database (_connection) and a command object (_command) that is used to execute a SQL command executed against this connection:

```
Public Class WXDBTraceListener
  Private _connection As SqlConnection
  Private _command As SqlCommand
```

The class also contains a data member that checks to see if the table written to (WXLog) exists and if the WXLog table does not exist, it creates it:

```
Private Const _setupCreateTable As String = _
    "IF NOT EXISTS (SELECT * " & _
                  "FROM dbo.sysobjects " & _
                  "WHERE id = object_id(N'[dbo].[WXLog]') AND " & _
                      "OBJECTPROPERTY(id, N'IsUserTable') = 1) " & _
    "CREATE TABLE [dbo].[WXLog] (" & _
        "[LogID] UNIQUEIDENTIFIER ROWGUIDCOL DEFAULT (NEWID()), " & _
        "[Message] [NVARCHAR] (4000) NOT NULL , " & _
        "[LogTime] AS (GETDATE()))"
```

The previous SQL seems a bit intricate but it is not. The IF NOT EXISTS portion checks to see if the table does not exist in the sysbobjects system table, if it doesn't the Create Table statement is executed. The LogID column contains a SQL Server generated GUID (hence the NEWID() function embedded in the CREATE TABLE statement). The Message column is a variable length Unicode (hence NVARCHAR where N stands for Unicode) that can contain up to 4,000 characters; this is why the WXDBTraceListener class checks the buffer length before inserting a new row (a new log entry) into the database. The LogTime column contains the current data and time as generated by SQL's GetDate() function.

The body of the constructor, New(), in its entirety is as follows:

```
Sub New()
    _connection = New SqlConnection("Data Source=localhost;" & _
                                    "Initial Catalog=northwind;" & _
                                    "User ID=sa;" & _
                                    "Password=sa;")
    _connection.Open()
    _command = New SqlCommand(_setupCreateTable, _connection)
    _command.ExecuteNonQuery()
    _closed = False
End Sub
```

The WXDBTraceListener class's constructor is used to ensure the WXLog table exists (using _setupCreateTable) in the database and that the connection to SQL Server is open. The connection to SQL Server is set up by creating an instance of type SqlConnection and assigning it to _connection. After this the Open() method of this data member is called, hence opening the connection to SQL Server. With the connection opened, a command can be created (New SqlCommand) and this command is associated with the connection. The ExecuteNonQuery() method of this SqlCommand is used to execute the previously described CREATE TABLE statement (which of course checked to make sure the table did not exist before executing).

The load parameter to the SqlConnection constructor is a connection string. The connection string refers to SQL Server running on the current machine (Data Source=localhost) and logs in using user, sa, (User ID=sa) with password, sa, (Password=sa). This represents SQL Server intrinsic security. A great many SQL Server installations uses intrinsic Windows security. Under this case the Windows account the application is running under serves as the security credential so the connection string does not require a User ID and Password. A better alternative in a real application would be to store the configuration details in an application configuration file.

The specific SQL Server database the connection is associated with is Northwind, since within the connection string Initial Catalog = Northwind. Most Access and SQL Server developers recognize Northwind as a sample database installed by default.

The Write() implementation is as follows where a Boolean data member, _closed, is used to prevent the trace listener from being written to after its Close() method has been called:

```
Private _buffer As String
Private _closed As Boolean

Public Overloads Overrides Sub Write(ByVal message As String)
  If _closed Then
    Throw New Exception("WXDBTraceListener closed")
  End If
  _buffer &= message
End Sub
```

The message to write will not be written to SQL Server until WriteLine() is invoked. For this reason the Write() method's message parameter is appended to the _buffer data member of the trace listener. It is the job of WriteLine() to use SQL (the language of SQL Server) in order to write the message to a table in SQL Server. This is achieved as follows:

```
Public Overloads Overrides Sub WriteLine(ByVal message As String)
  If _closed Then
    Throw New Exception("WXDBTraceListener closed")
  End If
```

```
        _buffer &= message
        If _buffer.Length > 4000 Then
          Throw New _
            OverflowException("message buffer exceeds 4000 bytes")
        End If
        _command.CommandText = String.Format( _
          "INSERT INTO WXLog (Message) VALUES ('{0}')", _buffer)
        _buffer = ""
        _command.ExecuteNonQuery()
      End Sub
    End Class
```

The previous code checks to ensure that the trace listener is not closed by checking the `_closed` data member. The message parameter passed to `WriteLine()` is then appended to the `_buffer` data member. This step ensures that the message written to `WriteLine()` will be appended to messages already appended to the `_buffer` by the `Write()` method. At this stage the size of the buffer is checked so it does not exceed 4,000 characters (the amount of space reserved in SQL Server for the data using the `NCHAR(4000)` data type). The `_buffer` is then associated with a SQL statement (`INSERT INTO`) and then the buffer can be emptied so the next set of `Write()` and `WriteLine()` invocations start with an empty buffer. The SQL command (`_command`, which is of type `SqlCommand`) can now be executed thus writing `_buffer` to the database.

The `Write()` and `WriteLine()` methods were quite simple. The complexity (about eight lines of code) is actually in connecting to the database, ensuring the table where to log entry is to be written exists, and closing the database.

# Run-time Debugger Configuration

When the application is built, the behavior of the `Assert()` method, the trace listeners and other debug mechanism might seem as if it is etched in stone. As it turns out, these items can be configured at run time using a particular application's configuration file. The idea is to use application configuration files instead of or in conjunction with programmatic setup. The application configuration files are XML-based and can contain all sorts of configuration information (security information, remoting settings, database connection strings, etc.) for information on how to create application configuration files see Appendix A.

*Developers, testers, and technical support staff can use application configuration files to enable any logging flags provide by your application. This feature has proved popular with many software engineering teams because of its flexibility and usefulness to numerous groups within a development project. Application configuration files are the way to go with respect to configuration logging and switches.*

In order to configure things in the `System.Diagnostics` namespace the following elements should be placed at the root level of the configuration file:

```
<configuration>
  <system.diagnostics>
  </system.diagnostics>
</configuration>
```

*Remember XML elements and attributes are case-sensitive. Each element discussed is lower-case and cannot be made upper-case or contain mixed case.*

The idea is that the configuration settings go within the `<configuration>` start and end tags. The `System.Diagnostics`, specific settings go between the correspondingly named start and end tags. Within the `<system.diagnostics>` tags the following elements are available for configuring the features of `System.Diagnostics`:

- `<assert>` – this element controls the behavior of the `Assert()` method exposed by the `Debug` and `Trace` classes. This was covered in the *Assert* and *Fail* sections of Chapter 4
- `<trace>` – this element controls the trace listeners associated with the `Debug` and `Trace` classes. If the `autoflush` attribute of `<trace>` is set to `true` then trace listeners auto-flush with each write so there is no need to call the `Flush()` method associated with a trace listener to actually get the log entries to their destination. By default, the `autoflush` attribute is set to `false` (no auto flush). The `indentdsize` attribute can be used to specify the number of spaces each log entry is indented with each level of indentation. If you set the indent level in your application's code that value will override the value set here. The following `<trace>` settings cause the listeners to auto-flush and set the indent size to two for all logs:

  ```
  <configuration>
    <system.diagnostics>
      <trace autoflush="true" indentsize="2"/>
    </system.diagnostics>
  </configuration>
  ```

- `<switches>` – specifies values for the switches used to control when tracing does and does not take place. The `<switches>` element will be presented in detail in the next section where the `Switch`, `BooleanSwitch`, and `TraceSwitch` classes are introduced.

The `<trace>` element can actually contain child elements, `<listeners>`. Within the `<listeners>` element, `<add>` can be used to add a trace listener to the `Listeners` property associated with `Debug` and `Trace`. The <add> element adds to both `Debug` and `Trace` at the same time; it is not possible to be selective. The `<remove>` element is also a child element of `<listeners>` and can be used to remove a trace listener from the `Listeners` property of both `Debug` and `Trace`.

The following configuration file demonstrate the use of the <add> and <remove> elements:

```
<configuration>
  <system.diagnostics>
    <trace>
      <listeners>
        <remove name="Default" />
        <add name="StockWroxListener"
             type="System.Diagnostics.EventLogTraceListener"
             initializeData="WXAnySource"/>
        <add name="StockWroxFileListener"
             type="System.Diagnostics.TextWriterTraceListener"
             initializeData="C:\WXLog.txt"/>
        <!-- Use custom trace listener -->
        <add name="CustomWroxListener"
             type=
         "WXDemoDebugAndTrace.WXDBTraceListener,WXDemoDebugAndTrace"/>
      </listeners>
    </trace>
  </system.diagnostics>
</configuration>
```

The previous configuration file uses the <remove> to remove the trace listener named "Default" (the default trace listener), hence the use of the name XML attribute. This value corresponds to the TraceListener's Name property:

Within the <add> elements the name XML attribute is used to associate a name with the trace listener being added (TraceListener.Name). The type XML attribute is a fully qualified name corresponding to the type of TraceListener to be added to the Listeners collection property. A fully qualified name is defined as follows:

```
Namespace.ClassName,AssemblyName
```

The <add> element also exposes the <initializeData> element. The text associated with this attribute is passed as the initData parameter to the constructor of the TraceListener being constructed (Sub New(ByVal initData As String)). The specific trace listeners added in the previous configuration file are as follows:

- StockWroxListener is an instance of type EventLogTraceListener that will access the WXAnySource event source.
- StockWroxFileListener is an instance of type TextWriterTraceListener that will write to the C:\WXLog.txt file.
- CustomWroxListener is an instance of the custom trace listener that was developed previously in this chapter. The namespace (WXDemoDebugAndTrace), class name (WXDBTraceListener), and assembly name (WXDemoDebugAndTrace) are used to fully qualify the TraceListener.

The values of each type attribute in the previous example of <add> are inconsistent. For the WXDBTraceListener custom trace listener, the assembly name had to be specified. For the instance of type TextWriterTraceListener and EventLogTraceListener there was no assembly required. This is because these classes are contained in mscorlib.dll, which is always available to a .NET application without specifically loading it

> *The examples in MSDN show the assembly being specified by adding* ",System" *to the end of the* type *attribute (corresponding to the* System.dll*). Specifying the assembly causes the* <add> *to fail for .NET native trace listeners.*

# Switches

By the term "switch" we mean the ability switch a feature on or off. .NET provides two classes, BooleanSwitch and TraceSwitch, (both derived from the Switch class) that are useful for switching logging functionality off. For BooleanSwitch the switch is on or off. With respect to TraceSwitch a specific trace level can be set (none, informational, warning, and error). The setting of both BooleanSwitch and TraceSwitch (the switch level) can be configured programmatically or using a configuration file as previously mentioned (the <switches> configuration element).

## *BooleanSwitch*

A BooleanSwitch instance is constructed by specifying a display name and a description corresponding to what the string represents:

```
Private _logDBStatistics As BooleanSwitch = _
  New BooleanSwitch("DBStats", "Monitor DB command execution times")
```

Once specified in the constructor these values can be retrieved using appropriately named properties exposed by the Switch base class:

```
Public ReadOnly Property DisplayName As String
Public ReadOnly Property Description As String
```

In order to determine if the switch is enabled (true or false) the Enabled property is exposed:

```
Public Property Enabled As Boolean
```

The following code snippet demonstrates using the _logDBStatistics BooleanSwitch instance to enable and disable calls to the Trace class's WriteLineIf method:

```
Private _logDBStatistics As BooleanSwitch = _
  New BooleanSwitch("DBStats", "Monitor DB command execution time")

Public Sub WXExecuteDatabaseCommand()
  Trace.WriteLineIf(_logDBStatistics.Enabled, _
                    "DB Command start time: " & DateTime.Now)
  ' execute database commands here
  Trace.WriteLineIf(_logDBStatistics.Enabled, _
                    "DB Command end time: " & DateTime.Now)
End Sub
```

The previous example is nifty but where is the `Enabled` property set? The previous code is associated with the `WXDemoSwitch` application. The `WXDemoSwitch.exe.config` configuration file is found in the same directory as this application and contains the following:

```
<configuration>
  <system.diagnostics>
    <switches>
      <add name="DBStats" value="0" />
      <add name="HRModule" value-"3" />
      <add name="StockOptionsModule" value="2" />
    </switches>
  </system.diagnostics>
</configuration>
```

The previous configuration file contains a `<switches>` element with three `<add>` child elements. The value associated with the `name` attribute of the `<add>` element contains the display name (`DisplayName` property) of a class derived from the `Switch` base class. Recall from the previous code snippet that the `_logDBStatistics` `BooleanSwitch` instance (derived from `Switch`) is named `DBStats`. The `value` attribute of the `<add>` element is used to specify whether the `BooleanSwitch`'s `Enabled` property is set to `True` (`value="1"`) or `False` (`value="0`).

## *TraceSwitch*

Following in the footsteps of the `BooleanSwitch` class, the `TraceSwitch` class also exposes a constructor that is used to specify a display name and description of the switch. Also exposed are the `DisplayName` and `Description` properties (type, `String`) to retrieve these values.

In order to determine what to trace, the `TraceSwitch` class exposes the `Level` get/set property of enumeration type `TraceLevel`. The permissible values for the `TraceLevel` enumeration indicate what information should be traced for a `TraceSwitch` instance. The `TraceLevel` enumeration values are defined as follows:

| Enumeration Value | Numeric Value |
|---|---|
| TraceLevel.Off | 0 |
| TraceLevel.Error | 1 |
| TraceLevel.Warning | 2 |
| TraceLevel.Info | 3 |
| TraceLevel.Verbose | 4 |

Zero is the default value but this being VB.NET that should not be a surprise.

Two TraceSwitch instances are declared in the WXDemoSwitch application as follows:

```
Private _hrModuleLogLevel As TraceSwitch = _
  New TraceSwitch("HRModule", "HR Package")
Private _stockOptionsModuleLogLevel As TraceSwitch = _
  New TraceSwitch("StockOptionsModule", "S.O. Package")
```

Recall that the WXDemoSwitch.exe.config configuration file contained two <add> child elements with <switches> elements that we didn't use before:

```
<add name="HRModule" value="3" />
<add name="StockOptionsModule" value="2" />
```

The HRModule TraceSwitch instance is set to a value of "3" which means that it is set to enable the displaying of informational messages (TraceLevel.Info). The StockOptionsModule TraceSwitch instance is set to enable the displaying of warning messages (value="2").

The TraceSwitch class exposes ReadOnly Boolean properties corresponding to the trace level enabled: TraceError, TraceWarning, TraceVerbose, and TraceInfo. Each of these Boolean properties corresponds to a specific enumeration setting and not a flag. What this means is that only one of the aforementioned Boolean properties can return True at any given time.

The following code snippet demonstrates the TraceSwitch instance, _hrModuleLogLevel, displaying a Debug message only if the Level property is set to TraceLevel.Info:

```
Debug.WriteLineIf(_hrModuleLogLevel.TraceInfo, _
                  "HR Module: Employee Remuneration Report Generated")
```

## Custom Switch

TraceSwitch exposes five levels of configuration while BooleanSwitch provides just two (on and off). If this does not meet an application's needs, a custom switch can be implemented by deriving from the Switch class. The constructor for Switch is Protected meaning the derived application must expose a means by which to construct the object.

The numeric value associated with the switch corresponds to the Switch base class's SwitchSetting property. This integer property is Protected so a derived application must expose a means by which to evaluate the SwitchLevel.

The following code from WXCustomSwitch.vb demonstrates a custom switch:

```
Public Class WXCustomSwitch
  Inherits Switch

  Public Sub New(ByVal displayName As String, _
                 ByVal description As String)
    MyBase.New(displayName, description)
  End Sub

  Public Function ToleranceExeeded(ByVal defects As Integer) _
                                                         As Boolean

    ' If the number of 'defects' exceeds SwitchSetting then
    ' the tolerance level is exceeded and the function is returned
    Return defects > SwitchSetting
  End Function

End Class
```

Notice in the constructor that MyBase.New is specified so that the constructor for the WXCustomSwitch class can construct the Switch base class. The SwitchSetting parameter is used by the ToleranceExceeded() method. This method takes a number of defects parameters (Integer) and compares the defects to the value of the SwitchSetting property. If there are too many defects then ToleranceExeeded() returns True.

The following code snippet demonstrates the custom switch in action displaying extra information if a pre-configured threshold is exceeded:

```
Private _fabLine4 As WXCustomSwitch = _
  New WXCustomSwitch("FabLine4", "Defects per lot")

Sub WXCheckLog(ByVal defectsCurrentLot4 As Integer)
  If _fabLine4.ToleranceExeeded(defectsCurrentLot4) Then
    ' display additional quality control information for lot
  End If
End Sub
```

The following snippet from an application configuration file sets the maximum number of defects for the `WXCustomSwitch` associated with `FabLine4` (`DisplayName` property) to `4` (`SwitchLevel` property):

```
<switches>
  <add name="FabLine4" value="4" />
</switches>
```

# Programmatic Debugger Interaction

Using the `Launch()` and `Break()` methods we can launch a debugger from running code or break execution if a debugger is already attached. In the same vein, an application can send specific text to the debugger using the `Log()` method and the application can determine if it is presently being debugged using the `IsAttached` property.

To understand how nifty the `Debugger` class is, consider the case of an extremely rare bug that occurs in an application. For release code you don't really want to launch a debugger, so you would want to handle the error in some way. However, you could use the `IsAttached` to see if we're debugging and break execution if the answer is true; that way you get the best of both worlds.

Notice that this is the *application choosing* when/how to interact with the debugger (hence the class name, `Debugger`). Usually applications are passive, letting debuggers attach or letting debuggers specify the breakpoints.

## Controlling the Debugger

If an application encounters an unhandled exception then (if a debugger is installed) we will get the opportunity to debug that process. Consider the case where an application encounters some other error state and you want the opportunity launch the debugger. This can be achieved using the `Debugger` class's `Launch()` method. An application can also force the debugger to break using the `Break()` method.

### Break

The `Break()` method (as previously mentioned) causes the debugger to break (pause but not terminate) when this method is executed. The signature for the `Break()` method is as follows:

Shared Sub Break()

If `Debugger.Break()` is executed and no debugger is available (when the application is running on a machine with just the .NET redistributable installed) an exception is generated. Clearly, this could be avoided by using the `Debugger` class's `IsAttached` property.

## Launch

Like `Break()`, `Launch()` causes a debugger to be launched if the application is currently not being debugged. The signature for the `Launch()` method is as follows:

```
Shared Sub Launch()
```

If the debugger launches successfully or if the application is already being debugged then `Launch()` returns `True`. If the debugger does not launch successfully then the `Launch()` method returns `False` and an exception is generated.

Although `Launch()` and `Break()` can both attach an application to a debugger, there is a difference. The `Launch()` method does cause the attached debugger to break the application when the debugger is initially loaded. However, if the debugger is already attached, then `Launch()` simply returns `True` and does not cause the debugger to break. The `Break()` method always causes the debugger to break when the `Break()` method is invoked even if the application is already attached to the debugger.

## Launching a Debugger

We know that if `Launch()` or `Break()` is executed when no debugger is attached, we'll get the option to attach one. There is a bit more to this, though; there may be several debuggers available and these can be launched in several different configurations. The `WXDemoDebugger` application can be used to demonstrate the debugging options when running an application from the command line, rather than from inside a development environment.

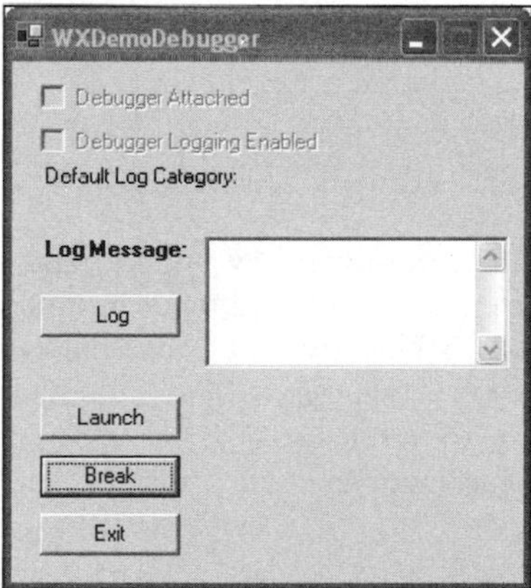


We won't bother to go through the application in laborious detail, it simply demonstrates the various debugging features we talk about in this chapter. The implementation is basically self explanatory but the code for this application is in the book's code download if you need it.

The following snippet from the WXDemoDebugger application demonstrates the scenario of causing the debugger to break if an extremely rare circumstance is encountered.

```
If _britWinsWimbledon And americaWinsWorldCup And _
  _franceMakesEnglishOfficialLanguage Then
  Debugger.Launch()
End If
```

After execution has begun, launch Visual Studio .NET and open the project for `WXDemoDebugger`. When `Debugger.Launch()` is called from inside `WXDemoDebugger.exe` (by clicking **Launch**), the following dialog is displayed, which enables selection of particular debugger flavors:

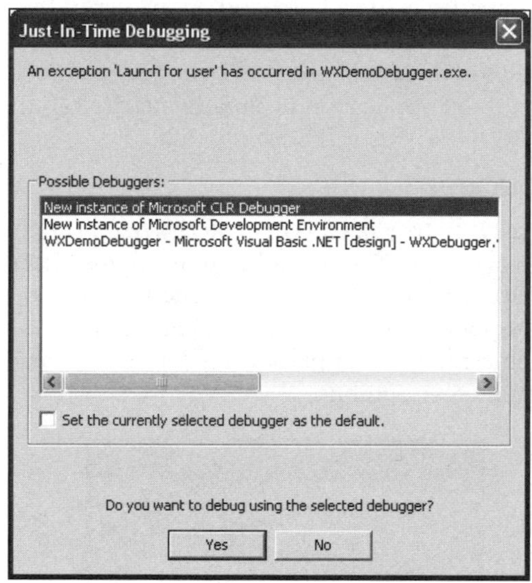


What appears in the **Possible Debuggers:** window will depend on what development tools are available on the current machine, and what instances of Visual studio are running. If you only had the .NET Framework SDK installed then you'd just see the first option, **New instance of Microsoft CLR Debugger**, which launches the `DBGCLR.exe` application. The second choice in the **Just-In-Time Debugging** dialog (**New Instance of Microsoft Development Environment**) launches a new instance of Visual Studio .NET.

> *The `DBGCLR.exe` debugger offers quite a few features, but Visual Studio .NET and its debugger come with more features (such as the ability to edit files, build projects, and manage solutions) so use that, if you have it.*

# Conditional Breaking

The Trace and Debug classes offer similar but enhanced functionality to Launch() and Break() with the Assert() and Fail() methods, which add built-in Boolean condition evaluation.

## Assert

The Assert() method tests a Boolean condition and if the condition evaluates to False an *assertion is raised,* which will display a message box. Ever had a coworker who always uses your code incorrectly or never sets up their environment in the right way? The Debug.Assert() method is a great way to inform them (politely) of their error and as a bonus, it is (typically) not part of the release build.

The Assert() method's signatures are as follows:

- Sub Assert(Boolean) – if the expression (type, Boolean) evaluates to False then the present call stack is displayed (a stack trace). A classic use for this type of assertion is to point out to coworkers using your methods that their parameters are incorrect:

```
Sub WXSomeMethod(ByVal keyData As String)
  Debug.Assert(If Not keyData Is Nothing)
  ' Rest of method implemented here
End Sub
```

- Sub Assert(Boolean, String) – behaves just like Assert(Boolean) save that in addition to the call stack a message (the value of the String parameter) is displayed. An example of this method is action is as follows:

```
Debug.Assert(Not File.Exists("C:\WXFiles\ExtraConfig.xml"), _
             "Hey, you forgot the config file!")
```

- Sub Assert(Boolean, String, String) – behaves just like the previously reviewed flavor of Assert(), except that a second String parameter is provided. The first String parameter specifies the message to be displayed (when the Boolean evaluates to False), while the second String parameter usually corresponds to a more detailed message that explains the first message. The parameter police will not arrest you if you do not use these String parameters for precisely this purpose. An example of this method strutting its stuff is as follows:

```
Debug.Assert(File.Exists("C:\WXFiles\ExtraConfig.xml"), _
  "Hey, you forgot the configuration file AGAIN!", _
  "An example is on my share drive \\YouKnuckleHead\StuffForBozo")
```

Thus far how the issue of how the stack trace and various message are to be displayed has not been presented. Recall from Chapter 4 that `Debug` and `Trace` are associated with a default listener. This default listener displays a message box when it encounters an `Assert()` method. This behavior can be modified by removing the default listener from the `Listeners` property of `Trace` and/or `Debug`. For other listeners (event log and text file) the parameters passed to `Assert()` will be passed as normal where the value of `Assert`'s parameter is prefixed by "Fail:":

```
Fail: message-string-parameter detail-message-string-parameter
```

An example of the message box displayed by the default listener for an assertion generated by invoking `Debug.Assert(Boolean, String, String)` is as follows:

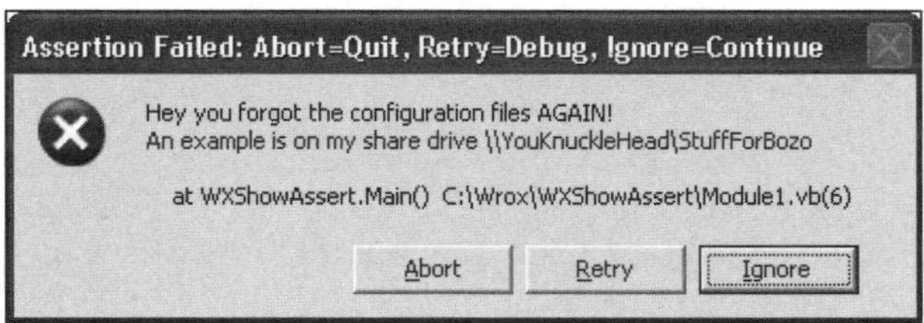


The buttons associated with the message box are:

- Abort – causes the application to be abort (execution ceases, game over, etc.).
- Ignore – ignores the assertion and continues execution. An example scenario where the use of Ignore is applicable is as follows:

```
Debug.Assert(Not bFileLockAcquired, _
             "Click 'Ignore' to keep trying to lock the file")
```

- Retry – either causes the Just-In-Time Debugging dialog to be displayed if the process is not presently be debugged or breaks at the line in question if we are debugging.

> **The examples have all shown `Debug.Assert()`. `Trace.Assert()` can cause an unhandled exception. This will occur if the user attempts to Retry on a production machine (a machine with no debugger). An unhandled exception causes garbage collection not to occur for the application and hence the objects might not get cleaned up (finalized) properly. One solution to this is to remove the default trace listener that causes the Assert message box to be displayed; since the other trace listeners provided simply log the string associated with the assertion as text they do not present a problem.**

Use `Assert()` at the beginning of a subroutine to test preconditions and at the end to test post-conditions prior to returning. Liberal use of `Assert()` can make a program more robust (meaning, more tolerant of how other programmers use your modules) and easier to maintain. An `Assert()` can be thought of as a means to have a program test itself, or to test how other programmers use your routines. It is a good way to explicitly state your assumptions in a way that cannot be easily overlooked. For example, a comment such as "Call this routine with 2 or more Points in the array..." might be ignored later when someone instead passes in a single point. The resulting error might be time-consuming to track down to passing in a single point. Instead, the line:

```
Debugger.Assert( numPoints >= 2, "Two or more Points are required." )
```

will not be ignored if indeed your constraint is violated.

### Fail

The `Fail()` method is closely related to the `Assert()` method but the `Fail()` asserts automatically since it is associated with no conditional test. The idea behind the `Fail()` method is to cause an assertion when there is no ambiguity (no Boolean required):

- `Sub Fail(String)` – behaves just like `Assert(False, string)` meaning that acts like `Assert` with a message parameter where the condition is `False` (hence the `Assert` always generates an assertion).
- `Sub Fail(String, String)` – behaves just like behaves just like `Assert(False, string, string)`.

# Logging to the Debugger

The `Log()` method sends logging-related information to the debugger. If a debugger is not attached then the `Log()` method does nothing. The signature for the `Log()` method is as follows:

```
Public Shared Sub Log(ByVal level As Integer, _
                      ByVal category As String, _
                      ByVal message As String)
```

The body of the message being logged is passed via the `message` parameter. The `level` parameter indicates the severity of the error and the `category` parameter indicates into which category the log message falls. Choosing appropriate categories and log levels is a task left up to the developer of the application being debugged. In order to demonstrate the effects category and level have on Visual Studio .NET's display of logging information consider the following code snippet from the `WXDemoDebugger` project:

```
Debugger.Log(1000000, "Error", _
              "This is quite important" & Environment.NewLine)
```

This code snippet uses the `Environment` class's `NewLine` property in order to provide a carriage-return/line-feed for the specific environment (meaning the carriage-return/line-feed does not have to be hard-coded as a particular numeric sequence). The importance (or lack there of) of the `level` and `category` parameters should be clear from the following screenshot of Visual Studio .NET's Output window (View | Other Windows | Output):

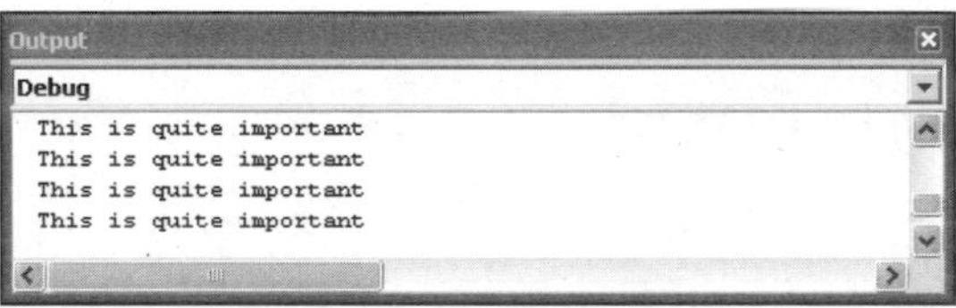


When Visual Studio .NET displays the message associated with `Debugger.Log()` ("This is quite important"), the `level` and `category` parameters have no effect on the output generated.

## The DefaultCategory Field

The `Debugger` class provides the `DefaultCategory` field, which provides an application with access to the default logging category used by the debugger. The signature for this field is as follows:

```
Public Shared ReadOnly DefaultCategory As String
```

The value returned when `DefaultCategory` is accessed is `Nothing`. This means that the `Debugger` class does not bother to provide a default category and given Visual Studio .NET does not display the category, the category parameter for the `Log()` method seems more like a feature that will be exploited in the future rather than the present.

## The Effect on Performance

Whenever a feature such as `Debugger.Log()` is provided, it is important to evaluate its impact on performance. Calling the `Log()` method inside code makes sense only if it doesn't seriously affect performance, obviously this process is complicated if the debugging techniques you use seriously affect performance themselves.

For this reason, the `WXDemoDebugger` application contains the following code that uses the contents of a Windows Forms `TextBox` (`TextBoxLogMessage.Text`) to generate a log message:

```
Dim count As Integer
Dim message As String = TextBoxLogMessage.Text & Environment.NewLine
Dim startTime As DateTime = DateTime.Now

For count = 1 To 10000
  Debugger.Log(10, "User error", message)
Next

LabelLogRate.Text = "Execution time: " & _
  DateTime.Now.Subtract(startTime).TotalMilliseconds
```

The message is passed ten thousand times using a `For` loop thus allowing the time taken to generate a message to be measured using the `DateTime` class's `Now` property (current time). The difference between the end time (after logging is completed) and the start time is displayed to a Windows Forms `Label` (`LabelLogRate.Text`). The time taken to display a log message is dependent on a variety of factors including the following:

- No debugger attached – each call to `Debugger.Log()` takes about ten microseconds (0.00001 seconds) if there is no debugger attached. This time can be viewed as inconsequential.
- `Debugger` attached but with no output window not displayed – each call to `Debugger.Log()` takes about one millisecond (0.001 seconds).
- Debugger attached and an output window displayed – each call to `Debugger.Log()` takes about fifteen milliseconds (0.015 seconds).

The lesson learned from this previous experiment is not that `Debugger.Log()` is slow (although 15 milliseconds is certainly not fast). The real lesson to be learned is that I/O sent to a window is extremely slow. Although it is convenient to display messages to the screen, do not go overboard (a `For` loop with ten thousand `Debugger.Log()` invocations is overboard). Web Services and Windows Services are not associated with a GUI for a reason – a GUI is inherently slow and how `Debugger.Log()` is used may slow down an application as it is running attached to a debugger.

# Testing the Debugger's Status

The signatures for the `Debugger` class's `IsAttached` property and the `IsLogging()` method are as follows:

```
Public Shared ReadOnly Property IsAttached As Boolean
Public Shared Function IsLogging() As Boolean
```

The `IsAttached` property returns `True` if the application is currently attached to a debugger and `False` if it is not attached to a debugger.

The IsLogging() method similarly returns True if the attached debugger is currently handling logging information sent form the application being debugged and False if logging information is not being handled. When an application is running under the most commonly used debugger, Visual Studio .NET, the value returned by the IsLogging() method is always True. This value is True whether Visual Studio .NET's Output window is open or closed. Clearly, the presence of the Output window is not a litmus test as to whether or not the Visual Studio .NET debugger has enabled logging or not for the application being debugged.

A crafty application can generate additional debugging information for use by the debugger if detects the debugger is running. An example of this is the following snippet from WXDemoDebugger where the application causes the application to break (Debugger.Break()) if it detects the debugger is present (Debugger.IsAttached) at the same time a certain, non-critical error condition is occurring:

```
If Debugger.IsAttached And _
  _annoyingHardToFindNonCriticalBugIsPresent Then
  Debugger.Break()
End If
```

An application can better direct the debug-related information it was producing when it is cognizant that logging is enabled. The following excerpt from WXDemoDebugger shows the application only creating a certain logging string in the event that the debugger is logging:

```
If Debugger.IsLogging Then
  Dim lotOfTimeToCompute As String = _
    String.Format("Percentages: sugar={0}, spice={1}, _
                  ChemicalX={2}", Sugar, Spice, ChemicalX)
  Debugger.Log(1, "Power Puff composition", lotOfTimeToCompute)
End If
```

In the previous example, the Debugger.IsLogging() may seem superfluous because Debugger.Log() would not log anything if there was no debugger logging. The string being logged is "lotOfTimeToCompute", which is a less-than-subtle hint that this string takes a significant amount of time to compute (based on retrieving the properties Sugar, Spice, and ChemicalX). The Debugger.IsLogging() suppresses the generation of this time-expensive string in the event that there is no debugger performing logging.

# Summary

This chapter presented the options for logging information. Courtesy of System.Diagnostics, writing to the system event log and managing specific logs and event sources has been dramatically simplified. The EventLog and EventLogEntry classes of the aforementioned namespace support logging and managing the system event log.

Also provided for the event log is a trace listener, `EventLogTraceListener`. This class (derived from `TraceListener`) works in conjunction with other trace listeners in order to allow `Debug` and `Trace` to log to multiple destinations. Other forms of trace listeners support the ability to log to a file (`TextWriteTraceListener`) and to the debugger associated with an application (`DefaultTraceListener`).

The configuration file associated with an application can also be used to configure switches (classes derived from the `Switch` base class). The `BooleanSwitch` class allows an on/off category to be specified (setting whether a feature on or is it off) while the `TraceSwitch` lets us specify a more granular category (off, error, warning, etc.).

The icing on the cake is that applications can develop custom version of the elements exposed by the `System.Diagnostics` namespace. Custom switches and custom trace listeners can be developed with minimal effort.

The ability to launch the debugger, break execution, raise an assert, or log messages from a programmer to the debugger can be a great boon. Imaginative use of these facilities can ease collaboration on large projects and help people who are using or extending your code base. While all these techniques can be useful in development code, it is important to consider the implications of using any of these techniques in release code. Some of them will raise exceptions, stall execution, or slow down your application – none of these results will please your customers.

Debugging using .NET is dramatically simpler than working with previous technologies. The configuration files are a boon, but also simplified is the use of the event log. It is now possible to perform these tasks from locations where it was previously taboo (services and serviced components). The `System.Diagnostics` namespace is so useful that developers must be cautioned not to add extra bugs to their code just to use this namespace's features. OK, the last sentence is blatantly untrue but `System.Diagnostics` is darn nifty.

VB.NET
Debugging
Handbook
5

# 5

# Debugging Web Applications

In this chapter, we will take an in-depth look at how to debug Web Applications. In most of the examples we will be using the debugger that is integrated with the new Visual Studio .NET IDE. It is very easy to use, and represents a great improvement over the capabilities previously available in Visual Interdev, which was Microsoft's IDE of choice for classic ASP development.

We will also spend a little time discussing how to use the SDK debugger. This would be relevant if you are **not** using the Visual Studio .NET IDE, but maybe venerable old 'Notepad' or the free Web Matrix development environment available from: http://www.asp.net/webmatrix/default.aspx.

Throughout this chapter, we will consider the different kinds of web applications that can be created using ASP .NET, and discuss various aspects of debugging them. The chapter outline is roughly as follows:

- Regular ASP.NET web application – first we will create a regular ASP.NET web application, and demonstrate how to debug it using the Visual Studio .NET IDE as well as the SDK Debugger.
- Stored Procedures – then we will modify the application to use a SQL Server stored procedure, and show how easy it is to debug these as well.
- Client-side script in a web application – we will then extend the application by adding client-side script and explore how we can debug that.
- Trace and Debug information – in this section, we will discuss how to insert trace and debug statements into the code so that we can track the execution of a running system. We will also see how to enable tracing at the page level and application level.

- Web Services – next we will look at debugging web services. These are a special case since you will often attach your debugger to the web service client, and then step from the client into the web service itself.
- Debugging ASP and ASP.NET side-by-side – another special case is the situation where your application contains legacy ASP pages as well as regular ASP.NET pages.
- Debugging an ASP .NET server control – in this section we will create an ASP.NET server control and a client application that uses it. We will then set up the debugger to start from the client application and step into the server control.
- Windows Forms Control – finally, we will show how to debug a Windows Forms control hosted in IE.

So, let's start the chapter by looking at a sample ASP.NET web application and then see how to set it up for debugging.

# Debugging ASP.NET Web Applications

In the previous versions of ASP, debugging has always been considered a difficult task. If you are an ASP developer, `Response.Write()` is probably the primary method of finding out what is happening in a program, as the script debugger was weak in comparison to the debuggers that Windows developers had for languages such as VB and Visual C++. All that has now changed with .NET, because the Common Language Runtime provides integrated debugging for all .NET applications. ASP.NET introduces modern debugging practices into web development: you can now step into your code, set breakpoints, have a watch window to observe the values of your variables, and so on.

In this section we will create a new ASP.NET Web Application in VB.NET. Initially the application will contain only one page (`Categories.aspx`), which displays details of all the categories in the categories table that is present in the Northwind database for SQL Server.

If you do not already have the Northwind database installed, you can find it on your SQL Server disk, and install it using the `osql` command-line utility. Assuming the install script is located at `d:\standard\install\instnwnd.sql`, and you have an `sa` account with administrator rights and no password, type the following from a command prompt:

```
> osql -Usa -P -id:\standard\install\instnwnd.sql
```

## Creating a Sample Web Application

Let's start off by creating a new Visual Basic .NET project in Visual Studio .NET: specifically an ASP.NET Web Application project. Name it DebuggingDemoApp (the location should be http://localhost/DebuggingDemoApp).

When Visual Studio .NET opens the new project, delete the default web form (`WebForm1.aspx`) and create a new web form called `Categories.aspx`. Right-click on the form, select Properties and set the Page Layout property to "Flow Layout".

Drag a `DataGrid` onto the form and use the property inspector to change its `Name` property to `gridCategories`. Switch to HTML View and make the additions shown below:

```
<%@ Page Language="vb" AutoEventWireup="false"
Codebehind="Categories.aspx.vb"
Inherits="DebuggingDemoApp.Categories"%>
<!DOCTYPE HTML PUBLIC "-//W3C//DTD HTML 4.0 Transitional//EN">
<HTML>
...
<body>
  <form id="Form1" method="post" runat="server">
    <h1>List of Categories</h1>
    <asp:DataGrid id="gridCategories"
                  runat="server"
                  AutoGenerateColumns="False">
      <Columns>
        <asp:BoundColumn
          DataField="CategoryName"
          HeaderText="Category Name">
        </asp:BoundColumn>
        <asp:BoundColumn
          DataField="Description"
          HeaderText="Description">
        </asp:BoundColumn>
        <asp:HyperLinkColumn
          Text="Show all Products"
          DataNavigateUrlField="CategoryID"
          DataNavigateUrlFormatString=
            "ProductListing.asp?categoryid={0}"
          HeaderText="Show all products in category">
        </asp:HyperLinkColumn>
      </Columns>
    </asp:DataGrid>
  </form>
</body>
...
</HTML>
```

Now switch to the code-behind page.

We will start by adding the following `Imports` statements at the top of the code-behind file of `Categories.aspx`:

```
Imports System.Data.SqlClient
```

Then add the following code to the `Page_Load()` method:

```
Private Sub Page_Load(ByVal sender As System.Object, _
                      ByVal e As System.EventArgs) _
                      Handles MyBase.Load
```

We start by retrieving the connection string from the `appSettings` element in `web.config` file (which we will review in a moment):

```
    Dim connString As String = _
        ConfigurationSettings.AppSettings.Item("connectionString")
```

The next couple of lines create a `SqlConnection` object and a `SqlDataAdapter`. The first parameter to the `sqlDataAdapter` is the SQL statement to be executed:

```
    Dim sqlConn As New SqlConnection(connString)
    Dim adapter As New SqlDataAdapter( _
        "Select CategoryID,CategoryName,Description from Categories", _
        sqlConn)
```

Then we invoke the `Fill()` method of the `SqlDataAdapter` object and fill the dataset with the results returned from the execution of the SQL query:

```
    'Create and fill a Dataset with the results of the executed query
    Dim dstCategories As New DataSet()
    adapter.Fill(dstCategories)
```

Finally, we bind the `DataView` to the `datagrid` control:

```
    gridCategories.DataSource = dstCategories.Tables(0).DefaultView
    gridCategories.DataBind()

    'Close the opened database connection
    sqlConn.Close()

End Sub
```

Now open up the `web.config` file and add the following at the bottom of the page:

```
...
</system.web>

<appSettings>
  <add key="ConnectionString"
   value="server=localhost;uid=sa;pwd=;database=Northwind"/>
</appSettings>

</configuration>
```

The `appSettings` element is a convenient place to store configuration data for our application. In this case, we specify the connection string, which will be used to access the database.

> **Obviously, in a real production environment, you would never use a blank administrator password, and you would never connect to the database using an administrator account, unless you were actually administering the database! However, we are focusing on debugging issues in this chapter, so we will use these connection parameters for simplicity's sake.**

Once you view the page (by selecting the `Categories.aspx` page in the Solution Explorer, right-clicking, and selecting Build and Browse), you should see this:

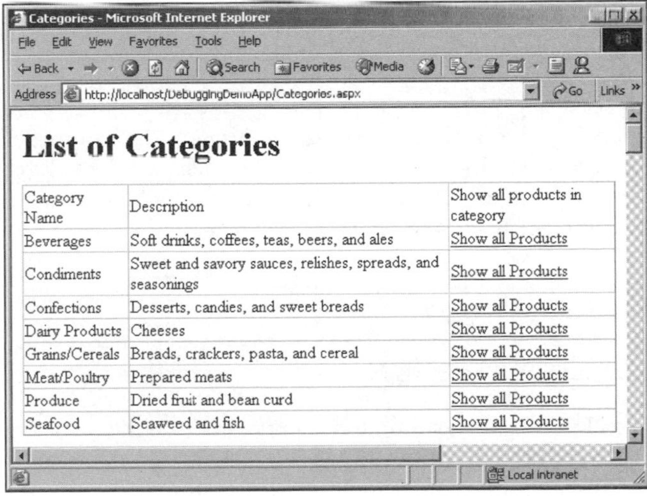

Now that we have looked at the code, let's find out how to debug the web application using Visual Studio .NET.

## Debugging in Visual Studio .NET

To debug the web application, we need to se tup breakpoints in code. Navigate to the line shown in the screenshot below and press *F9* (alternatively, you may simply click the left margin of the designer):

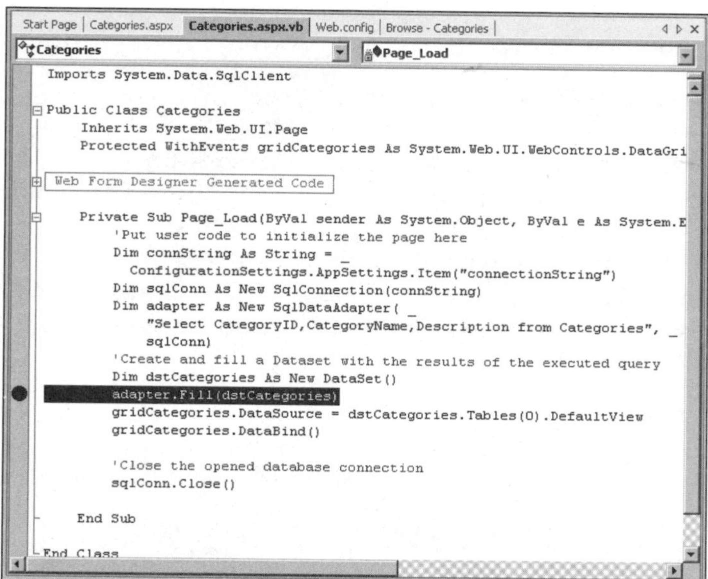


You then need to set a start page for the project. Right-click on the `Categories.aspx` page in the Solution Explorer and select Set As Start Page... Then press *F5* to build the application and start it within the IDE debugger. Because we selected the `Categories.aspx` page as the start page, the application will automatically stop and bring up the IDE debugger when the breakpoint is reached:

```
Dim dstCategories As New DataSet()
adapter.Fill(dstCategories)
gridCategories.DataSource = dstCategories.Tables(0).DefaultView
gridCategories.DataBind()
```

Once it hits the breakpoint, we can step through the code in the same way as we do with any other .NET application. At this point, we have all the debugging features of Visual Studio.NET available to us as we debug the web form.

> **You should note that this only worked because the IDE automatically sets up a new project with the Debug configuration.**

You can switch between configurations using the drop-down listbox at the top of the IDE:

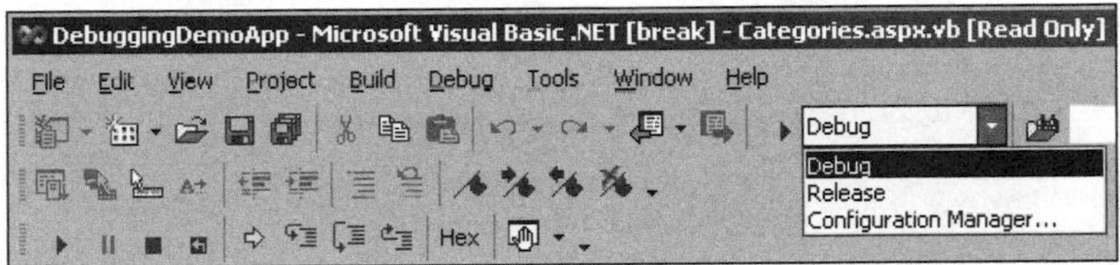


## Debugging with the SDK Debugger

The SDK Debugger (`DbgClr.exe`) comes bundled with the .NET Framework SDK. By default its location is:

```
<DriveName>:\Program Files\Microsoft.NET\FrameworkSDK\GuiDebug
```

or, if Visual Studio .NET is installed:

```
<DriveName>:\Program Files\Microsoft Visual Studio.NET\
             FrameworkSDK\GuiDebug
```

Before we start using it, it is worth noting that the SDK debugger (often also referred to as the `CLRDebugger`) has the following limitations:

- It does not provide support for remote debugging
- It does not provide context-sensitive help

Let us now debug our web application using the SDK debugger. We will start by launching the debugger (`DbgClr.exe`). After that, we will select Tools | Debug Processes to show the following dialog:

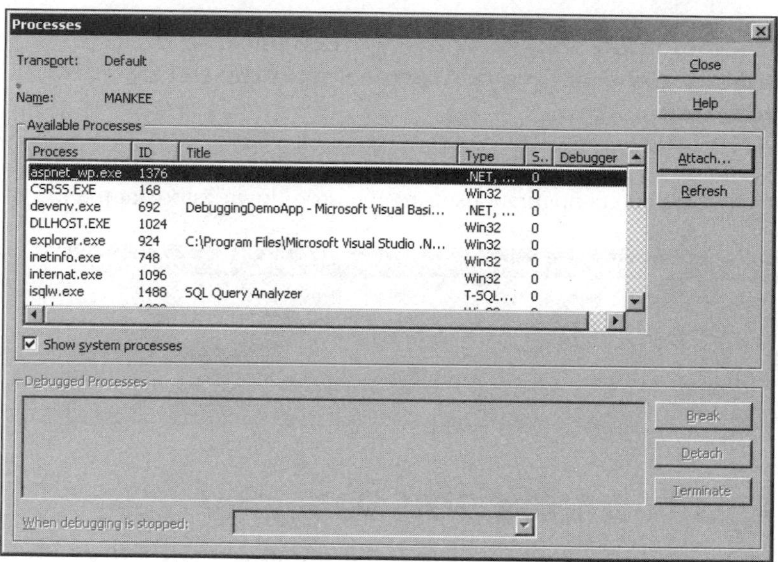


The above dialog box shows the list of processes that we can pick to debug. Make sure the Show System Processes checkbox is selected, and then pick aspnet_wp.exe, which is the ASP.NET worker process. We then click the Attach... button to attach the debugger to the process, and close the dialog. Note that you can only attach one debugger at a time to a process. The above would therefore fail if you were still debugging using the integrated Visual Studio .NET debugger, as we did in the previous section.

Now that we have attached the debugger to the process, we must set the breakpoint(s). Select File | Open | File... and navigate to the web application directory that has the `Categories.aspx.vb` file. Then navigate to the line:

```
adapter.Fill(dstCategories)
```

and click in the left margin to set the breakpoint.

Now if you open up a browser and make a request for the `Categories.aspx` page, you will automatically hit the above breakpoint. After that, we can debug the application in a similar way to how we did with the Visual Studio.NET debugger.

# Debugging SQL Stored Procedures

The Visual Studio IDE makes it very easy to debug SQL stored procedures. To explore this, let's create a copy of the `Categories.aspx` page, and modify the code to use a stored procedure.

1. Open the DemoDebuggingApp solution in Visual Studio.NET.
2. Select the `Categories.aspx` page in the Solution Explorer. Right-click and select Copy.
3. Right-click on the DemoDebuggingApp project in the Solution Explorer, and select Paste. This creates a new file (`Copy of Categories.aspx`).
4. Rename this file to `CategoriesSp.aspx`.
5. Open up the `CategoriesSp.aspx` file and change the `Inherits` attribute in the first line from `Categories` to `CategoriesSp`.
6. Open up the `CategoriesSp.aspx.vb` file and change the classname `Categories` to `CategoriesSp`.

You now have a `CategoriesSp` page with the same functionality as the `Categories` page from the previous chapter. Right-click on the `CategoriesSp.aspx` page, select Set as Start Page, and then press *F5* to run the page and verify that it works.

## Modifying the Code

We now need to modify the code to use a stored procedure. Open up the `CategoriesSp.aspx.vb` file and make the following modifications:

```
Private Sub Page_Load(ByVal sender As System.Object, _
        ByVal e As System.EventArgs) Handles MyBase.Load

  Dim connString As String = ConfigurationSettings.AppSettings. _
      Item("connectionString")

  Dim sqlConn As New SqlConnection(connString)

  'specify stored procedure command
  Dim sqlCmd As New SqlCommand("GetCategories", sqlConn)
  sqlCmd.CommandType = CommandType.StoredProcedure
```

As you can see, the first couple of lines create a command object and tie it to the connection object, specifying that we want to invoke a stored procedure. We then specify one parameter that will be forwarded to the stored procedure:

```
  'add one parameter to pass to the stored procedure
  Dim sqlParam As SqlParameter
  sqlParam = sqlCmd.Parameters.Add( New _
             SqlParameter("@CategoryNameCriteria", _
             SqlDbType.VarChar, 50))
  sqlParam.Direction = ParameterDirection.Input
```

Then we set the parameter's value. In a more realistic example, this would be created after input from the user:

```
    sqlParam.Value = "C%"
```

Finally, we hook up the command with the data adapter, and use the data adapter to fill the dataset as before:

```
    Dim adapter As New SqlDataAdapter(sqlCmd)

    'Create and fill the Dataset
    Dim dstCategories As New DataSet()
    adapter.Fill(dstCategories)
    gridCategories.DataSource = dstCategories.Tables(0).DefaultView
    gridCategories.DataBind()

    'Close the opened database connection
    sqlConn.Close()
  End Sub
```

## Creating the Stored Procedure

To create the stored procedure, select the Server Explorer on the left side of the IDE. Select the SQL server where the database resides, find the Stored Procedures tree of the database, and then right-click and select New Stored Procedure.

Modify the default procedure so that it looks like the screenshot below:

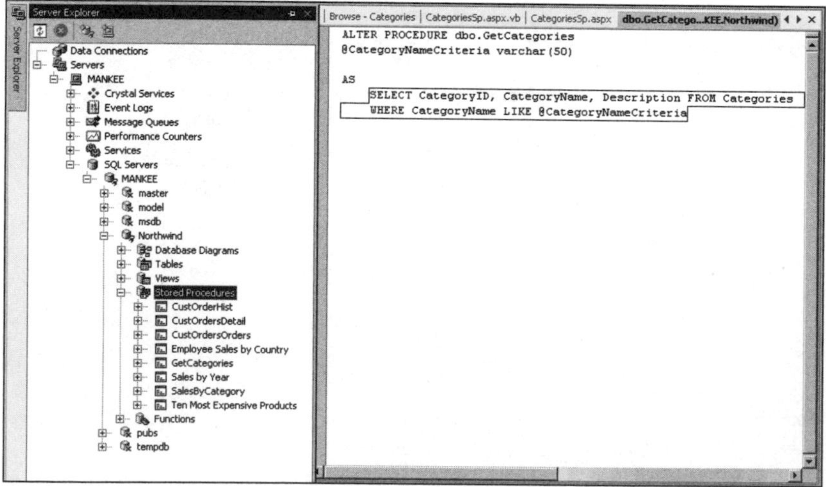

As you can see, the procedure is very simple. It returns `CategoryID`, `CategoryName`, and `Description` from the `Categories` table, where the category name matches the criteria passed into the stored procedure.

Finally, click in the left margin to set a breakpoint in the stored procedure.

## Debugging the Stored Procedure in Visual Studio .NET

You are now in almost ready to go. The last thing you need to do is to enable SQL debugging in the project. This is done in the Property Manager for the project. Right-click DebuggingDemoApp in the Solution Explorer, select Properties, and then select Configuration Properties | Debugging from the treeview. You will see an option called SQL Server debugging. Check the checkbox and click OK.

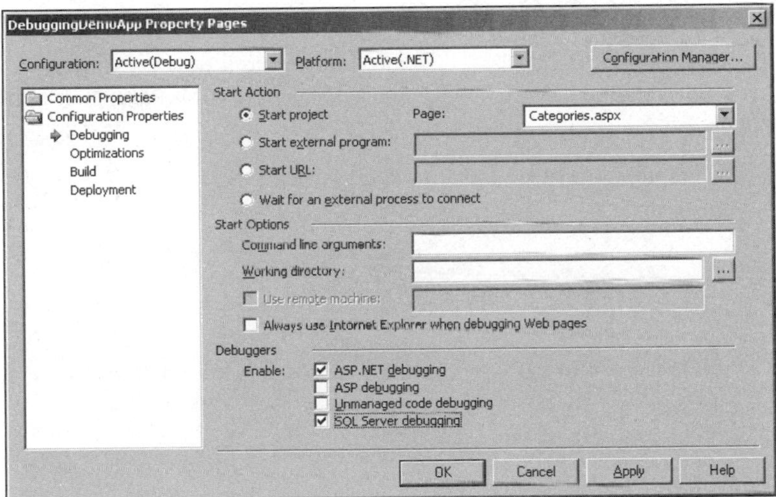


Now you are ready to go. Press *F5*, and watch the debugger hit the break point in the stored procedure. If you open up the Locals window at the bottom of the IDE you can inspect the value of the supplied parameter `@CategoryNameCriteria`.

**You cannot debug into a stored procedure using the SDK debugger!**

# Debugging Client-Side Script

So far, we have seen how to debug server-side script (code that gets executed on the server). In this section, we will see how to set up debugging for client-side scripts. Typically, client-side script is written using languages such as JScript and VBScript, with JScript being the most commonly-used language, as it is also supported by non-Microsoft browsers. Such client-side script could be embedded inside an `.html`, `.asp` or `.aspx` page loaded in Internet Explorer, or it could reside inside a `.js` or `.vbs` file loaded into `wscript.exe`, `cscript.exe`, or some other script host.

Since client-side script is totally independent from server-side script, we can create a simple HTML page to illustrate how this works. The page we will create will allow the user to select either of our two `Categories.aspx` pages, but only if they can make up their mind within 10 seconds.

## Creating the HTML Page

Open up the DebuggingDemoApp solution again, and create a new page by right-clicking on the Solution Explorer, and selecting Add | Add New Item... | HTML Page. Name the page DemoMenu.html.

Switch to HTML view and replace the template text with this:

```
<html>
  <head>
    <script language="javascript">
      <!--
```

In the top of the Javascript block we define a variable `intTimeOut` and set it to the value `11`:

```
        var intTimeOut=11

        function WaitForDecision()
        {
```

When the function `fnWaitForDecision` is called, it checks if `intTimeOut` is `>0`. If so, it decrements `intTimeOut`, updates the text to be displayed and sets a timer to call the function again one second later:

```
          if (intTimeOut>0) {
            intTimeOut-=1;
            setTimeout("WaitForDecision()",1000);
            counter.innerHTML="You have <b> "+ intTimeOut +
              " </b> seconds left!";
          }
```

If on the other hand, the counter is 0, the user has procrastinated and is rewarded. The function pops up a message box and then redirects the browser to Wrox's home page:

```
        else {
          //Too late, redirect user to wrox site!
          var alertMessage = "Procrastination pays! You will now be"
                           + " redirected to the Wrox home page.";
          alert(alertMessage);
          location.href="http://www.wrox.com";
        }
      }
    //-->
    </script>

    <title>DemoMenu</title>

  </head>
```

Our function is called the first time because of the `onload="WaitForDecision"` attribute in the `<body>` tag:

```
  <body onload="WaitForDecision()">
    <h1>Make your selection now!</h1>
```

Finally, the `<Div id="counter">` tag is used to identify the location where the `fnWaitForDecision` should insert the timing information:

```
    <div id="counter"
         style="display:block;
                background-color: black;
                font-family: Arial,font-size:20pt;
                color: white;">
    </div>
    <a href="categories.aspx">Pick the Categories.aspx page</a>
    <br>
    <a href="categoriessp.aspx">Pick the CategoriesSp.aspx page</a>
    <br>
  </body>
</html>
```

A screenshot of the application running under IE 6.0 is shown overleaf:

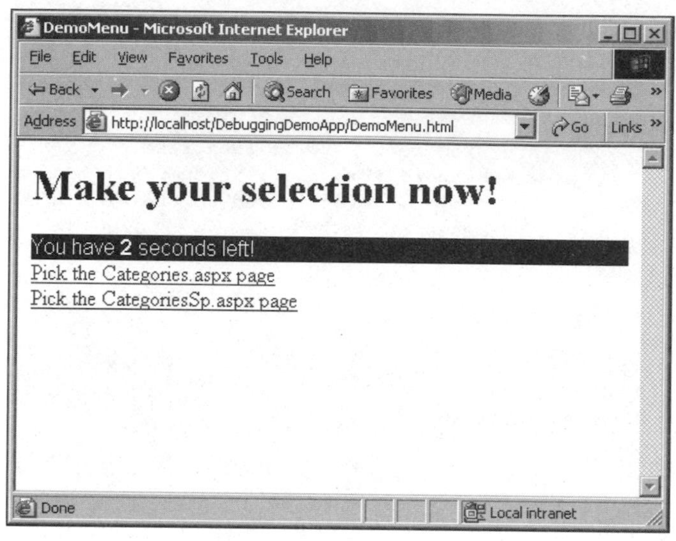


## Debugging Client-Side Script

Before we look at the steps to be followed for debugging client-side script, we need to ensure that the Disable Script Debugging checkbox is not checked in Internet Explorer. The following dialog box (that can be accessed by selecting Tools | Internet Options... in Internet Explorer 6) shows how to enable client-side debugging:

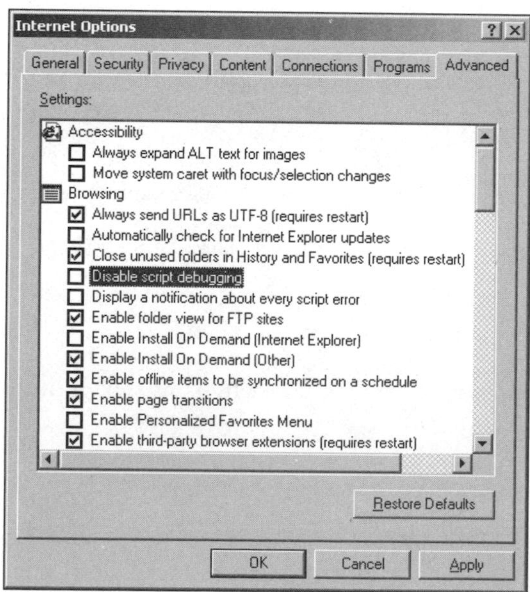

Click Apply and OK and close IE6 again, to ensure the new settings are stored properly.

If you are debugging an HTML page without server-side script (which is the case here), the steps required should be pretty familiar. Set DemoMenu.html as the start page, set a break point anywhere in the client-side script of the page, and hit *F5*.

The screenshot below shows that the debugger has correctly stopped in our `fnWaitForDecision` function:

```
if (intTimeOut>0) {
  intTimeOut-=1;
  setTimeout("WaitForDecision()",1000);
  counter.innerHTML="You have <b> "+ intTimeOut +
    " </b> seconds left!";
}
```

However, if you are debugging client-side script embedded in an ASP.NET server page, this approach will not work. In this case, you need to do the following:

1. Run the ASP.NET web application that contains the client-side script by pressing *F5*. When you do that, the debugger will be automatically attached to Internet Explorer.
2. Go back to the IDE and select Debug | Windows | Running Documents. Now, in the Solution Explorer, you will see the currently running `.aspx` file listed.
3. Double-click on that file to open up the code. Set up breakpoints in that file, go back to the browser, and execute some code that hits the breakpoint that you have already set up.
4. It will automatically hit the breakpoint in the IDE and now you can start debugging the client-side script using the debugging features of Visual Studio .NET.

# ASP.NET Trace and Debug Output

We have seen how you can easily follow the execution of an application by stepping though it with the debugger. There are, however, situations where it is more convenient to get a summary of values of some key variables as the application progresses. This is called "tracing".

ASP.NET and the .NET framework provide a number of classes and solutions that make tracing elegant and easy.

## The TraceContext Class

One of the properties of the `Page` class – from which all `.aspx` pages are derived – is called `Trace`. The `Trace` property actually returns a `System.Web.TraceContext` object that lets you send trace messages.

The `TraceContext` class exposes the following two methods:

- `Write()` – allows us to write an informational message to the page
- `Warn()` – similar to `Write()` except that it writes out the messages in red

and the following properties:

- `IsEnabled` – returns `true` or `false` based on whether tracing is enabled on the page or for the application
- `TraceMode` – allows us to get or set the sorting mode that tracing uses internally to sort tracing messages. Values are either `SortByCategory` or `SortByTime`.

You can call the methods by calling `Trace.Write()` and `Trace.Warn()`, just as you would have used `Response.Write()` in the past to output relevant text. However, with the `Trace.Write()` and `Trace.Warn()` methods, their output only appears when tracing is enabled. We will see how to enable and disable tracing in a moment.

## Enabling Tracing at the Page Level

All it takes to turn on (or off) page-level tracing is the setting of the `Trace` attribute in the `@ Page` directive:

```
<%@ Page Trace="[true/false]" %>
```

When tracing is enabled, we automatically get a plethora of information on the ASP.NET web page. The information will appear neatly at the bottom of the page, unless you have designed a web page where the HTML elements have absolute positioning (this would be the case if you were using `GridLayout` when designing the page).

The following list describes the kind of information that we get by enabling tracing:

- Request Details – such as Session ID, Request time, type, and encoding; and status code.

- Trace Information – Page-level ASP.NET messages that you specify via `Trace.Write()` and `Trace.Warn()`.
- Control Tree – a listing of the web controls on the ASP.NET web page, and how they relate to one another. In addition we get the sizes of the HTML sent to the client and the data stored in the `ViewState`.
- Cookies Collection – all of the cookies.
- Headers Collection – a listing of the entire HTTP headers.
- Server Variables – a listing of all of the server variables.

Let's now use our DebuggingDemoApp example to demonstrate how to use tracing in Visual Studio .NET. Open it up and select the `Categories.aspx` file.

Switch to HTML view and change the first line so it looks like this:

```
<%@ Page Language="vb" AutoEventWireup="false"
   Codebehind="Categories.aspx.vb"
   Inherits="DebuggingDemoApp.Categories"
   Trace=true%>
```

This enables tracing for this page only.

Now select the code-behind file (`Categories.aspx.vb`) and insert `Trace.Warn()` and a `Trace.Write()` statementsmethod, method, in the `Page_Load()` method, as illustrated below:

```
Private Sub Page_Load(ByVal sender As System.Object, _
                      ByVal e As System.EventArgs) Handles _
                      MyBase.Load

  Dim connString As String = _
      ConfigurationSettings.AppSettings.Item("connectionString")

  Trace.Warn("The ConnectionString is:" + connString)

  Dim sqlConn As New SqlConnection(connString)
  Dim adapter As New SqlDataAdapter( _
      "Select CategoryID,CategoryName,Description from Categories", _
      sqlConn)

  'Create and fill the Dataset...
  Dim dstCategories As New DataSet()
  adapter.Fill(dstCategories)

  Trace.Write("Number of rows returned from query is " + _
            dstCategories.Tables(0).Rows.Count.ToString())

  gridCategories.DataSource = dstCategories.Tables(0).DefaultView
  gridCategories.DataBind()
```

```
    'Close the opened database connection
    sqlConn.Close()
  End Sub
```

Now that we have added `Trace.Warn()` and `Trace.Write()` statements to the code, let's view the page in the browser:

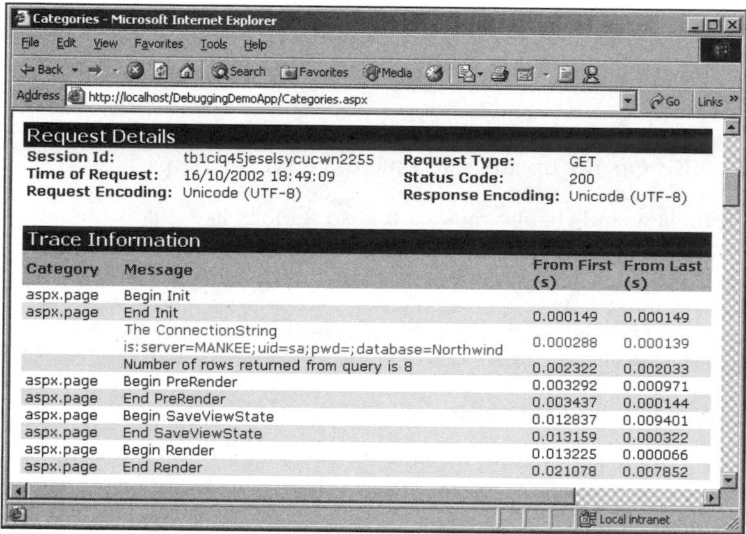

As you can see, our two trace messages are neatly displayed, along with a lot of other information below the table that is output by our regular server code.

> **Before you get over-excited and enable tracing on all your pages, note that this trace information is very useful to any hacker. Even if we don't explicitly write out the value of the connection string, there is so much additional information that it makes your application very vulnerable. So be careful!**

## Enabling Tracing at the Application Level

By turning tracing on and off at page level, we still have some of the inherent disadvantages found with using the `Response.Write()` approach. For example, when we want to disable tracing, we must go through each page and set `Trace` to `False`. Also – as we warned you – if you wish to turn on tracing for a live web site, every visitor will see the tracing output at the bottom of the page.

Fortunately ASP.NET alleviates these worries by providing us with the opportunity to turn on (and off) tracing for an entire web application. To do this, we need to use the `trace` setting in `Web.config`. The `trace` setting accepts the following parameters:

```
<trace enabled="[true|false]"
       localOnly="[true|false]"
       pageOutput="[true|false]"
       requestLimit="[number]"
       traceMode="[SortByTime|SortByCategory]" />
```

Let's briefly review the above attributes:

- `enabled` – can be set to `true` or `false`, indicating that tracing is either enabled or disabled at the application level. The default value is `false`.
- `localonly` – specifies if trace information is only displayed on local clients (in other words, the machine where IIS is running), or if it can be seen by remote users as well. The default value is `true`.
- `requestlimit` – specifies the total number of trace requests to keep cached in memory on a per-application basis. When this limit is exceeded the first trace request is deleted. The default value is `10`.
- `pageOutput` – specifies if the trace details are also written at the bottom of every page, in addition to being stored in the cache. The default value is `false`.
- `traceMode` – allows us to specify how we want the trace detail information to be displayed. The tracing information can be sorted by either category or by time. We specify them by using any one of the following values – `SortByCategory` or `SortByTime`. The default value is `SortByTime`.

To enable tracing output on our ASP.NET web pages for the entire web application, we simply set `enabled` to `true` and `pageOutput` to `true`. If you are working on a live site, make sure you set `localOnly` to `true`, meaning that only those hitting the site through http://localhost will see the tracing information. The settings in the `web.config` file simply specify the default behavior; that is, what is to happen if no page-level directive for tracing is specified. It is also possible to override these settings on a page-level by explicitly setting the trace page-directive to `true` or `false`.

When you set the `pageOutput` attribute to `false`, the tracing information will be displayed only in the application trace viewer. The trace viewer is identified by the special application called `Trace.axd`. When requested, the viewer will display a trace log of the last 10 requests assuming that the `requestLimit` is set to `10` in the `web.config` file).

Let's now add these trace-related entries to the `web.config` file to enable application-level tracing. To do this, we need to add (or modify) the following `trace` element under the `system.web` element:

```
<trace enabled="true"
       localOnly="true"
       pageOutput="false"
       requestLimit="10"
       traceMode="SortByTime" />
```

Now if you navigate to the `Categories.aspx` page a few times and then open up the trace viewer, you will see something similar to the following in your browser.

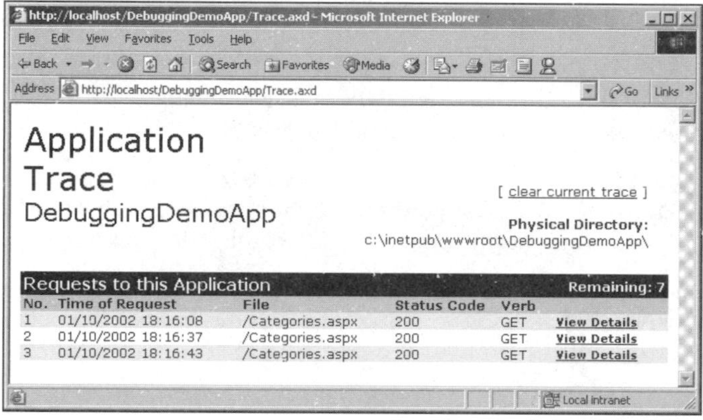


As you can see from the above, the trace viewer displays the list of requests made to the DebuggingDemoApp. We can also get more details about a specific request by clicking on the hyperlink View Details. It is also possible to clear all the trace information stored in the trace viewer by clicking on the hyperlink clear current trace.

# ASP.NET Web Service Debugging

Debugging a web service is similar to debugging an ASP.NET web application. The important difference is that while you set your break points in the web service code, you must invoke some kind of client to get that code called.

To demonstrate, let's add a simple web service to our application.

## Creating the Web Service

Open the DebuggingDemoApp solution in Visual Studio .NET. Right-click on the DebuggingDemoApp project and select Add | Add WebService. Then name the service `NorthwindWebService.asmx`.

The NorthwindWebService will contain one method, which returns details about all the categories in the Northwind database.

Click on the `NorthwindWebService.asmx` file in the Solution Explorer and press *F7* to get to the code. Remove the commented out default method, and then modify the contents to the following:

```
Imports System.Web.Services
Imports System.Data.SqlClient
```

We start by importing the `System.Data.SqlClient` at the top of the web service code-behind file. Next, we give the web service a proper name, instead of the default `tempuri.org`:

```
<WebService(Namespace:="http://Wrox.com/vbdebugging")> _
Public Class NorthwindWebService
    Inherits System.Web.Services.WebService
```

Then we declare the web method and start implementing it:

```
<WebMethod()> _
  Public Function GetCategories() As DataSet

    Dim connString As String = _
        ConfigurationSettings.AppSettings.Item("connectionString")
    Dim sqlConn As New SqlConnection(connString)
    Dim adapter As New SqlDataAdapter( _
    "Select CategoryID,CategoryName,Description from Categories", _
        sqlConn)

    'Create and fill the Dataset query
    Dim dstCategories As New DataSet()
    adapter.Fill(dstCategories)
```

This code is equivalent to the code we developed previously for the `Categories.aspx` file. We open a `Connection`, create a `DataAdapter` and used it to fill the `dstCategories` `DataSet`.

Finally, we return the `dstCategories` from the method, and close the connection:

```
        'Return data set to caller
        GetCategories = dstCategories

        'Close the opened database connection
        sqlConn.Close()
    End Function

End Class
```

## Debugging the Web Service using Visual Studio .NET

To debug the web service, we need to set up breakpoints in the web service code. To perform this, open up the code-behind file of the NorthwindWebService web service and then set breakpoints as shown in the following screenshot:

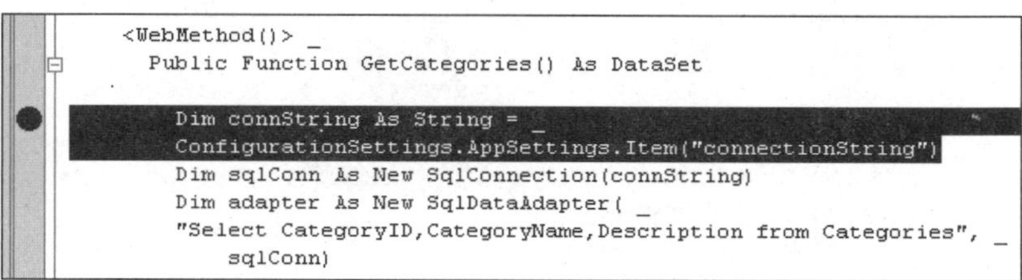

```
<WebMethod()> _
  Public Function GetCategories() As DataSet

    Dim connString As String = _
    ConfigurationSettings.AppSettings.Item("connectionString")
    Dim sqlConn As New SqlConnection(connString)
    Dim adapter As New SqlDataAdapter( _
    "Select CategoryID,CategoryName,Description from Categories", _
        sqlConn)
```

Use the Solution Explorer to set the `NorthwindWebService.asmx` file to be the project start page (select Set as Start Page). Then press *F5* to build the application and run it in the debugger:

In the above window, if you click on GetCategories, you will see the following screen:

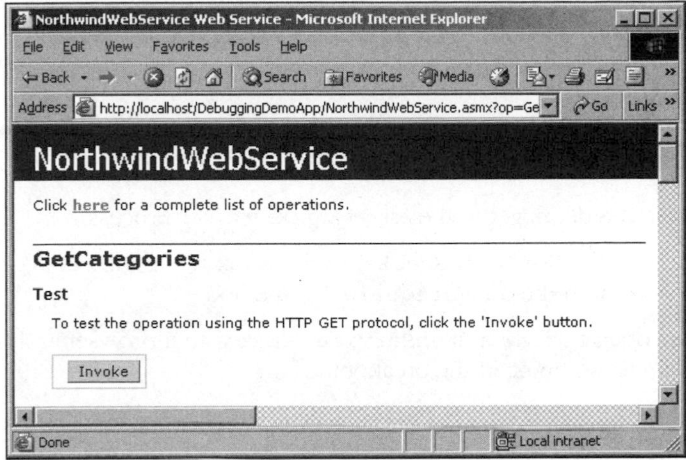


When you click the Invoke button, the web service will actually be invoked, and the result displayed on the screen. However, since we have set up a breakpoint in the web service, the debugger will automatically stop at the line where we have set the breakpoint.

Once it hits the breakpoint, then we can step through the code as with any other .NET application. At this point, we have all the debugging features of Visual Studio.NET available to us to debug the web service. After debugging the code, when you run the application, you will get the following window where the result of the web service execution is displayed:

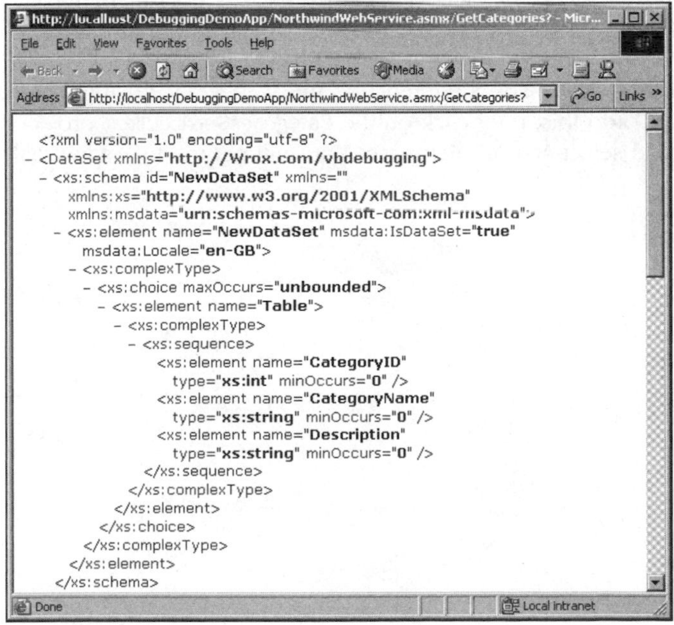

## Debugging a Web Service using the SDK Debugger

As you probably guessed, the steps for debugging the web service using the SDK Debugger are very similar to what we did earlier for the web application:

1. Attach the debugger to the aspnet_wp.exe worker process.
2. Open up the `NorthwindWebService.asmx` file in the debugger and set a breakpoint in the `GetCategories()` method.
3. Now open `NorthwindWebService.asmx` with a browser and notice the debugger stopping at the breakpoint.

## Debugging the Web Service from a Windows Forms Client using Visual Studio .NET

In this example, we will write a Windows Forms client application for our web service, and then see how to debug the web service from the client application.

### Creating a Web Service Client

We will need to add a new Windows Application project to our existing DebuggingDemoApp solution. To do this, right-click on the solution from the Solution Explorer and then select Add | New Project. In the Add New Project dialogue, specify a new Windows Application project named CategoriesServiceClient and then hit OK.

Once the project is created, add a reference to the web service using the Add Web Reference dialog. To do this, right-click on the CategoriesServiceClient project from the Solution Explorer and select Add Web Reference. You will get the following dialog:

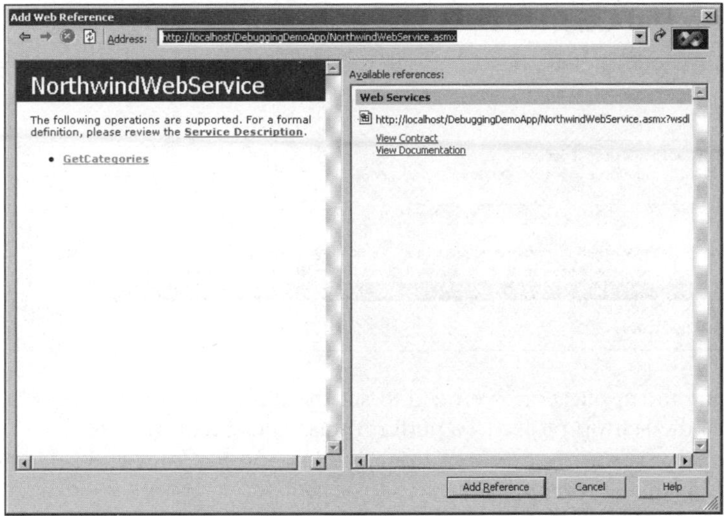


In the address bar, enter the location and filename of the web service and then hit *Enter*. In the above dialog, when you click the Add Reference button, Visual Studio.NET automatically creates the proxy class that is required for communicating with the web service. The code for the proxy is not directly included in the Solution Explorer, but if you are interested, you can find it under a `WebReference` folder created in the solution's directory. This now contains a `localhost` subdirectory, which includes a number of files, one of which is `Reference.vb`, where the proxy code resides. For a detailed description of these refer to Wrox' *Professional ASP.NET Web Services with VB.NET* (ISBN 1-86100-775-2).

Now that we have added a reference to the web service, let's open the form in the designer and add a `Datagrid` control and a `Button`. Name them as `grdCategories` and `cmdGetCategories` respectively. In the click event handler of the button, add the following lines of code:

```
Private Sub cmdGetCategories_Click(ByVal sender As System.Object, _
                                  ByVal e As System.EventArgs) _
                                  Handles cmdGetCategories.Click
  Dim categoriesSvc As New localhost.NorthwindWebService()
  grdCategories.DataSource = categoriesSvc.GetCategories()
End Sub
```

Here we simply create an instance of the web service proxy class, and then invoke the `GetCategories()` method.

In this situation, the proxy is named `localhost` because we have located the web service on our local machine to keep things simple. In a more realistic scenario, the web service would be located on a remote server, and the proxy name would be the name/URL of that server. We would still be able to debug into that server, provided the remote debugging components are installed on the remote server, and you have Administrator privileges on the remote machine.

### Debugging the Client in Visual Studio .NET

While still in the editor, set a breakpoint in the code, as shown in the following screenshot:

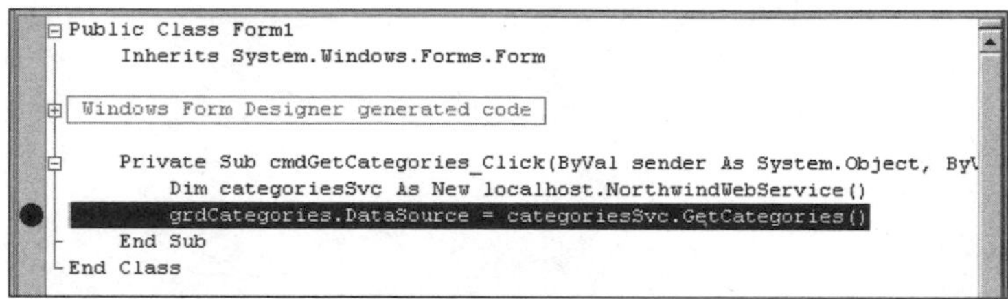

Before running the application, we need to set the `CategoriesServiceClient` application as the startup project. To perform this, right-click on the `CategoriesServiceClient` project from the Solution Explorer and select **Set as Startup Project** from the context menu.

Now run the application by pressing *F5*. When we click the button, we will hit the breakpoint that we have already set up. At this point, if we select **Debug | Step Into** from the menu or press *F11*, we can step into the web service code and start debugging.

# Debugging ASP and ASP.NET Side by Side

In this section, we will see how to debug ASP and ASP.NET pages side by side using Visual Studio .NET. We will also see how an ASP page and an ASP.NET web form can seamlessly coexist and exchange limited information. Remember that ASP and ASP.NET run in two different processes and are executed by completely different ISAPI DLLs, which means that they do not share `Application` and `Session` variables. They can, however, still reside in the same project.

## *Creating the ASP Page*

For this demonstration, we will use our previously created solution DebuggingDemoApp. Select the DebuggingDemoApp project in the Solution Explorer and reset it to be the startup application again.

Then right-click on the project and select **Add | Add New Item**, select **Text File**, and set the file name to `ProductListing.asp`.

We will implement `ProductListing.asp` to display all of the products within a specified category. The caller must specify the category in the query string, as shown below:

http://localhost/DebuggingDemoApp/ProductListing.asp?CategoryId=3

```
<%@ Language=VBScript %>
<% Option Explicit %>
<%
  Dim objProducts
  Dim rstProducts
  Dim lngCategoryID
  Dim strSql
  Dim strConnectionString
  strConnectionString = _
    "provider=SQLOLEDB;server=localhost;uid=sa;pwd=;" _
    + "database=Northwind"
  'Get the CategoryID from the Querystring
  lngCategoryID = CLng(Request.QueryString("CategoryID"))
  strSql = "Select * from Products Where CategoryID = " & _
    lngCategoryID
  'Create an instance of the recordset object
  Set rstProducts = Server.CreateObject("ADODB.Recordset")
  'Open the recordset passing in the required arguments
  rstProducts.Open strSql,strConnectionString,0
%>
<HTML>
<HEAD>
<TITLE>Northwind Web Application</TITLE>
<LINK rel='Stylesheet' type='text/css' href='Styles.css' />
</HEAD>
<body>
<table cellSpacing='0' cellPadding='0'
       width='600' border='0' ID="Table1">
  <tr>
    <td class='lightAccent'>
      <IMG height='10' src='images/spacer.gif' width='1' />
    </td>
  </tr>
  <tr>
    <td class='accentColor'>
      <IMG height='1' src='images/spacer.gif' width='1' />
    </td>
  </tr>
  <tr>
    <td align='middle' vAlign='top'>List Of Products<br></br>
      <table height='311' cellSpacing='0' cellPadding='1'
       width='722' border='0' ID="Table2">
        <tr>
          <td width='631' colSpan='3' height='21'>
            <hr class='hr' />
          </td>
```

```
          </tr>
          <%
            Do While Not rstProducts.EOF
          %>
          <tr>
            <td class="CartListItem"
                style="background-color:buttonface;"
                align='middle' width='631' colSpan='1' height='15'>
              <p>
                <%=rstProducts("ProductName")%>
              </p>
            </td>
            <td class="CartListItem"
                style="background-color:buttonface;"
                width='631' height='15' colspan="2">
              <%=rstProducts("QuantityPerUnit")%>
            </td>
          </tr>
          <tr>
            <td colspan="3"> </td>
          </tr>
          <%
            rstProducts.MoveNext
            Loop
            rstProducts.Close()
            Set rstProducts = Nothing
          %>
        </table>
      </td>
    </tr>
  </table>
  </body>
  </HTML>
```

In the above lines of code, we start by retrieving the category ID that is passed in the `querystring`. Note that this `querystring` is passed from the `Categories.aspx` page, when the user presses the Show all Products link. After that, we get the list of products for that specific category ID. We do this by executing a SQL statement using the ADO `Recordset` object. Once we get the `Recordset`, we then loop though its contents and display them in the page.

Now that we have completed the ASP page, let us see what it takes to debug the ASP page in the Visual Studio .NET IDE. To debug the ASP page, all we need to do is to set the ASP debugging property to `true`. We can do this by right-clicking on the DebuggingDemoApp from the Solution Explorer and selecting Properties. In the property pages window, select Configuration Properties | Debugging from the treeview; you will see an option called ASP debugging. Check the checkbox and click OK.

Now open up the `ProductListing.asp` file ASP page and set up breakpoints in places that you want to monitor. Set the `Categories.aspx` page to be the start up page for the solution, and press *F5* to run the application in the debugger.

You will be prompted to enter the user name and password of a user with administrative rights to configure IIS on your machine:

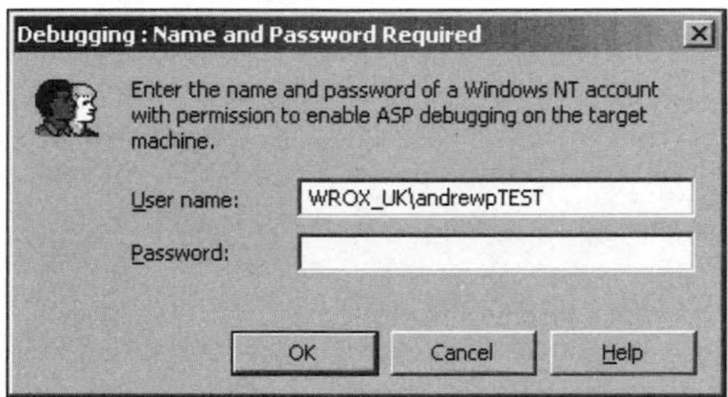


After you provide this information, the Visual Studio .NET debugger will attach automatically to the ASP worker process and continue with loading the page. Now you will get the categories page, where all the categories in the Northwind database will be displayed. If you select the hyperlink Show all Products, it will navigate to the `ProductListing.asp` file and then you will hit the breakpoint. Now you can debug your ASP page using all the features of the Visual Studio .NET IDE.

# Debugging ASP.NET Server Controls

In this section, we will see how to debug ASP.NET server controls using Visual Studio .NET. For this example, we will create an ASP.NET Server Control called `MyDataGridControl` that is capable of displaying data from a SQL Server database in a grid format.

Start by creating a new Visual Basic Web Control Library project named ServerControlDemo. Then delete the default class (`WebCustomControl1`) and create a new one called `MyDataGridControl`, by right-clicking in the Solution Explorer and selecting Add | Add New... Web Custom Control:

To be able to display the data in table format, the `MyDataGridControl` requires the following two important properties:

- Connection string – allows us to specify the database to connect to
- SQL query – allows us to specify the `SELECT` query to be executed

The control also exposes public properties such as `TableBorder`, `TableHeight`, `TableWidth`, `BGColor`, and `HeaderColor`.

Here is the code listing for the `MyDataGridControl`. Start by removing the default `Render()` method and default "`text`" property and field. Then we start by adding an import for the `System.Data.SqlClient` namespace. We also change the value for the `DefaultProperty` from "`text`" to "`ConnectionString`". This defines which property will be selected by default in the IDE's property browser, once the control is used on a form:

```
Imports System.ComponentModel
Imports System.Web.UI
Imports System.Data.SqlClient

<DefaultProperty("ConnectionString"), _
  ToolboxData("<{0}:MyDataGridControl _
  runat=server></{0}:MyDataGridControl>")> _
Public Class MyDataGridControl
    Inherits System.Web.UI.WebControls.WebControl
```

In the constructor of the `MyDataGridControl`, we pass in an `HtmlTextWriterTag.Table` element as an argument to the base class (`WebControl`). By doing this, we indicate that we want to render the HTML table element as part of the server control. Once we specify the HTML Table element as part of the constructor, we can then add attributes to the `Table` element by overriding the `AddAttributesToRender()` method. We will look at the code for the `AddAttributesToRender()` method in a moment.

```
  Public Sub New()
    MyBase.New(HtmlTextWriterTag.Table)
  End Sub

  Private connString As String
  Private backGroundColor As String
  Private header As String
  Private sql As String
  Private border As Integer
  Private controlHeight As Integer
  Private controlWidth As Integer

  Public Property ConnectionString() As String
    Get
      Return connString
    End Get

    Set(ByVal Value As String)
      connString = Value
    End Set
  End Property
```

```
Public Property SqlQuery() As String
  Get
    Return sql
  End Get

  Set(ByVal Value As String)
    sql = Value
  End Set
End Property

Public Property TableBorder() As Integer
  Get
    Return border
  End Get

  Set(ByVal Value As Integer)
    border = Value
  End Set
End Property

Public Property TableHeight() As Integer
  Get
    Return controlHeight
  End Get

  Set(ByVal Value As Integer)
    controlHeight = Value
  End Set
End Property

Public Property TableWidth() As Integer
  Get
    Return controlWidth
  End Get

  Set(ByVal Value As Integer)
    controlWidth = Value
  End Set
End Property

Public Property BGColor() As String
  Get
    Return backGroundColor
  End Get

  Set(ByVal Value As String)
    backGroundColor = Value
  End Set
End Property

Public Property HeaderColor() As String
  Get
```

```
        Return header
      End Get

      Set(ByVal Value As String)
        header = Value
      End Set
    End Property
```

As you can see from the above code listing, we expose the following public properties from our control: `ConnectionString`, `SqlQuery`, `TableHeight`, `TableWidth`, `TableBorder`, `BGColor`, and `HeaderColor`. By setting these properties to appropriate values, the consumers of our server control can control the output generated.

In the `AddAttributesToRender()` method, we set the attributes for the `<Table>` element that was passed to the constructor of our control class:

```
  Protected Overrides Sub AddAttributesToRender( _
                            ByVal output As System.Web.UI.HtmlTextWriter)
    output.AddAttribute(HtmlTextWriterAttribute.Border, _
                        border.ToString())
    output.AddAttribute(HtmlTextWriterAttribute.Bgcolor, BGColor)
    output.AddAttribute(HtmlTextWriterAttribute.Height, _
                        Height.ToString())
    output.AddAttribute(HtmlTextWriterAttribute.Width, Width.ToString())
    MyBase.AddAttributesToRender(output)
  End Sub
```

In the `RenderContents()` method, we specify the contents that we want our server control to render:

```
  Protected Overrides Sub RenderContents( _
                  ByVal output As System.Web.UI.HtmlTextWriter)
    Dim value As String
    Dim i As Integer
    Dim sqlConn As SqlConnection = _
      New SqlConnection(ConnectionString)
    sqlConn.Open()
    Dim sqlComm As SqlCommand = New SqlCommand(SqlQuery, sqlConn)
    Dim sqlReader As SqlDataReader = _
      sqlComm.ExecuteReader(CommandBehavior.CloseConnection)
    Dim fieldCount As Integer = sqlReader.FieldCount
    'Start rendering all the tags
    output.RenderBeginTag(HtmlTextWriterTag.Tr)
    output.AddAttribute(HtmlTextWriterAttribute.Colspan, _
                        fieldCount.ToString())
    output.AddAttribute(HtmlTextWriterAttribute.Align, "Center")
    output.AddAttribute(HtmlTextWriterAttribute.Bgcolor, "DodgerBlue")
    output.RenderBeginTag(HtmlTextWriterTag.Td)
    output.RenderBeginTag(HtmlTextWriterTag.B)
    output.Write("Wrox DataGrid Control")
```

```
    'Close the b tag
    output.RenderEndTag()
    'Close the TD tag
    output.RenderEndTag()
    'Close the TR tag
    output.RenderEndTag()
    'Specify the BGColor of the column headers
    output.AddAttribute(HtmlTextWriterAttribute.Bgcolor, header)
    'Add the column headers
    output.RenderBeginTag(HtmlTextWriterTag.Tr)
    'Loop thru all the columns and display their title
    For i = 0 To fieldCount - 1
      output.RenderBeginTag(HtmlTextWriterTag.Td)
      output.Write(sqlReader.GetName(i).ToUpper())
      output.RenderEndTag()
    Next i
    output.RenderEndTag()
    While (sqlReader.Read())
      output.RenderBeginTag(HtmlTextWriterTag.Tr)
      'Loop through all the fields in the SqlDataReader
      For i = 0 To fieldCount - 1
        output.RenderBeginTag(HtmlTextWriterTag.Td)
        If (sqlReader.IsDBNull(i)) Then
          value = ""
        Else
          Select Case (sqlReader.GetFieldType(i).ToString())
            Case "System.Int16"
              value = sqlReader.GetInt16(i).ToString()
            Case "System.Int32"
              value = sqlReader.GetInt32(i).ToString()
            Case "System.Int64"
              value = sqlReader.GetInt64(i).ToString()
            Case "System.Decimal"
              value = sqlReader.GetDecimal(i).ToString()
            Case "System.DateTime"
              value = sqlReader.GetDateTime(i).ToString()
            Case "System.String"
              value = sqlReader.GetString(i).ToString()
            Case "System.Boolean"
              value = sqlReader.GetBoolean(i).ToString()
            Case "System.Guid"
              value = sqlReader.GetGuid(i).ToString()
            Case "System.Double"
              value = sqlReader.GetDouble(i).ToString()
            Case "System.Byte"
              value = sqlReader.GetByte(i).ToString()
          End Select
        End If
        output.Write(value)
        output.RenderEndTag()
      Next i
        output.RenderEndTag()
```

```
        End While

        MyBase.RenderContents(output)

      End Sub
    End Class
```

In the above lines of code, we start by executing a query against the SQL server database. We also add various elements and attributes to our control by using the `RenderBeginTag()`, `RenderEndTag()`, and `AddAttribute()` methods. We then loop through all the columns contained in the `SqlDataReader` object and display them as sub-headings. Once the column names are rendered properly, we then render the actual contents from the `SqlDataReader` object. To accomplish this, we enumerate the `SqlDataReader` object by calling its `Read()` method. While enumerating the contents, we also check to see if a column contains a null value, and if it does then we assign an empty string to the local variable; otherwise we invoke the appropriate `GetXXX()` method based on the data type of the returned column.

## Creating a Client to Host the Server Control

Now that we have created the control, let's look at the code required for hosting our control in an ASP.NET page. For this, we will add a new ASP.NET Web Application project named ServerControlDemoClient to the ServerControlDemo solution. By now, you should know the drill. Right-click on the ServerControlDemo solution and select Add | New Project... to bring up the dialog box, and then select ASP.NET Web Application and name it ServerControlDemoClient.

Delete the default web form (WebForm1.aspx) from the project and create a new one called MyDataGridControlClient.aspx, using Add | Add WebForm in the Solution Explorer. Open up the designer for the form.

We will now add the server control to the toolbox. Right-click on the toolbox and select Add Tab. Name the tab "WroxServerControls". Click on the tab and then right-click on the toolbox again. Now select Customize Toolbox....

The Customize Toolbox dialog has two tabs. Select the one called .NET Framework Components. Then click Browse and locate the assembly we just created. This should be located under the `obj\debug\bin` directory:

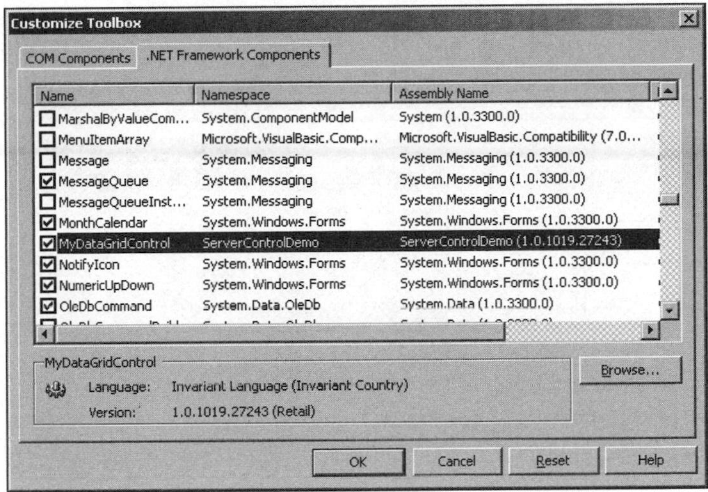


Once you click OK, the control will become available in the toolbox:

You can now drag the control onto the web form and use the property inspector to set the correct values, shown in the table below:

| **Property** | **Value** |
|---|---|
| `BgColor` | `Lavender` |
| `ConnectionString` | `server=localhost;database=northwind;uid=sa;pwd=` |
| `HeaderColor` | `Dodgerblue` |
| `SqlQuery` | `Select * from products` |
| `TableBorder` | `1` |
| `TableHeight` | `800` |
| `TableWidth` | `900` |

Now if you build the client and navigate to it in a browser, you'll see something like this:

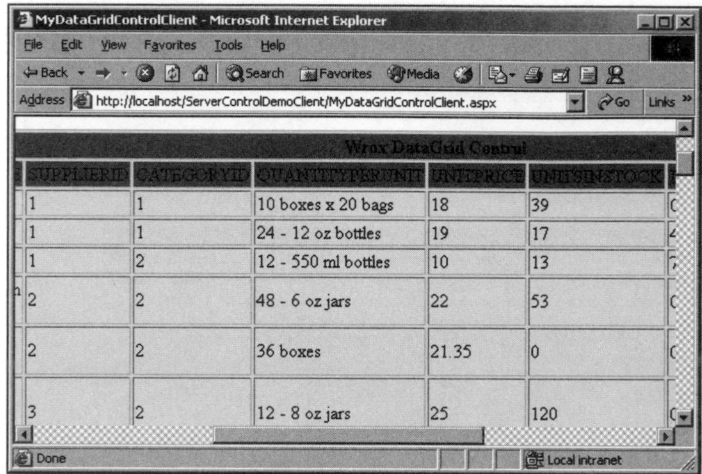


## *Debugging the ASP.NET Server Control*

To debug the server control from Visual Studio.NET, all you need to do is to set breakpoints in various places in the `MyDataGridControl` class. Right-click on the ServerControlDemoClient project from the Solution Explorer and select Set as Startup Project from the context menu. Then right-click on the `MyDataGridControlClient.aspx` file from the Solution Explorer and select Set as Start Page. After that, if you run the application by pressing *F5*, you will see that the browser will automatically hit the breakpoint that you have set in your `MyDataGridControl` class. Now you can debug the server control by stepping into it, monitoring variables, and so on.

# Windows Forms Controls in IE

In this section, we will see how to host a Windows Form control in Internet Explorer. From the control, we will also access a web service and display data returned from the web service. While performing all these operations, we will also demonstrate how to set up debugging and step through the code.

One of the great features of .NET is the seamless integration it provides with Internet Explorer. For example, we can activate a Windows Forms control from IE without even prompting the user. Also this is accomplished without having to do any registration but still utilizing all the features of Code Access Security provided by the CLR. The following list describes the five steps that we need to follow to activate a Windows Forms control within IE.

1. Create a Windows Forms control.
2. Create a HTML document with an object tag that identifies the Windows Forms control.
3. Configure the virtual directory for proper activation of the control.
4. Configure Code Access Permissions.
5. Run the control.

Now we will look at each of the above steps in detail.

## Creating a Windows Forms Control

In this step, we will create a simple Windows Forms control. This control will be very similar in functionality to the Windows Application (`CategoriesServiceClient`) that we created in the previous section. Start by creating a new Visual Basic .NET Windows Control Library project named CategoriesWebServiceClientControl.

Once the project is created, rename the default user control (`UserControl1.vb`) to `Categories.vb`. Also add a `DataGrid` control and a `Button` to the user control designer. These will be called `grdCategories` and `cmdGetCategories` respectively.

Since the controls need access to the `NorthwindWebService` that we created earlier, add a web reference to the web service (http://localhost/DebuggingDemoApp/NorthwindWebService.asmx) using the Add Web Reference dialog box. After that, in the click event handler of the button, we need to add code to retrieve the categories information from the web service and display it in a `Datagrid` control:

```
Private Sub cmdGetCategories_Click(ByVal sender As System.Object, _
                                   ByVal e As System.EventArgs)
                                   Handles cmdGetCategories.Click
  Me.Cursor = Cursors.WaitCursor
  Dim categoriesSvc As New localhost.NorthWindWebService()
  grdCategories.DataSource = categoriesSvc.GetCategories()
  Me.Cursor = Cursors.Default
End Sub
```

Finally, go to the top of the page and rename the class from `UserControl1` to `Categories`.

Now that we have created the control, we need to create a simple HTML page that will host our categories control.

## Creating an HTML Page

In this step, we will create an HTML document (CategoriesDisplay.htm) containing an object tag that is used to activate the Windows Forms control. The HTML page looks like the following:

```
<html>
  <body>
    <p>Categories Web Service Client Control<br> <br>
  </body>
  <object id="CategoriesControl1"
    classid="http:CategoriesWebServiceClientControl.dll#
             CategoriesWebServiceClientControl.Categories"
    height="500"
    width="500" VIEWASTEXT>
  </object>
  <br> <br>
</html>
```

In the classid attribute of the object tag, we specify the path to the control library and the fully qualified name of the control, separated by the # symbol. The combination of these two parameters serves as the unique identifier to identify the control. It is also possible to write client-side script against the control since it is identified by the unique id CategoriesControl1.

## Configuration of the Virtual Directory

Now that we have created the HTML page, let's create a new virtual directory and populate it with both the control (CategoriesWebServiceClientControl.dll) and the HTML document (CategoriesDisplay.htm). While configuring the virtual directory, it is important to set the execution permissions on the virtual directory to scripts. The control will not be properly activated if the execution permissions are set to scripts and executables.

## Configuration of Code Access Permissions

If our control is run from an intranet site, it will execute correctly. However, if the control needs to be run from an Internet site, we then need to configure Internet Explorer or alter security policy to allow it to run. We can do this by identifying our hosting page as belonging to the Trusted Sites zone. This will enable our web site for control download and execution of the code.

To set your site as part of the Trusted Sites zone, from IE choose Tools | Options | Security | Trusted Sites, add your site to the list, and then click OK. Next time, when you browse to that page, it should be in the Trusted Sites zone that has the Internet permission set by default.

## Running the Control

To run the control, all we need to do is to navigate to the HTML page that hosts our control from the browser. In the displayed HTML page, if you click on the GetCategories command button, the control connects to the web service, retrieves the categories information, and displays the categories information in the `DataGrid` control:

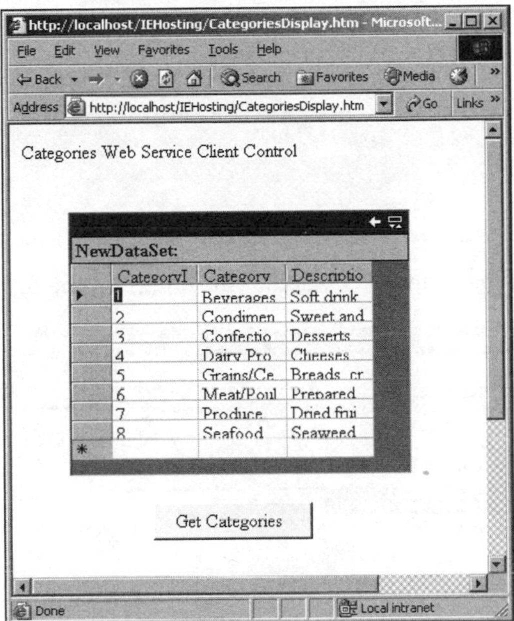


## Debugging the Windows Forms Control

The easiest way to debug the Windows Forms control is to attach the debugger to an instance of Internet Explorer, which we then subsequently use to open the HTML page. This can be done using the following steps in Visual Studio .NET, assuming Internet Explorer is already started:

1. Select Tools | Debug Processes... to bring up the Processes window:

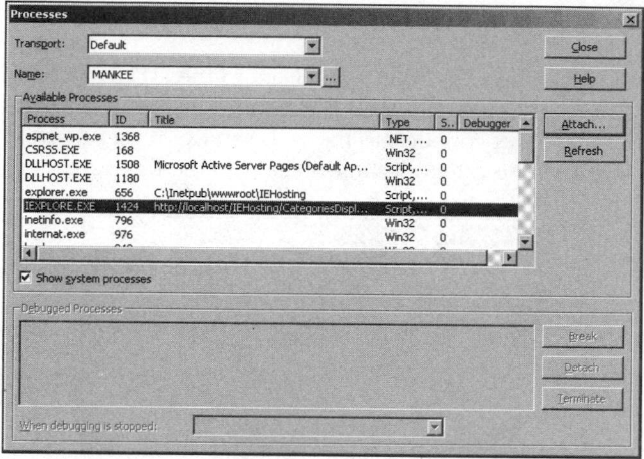


2. Select iexplore.exe and click Attach. This brings up the following dialog:

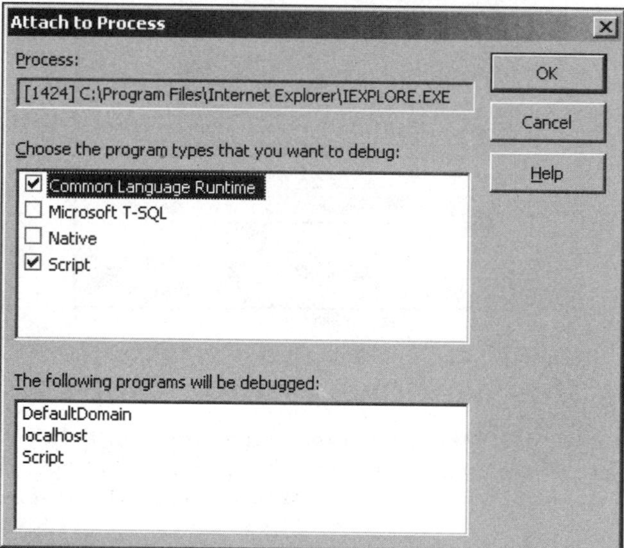


3. Make sure that Script is selected and press OK.
4. Now set a break point in the control code. Then switch to Internet Explorer, open the HTML file, and press the button.

You are now in the Windows Forms control and have access to all the regular features of the debugger. The procedure for debugging using the SDK Debugger would be almost exactly the same as shown for the Visual Studio IDE, except that you have to manually load the `.vb` file.

# Summary

In this chapter, we have seen how to debug web applications using the rich debugging support provided by Visual Studio .NET. Specifically we covered:

- How to debug an ASP.NET web application using the SDK Debugger and Visual Studio .NET
- Important features of instrumentation, and how to use tracing to effectively debug web applications
- How to debug an ASP.NET web service application using ASP.NET features, as well as from the web service consumer application
- How to debug an ASP.NET Server control from the client application using Visual Studio .NET
- How to debug ASP and ASP.NET pages side by side
- How to host a Windows Forms control in IE, and debug it

VB.NET

Debugging

Handbook

6

# 6

# Advanced Debugging Scenarios

Most of the time, the tasks associated with debugging are mundane in nature: call a class library from a Windows Forms application and examine the contents of a string. This chapter introduces several practical debugging scenarios that are anything but mundane. Much like a video game where you spend the first few levels honing your skills, this chapter uses those finally honed skills in order to debug several intricate applications.

The first application presented is a remoted application (WXServer and WXClient). Remoting is a one way to implement client-server applications in .NET and when you say "client-server", you should automatically think "inter-process control". This example will demonstrate how to debug multiple processes as part of a single application. These processes (client and server) can run on separate machines and hence serve as ways to introduce remote debugging. The idea behind remoting debugging is to control a process on a remote machine with a debugger running locally. This lets you use one machine to debug client and server applications even if the server is running off on another network host. An ancillary topic presented in conjunction with remoting is configuration files; these are boon to debugging, rating up there with Jonas Salk's invention of the Polio vaccine. OK, maybe that is a bit of exaggeration but configuration files are very useful.

The next application presented demonstrates a legacy Visual Basic GUI application (VB6) accessing a Windows Forms dialog. Clearly one of the themes discussed in this application is that of debugging mixed-mode applications that use unmanaged (VB6) and managed code (VB.NET). This application has a nice plot twist in that it requires (for reasons to we'll see latter) the spawning of a thread in order to solve a bug associated with the application. The overall gist of this debugging exercise is interoperability and multi-threaded debugging.

The last application presented extends the interoperability theme in demonstrating a VB.NET application calling an unmanaged COM Server written in C++. We use a C++ COM server because the application determines the application domains deployed within .NET processes. This information is not available through a managed API so therefore unmanaged C++ was used to access this information and make it available to a managed application VB.NET. A lesser theme of this application is cross-language debugging. The only problem with cross-language debugging is that it works with no setup required. There are not many lessons to be learned by a Visual Studio .NET feature (cross language debugging) that works just by debugging the assemblies/modules written in different languages.

Of course, all the aforementioned applications will be available for download with all of the source code for this book.

# Debugging Remote Applications

Before we can debug a remote application, we need to create one. This application consists of several parts:

- A client (`WXClient.exe`) – the client is a Windows Forms application. It calls a method exposed by the `WXAPIToRemote` class library and displays the results to the screen. The `WXAPIToRemote` class library is actually running inside the server process (`WXServer.exe`).
- A server (`WXServer.exe`) – the server is a Windows Forms application whose sole job is to expose a set of methods from a class library (`WXAPIToRemote.dll`) for consumption by one or more clients.
- Class library (`WXAPIToRemote.DLL`) – the class library contains a lone public class (`WXAPI`). The `WXAPI` class contains a lone method, `GetSomeInformation()`.

Although it is possible to run both `WXClient.exe` and `WXServer.exe` on the same host, it will be more interesting to debug the application on multiple machines. In the real world, servers quite often offload their display-related tasks to clients so this is a rather typical approach to deployment. The following diagram demonstrates the deployment of `WXClient.exe` and `WXServer.exe`:

**Figure 1**

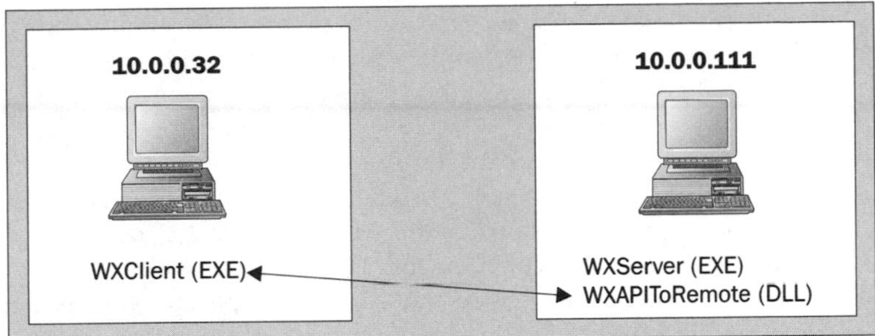


The diagram above shows that the client will run on a machine with the IP address `10.0.0.32`, and the sever components will run on a machine with IP address `10.0.0.111`. An XML-based application configuration file contains the information that allows each part of the application to find the other so these relationships do not need to be hard-coded into the application.

The structure of this application allows the demonstration of the following debugging scenarios:

- Debugging a class library (DLL) by specifying an executable to load the class library.
- Debugging two applications (`WXClient.exe` and `WXServer.exe`) in the same instance of Visual Studio .NET. This shows that Visual Studio .NET is capable of debugging multiple processes in a single running instance of Visual Studio .NET. Under this scenario, the client and server will run on the same machine.
- Debugging an application running on a remote machine where the remote application is launched from Visual Studio .NET running locally. The server (`WXServer.exe`) and client (`WXClient.exe`) will be debugged on the same host (the host running the client) but in separate instances of Visual Studio .NET.
- Debugging an application running on a remote machine where the remote application is already running and is attached to Visual Studio .NET running locally. The application already executing will be the server (`WXServer.exe`). Client and server will be debugged in separate instances of Visual Studio .NET.

Yes, there are variations that we could explore, but the techniques demonstrated are generally applicable.

## Application Domains

In the past, you could think of the communication between the separate parts of a client-server application as Inter-Process Communication (IPC). This term (IPC) made sense when process addresses spaces were the boundaries between applications. What is a process address space? In the era of Windows 3.1 (a decade ago), applications could actually share an address. This meant that your spreadsheet could (by default) share memory with your word processor. It also meant that your spreadsheet could corrupt your word processor's address space and cause it to crash. True processes – available in Windows as of Win32, (which means Windows NT, Windows 95, and above) – provide separate address spaces so that different applications were kept completely separate and hence unable to corrupt each other's memory.

In the era of Win32 development, the process boundary was the safe way to partition applications. Running multiple applications inside the same address space could cause problems if one application (say the client) behaved maliciously and corrupted the addresses used by another application (say the server) running in the same process. In .NET, however, two or more applications can safely share a process. The verification process managed code must go through ensures that a managed application can in no way be malicious with respect to another application's address space.

In the managed code world, application domains are the boundaries between applications and multiple applications can run in one Windows process. To pass data from client to server or vice-versa, the data must pass between application domains, which may or may not reside in the same process. Application domains are mentioned here because a client-server example application is about to be described in detail. The client and server applications presented each run in separate processes and separate process contains a single application domain. In this case, the term process is synonymous with the term application domain. Be aware that in a more sophisticated application with multiple application domains running in a process, the term process in not so readily interchanged with the term application domain.

## Application Setup

There are many different ways to implement a client-server application using the .NET Framework (Serviced COM+ Components implemented using the `System.EnterpriseServices` namespace, ASP.NET Web services, and raw sockets using the `System.Network.Sockets` namespace) but our choice is remoting. This approach is particularly interesting as it is new and it makes it simple to:

- Debug the client and class library in the same process address space without using the server process.
- Debug the client and server on the same host
- Debug the client and server on different hosts.

In fact, courtesy of XML-based configuration files you can run all these scenarios without altering a single line of source code. Although we used remoting, similar flexibility is available when using serviced components. There is no one right solution when deploying a client-server application (remoting, ASP.NET Web Services or service components). Each has pros and cons but the major advantage of using remoting is its configuration files that are readily editable using any text editor.

This section of the text discusses the implementation of the class library, client, and server. It is not meant to be a comprehensive tutorial on remoting but should serve to get developers up and running in a client-server deployment.

## Class Library (WXAPIToRemote.dll)

Creating a class library such as `WXAPIToRemote.dll` is a simple matter of File | New | Project | Visual Basic Projects | Class Library. The `WXAPIToRemote.dll`'s lone class and the lone method for this class is as follows:

```
Public Class WXAPI
  Function GetSomeInformation() As String
    Return "Information retrieved, Machine: " & _
           Environment.MachineName & ", When: " & DateTime.Now
  End Function
End Class
```

The `GetSomeInformation()` method simply returns a `String` containing:

- The machine (`Environment.MachineName`) on which we execute the method, to prove it is a method called from client to sever.
- The current time, to show when the client to server method was invoked.

There was nothing radical or unusual about the implementation of the `WXAPI` class, nothing that said, "This is remoted". The only data passing between client and server is of type `String` (passed from server to client as the function's return value). The definition for the `String` class is as follows:

```
<Serializable> _
NotInheritable Public Class String
  Implements IComparable, ICloneable, IConvertible, IEnumerable
```

Notice that the `<Serializable>` attribute, prefixes the `String` class. Without getting into specifics (since this is not a text on remoting), the `<Serializable>` attribute says the class can (among other things) pass between application domains. If you wanted to pass a different class from client-to-server or from server-to-client this class must be defined with the `<Serializable>` attribute as in the following example:

```
<Serializable()> _
Public Class MovesBetweenClientAndServer
  ' put body of class here
End Class
```

In spite of all this mumbo jumbo about remoting, there is nothing in the definition of the WXAPI class that prevents it from being tested as a simply DLL called from any executable. This is a great way to get the bugs out before deploying in a true client-server scenario. For detailed information on serialization and remoting, see the *Visual Basic Remoting Handbook* (Wrox Press, ISBN 1-86100-740-X) and the *Visual Basic .NET Serialization Handbook* (Wrox Press, ISBN 1-86100-800-7) respectively.

## Server (WXServer.exe)

On the surface our sever application appears to be trivial but in actuality it is more powerful than it first seems, since this humble application is a server that remotes every class (all one of them) and every method (again, all one of them) contained in the WXAPIToRemote.dll class library. From a visual perspective, the WXServer is as follows:

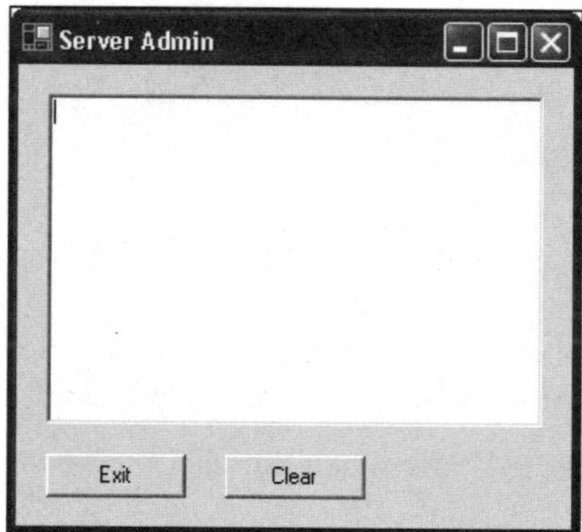


The WXServer.exe's dialog contains:

- TextBoxError – a TextBox class instance used to display any errors encountered by the application
- Exit button – a Button instance that exits the application
- Clear button – a Button instance that clears the contents of TextBoxError

In support of the WXServer.exe's mild mannered persona is its source code, which is as follows:

```
Imports System.Runtime.Remoting

Public Class FormServerAdmin
  Inherits System.Windows.Forms.Form
```

```
    Private Sub FormServerAdmin_Load(ByVal sender As System.Object, _
                                     ByVal e As System.EventArgs) _
                                     Handles MyBase.Load
      Try
        RemotingConfiguration.Configure( _
                                   "..\config\HTTPRemotingServer.config")
      Catch ex As Exception
        TextBoxError.Text = ex.ToString()
      End Try
    End Sub

    Private Sub ButtonExit_Click(ByVal sender As System.Object, _
                                 ByVal e As System.EventArgs) _
                                   Handles ButtonExit.Click
      Me.Close()
    End Sub

    Private Sub ButtonClear_Click(ByVal sender As System.Object, _
                                  ByVal e As System.EventArgs) _
                                    Handles ButtonClear.Click
      TextBoxError.Clear()
    End Sub

    ' Windows Forms specific infrastructure implemented here -
    ' not shown for reasons of brevity

  End Class
```

The previous code snippet is the bulk of `WXServer.exe`'s implementation excluding the Windows Forms designer generated code.

The `FormServerAdmin_Load()` method of the WXServer application is called when the Windows Form is loaded. This method is therefore a good place to perform application configuration. For this reason the `FormServerAdmin_Load()` method invokes the call to `RemotingConfiguration.Configure` that ultimately loads remoting settings for the server.

In the code above, the lines applicable to remoting are highlighted:

- `Imports System.Runtime.Remoting` – this namespace contains the `RemotingConfiguration` class. The aforementioned class is in the `mscorlib.dll` assembly, which is automatically available to all .NET applications, so there is no need to create a reference from the WXServer project to a special assembly that supports remoting.
- `RemotingConfiguration.Configure(filename)` – the server application (`WXServer.exe`) has no direct knowledge of the classes it is remoting. This information is contained in an XML-based configuration file (`..\config\HTTPRemotingServer.config`). This file dictates that the `WXAPIToRemote.dll` class library will expose its `WXAPI` class for remoting.

One reference does need to be set up; the WXServer project must reference the `WXAPIToRemote.dll` class library. A reference is set up by right-clicking on a project's References folder in the Solution Explorer windows. This displays a context menu that contains an Add Reference menu item.

The true "excitement" of the WXServer project is that the executable it builds acts as the server side of a remoted application. This server's use of the `RemotingConfiguration.Configure()` method can be summed up as extremely elegant. The elegance of the XML-based configuration file the previous method loads is that you can change the remoting behavior of the server application without rebuilding it. When deployed at a customer site, new classes can be remoted by modifying the configuration file. New assemblies containing classes to be remoted can be specified using the configuration file as can new remoting configuration settings, including different remoting protocols (HTTP, TCP/IP, etc.).

#### Server-side Configuration File: HTTPRemotingServer.config

The contents of the `..\config\HTTPRemotingServer.config` configuration file is as follows:

```
<configuration>
  <system.runtime.remoting>
    <application>
      <service>
        <wellknown mode="Singleton"
                   type="WXAPIToRemote.WXAPI,WXAPIToRemote"
                   objectUri="WXRemoteStuff" />
      </service>
      <channels>
        <channel ref="http" port="8999" />
      </channels>
    </application>
  </system.runtime.remoting>
</configuration>
```

Without decomposing every XML element, let's focus on the highlighted elements relevant to the remoting configuration:

- `<wellknown>` – specifies that the `WXAPIToRemote.WXAPI` class (the type to remote) will be exposed from `WXAPIToRemote` assembly. The `type` attribute is used to specify the API to remote (`Namespace.ClassName, AssemblyName`) where the assembly name is specified without the DLL extension. The `objectUri` XML attribute represents the name that the client will use in order to access the class remoted. This name is arbitrary (`WXRemoteStuff`) but clearly, in reality, the name should make logical sense.

- `<channel>` – configures the communication channel over which the server will remote its object or objects. In the previous configuration file, the `ref` XML attribute indicates the type of channel, `http` (Hypertext Transfer Protocol) and the `port` attribute indicates that the port is `8999`.
- The `objectUri` XML attribute specifies a Universal Resource Identifier (URI) and used to identify a resource. In this case, the resource is the class (type) to be remoted by the server.

The HTTP protocol is used by the channel over which WXServer remotes the `WXAPI` class. To use IIS is installable on the following platforms: Windows NT 4.0 (with the NT option pack or with IIS installed separately), Windows 2000 Professional (and above), Windows XP Professional, and the various versions of .NET Server. For environments such as Windows 2000 and Windows XP Professional, an extra installation step may be required in order to install IIS: Start Menu | Control Panel | Add and Remote Programs | Add and Remove Windows Components tab. Performing the following steps displays a dialog which on Windows XP Professional is entitled Windows Components Wizard. Check the Internet Information Server (IIS) option and install away in order to support the HTTP protocol.

## Client (WXClient.exe)

The client application, `WXClient.exe`, is a Windows Forms application that appears as follows:

The `WXClient.exe` dialog contains:

- `TextBoxRemoteResults` – a `TextBox` class instance that displays the return value of the remote method called
- `TextBoxError` – a `TextBox` class instance used to display any errors encountered by the application
- Exit button – a `Button` instance that exits the application
- Run Remote button – a `Button` instance that invokes the remote method hence writing results to `TextBoxRemoteResults`

The WXClient.exe application is fundamentally implemented as follows:

```
Imports System.Runtime.Remoting

Public Class WXClientAdmin
  Inherits System.Windows.Forms.Form

  ' Windows Forms specific infrastructure implemented here --
  ' not shown for reasons of brevity

  Private Sub ButtonRunRemote_Click(ByVal sender As System.Object, _
                                    ByVal e As System.EventArgs) _
                                    Handles ButtonRunRemote.Click
    Try
      Dim remoteAPI As New WXAPIToRemote.WXAPI()
      TextBoxRemoteResults.Text = _
      remoteAPI.GetSomeInformation()
    Catch ex As Exception
      TextBoxErrors.Text = ex.ToString()
    End Try
  End Sub

  Private Sub WXClientAdmin_Load(ByVal sender As System.Object, _
                                 ByVal e As System.EventArgs) _
                                   Handles MyBase.Load
    Try
      RemotingConfiguration.Configure( _
        "..\config\HTTPRemotingClient.config")
    Catch ex As Exception
      TextBoxErrors.Text = ex.ToString()
    End Try
  End Sub
  Private Sub ButtonExit_Click(ByVal sender As System.Object, _
                               ByVal e As System.EventArgs) _
                                 Handles ButtonExit.Click
    Me.Close()
  End Sub
End Class
```

The code above is pleasingly reminiscent of the server side of our application. As was the case with the WXServer project, the WXClient project uses an Imports declaration to expose the contents of the System.Runtime.Remoting namespace. Again, following the server-side model, the form load method, WXClientAdmin_Load, is used to load the configuration file used to specify client-side remoting settings (..\config\HTTPRemotingClient.config).

The ButtonRunRemote_Click() method of the WXClient project is triggered when a button on the GUI is pushed (the Run Remote button). The contents of this method are straightforward:

- Create an instance of the `WXAPIToRemote.WXAPI` class:

```
Dim remoteAPI As New WXAPIToRemote.WXAPI()
```

- Invoke the `GetSomeInformation()` method and associate the results it returned with a textbox displayed on the GUI:

```
TextBoxRemoteResults.Text = _
  remoteAPI.GetSomeInformation()
```

There is nothing in the previous two lines of code (create the `WXAPI` instance and invoke the `GetSomeInformation()` method) that indicates the method called is remoted. The knowledge that this is a remoted method comes from the configuration file loaded when we call `RemotingConfiguration.Configure()`. Just as with WXServer, the WXClient executable can have its remoting behavior modified without rebuilding the project.

Worth mentioning is that the `WXClient` project contains a reference to the `WXAPIToRemote` assembly. This does not mean that the `WXClient` will access this assembly by loading it into the same process address space as `WXClient.exe` (not accessing through remoting). Each assembly (for example the class library) contains metadata that describes the contents of that assembly (information describing the namespaces, class, methods, etc. exposed by the assembly). This metadata is what `WXClient.exe` uses in order to know that it is creating an instance of `WXAPIToRemote.WXAPI` and that it can invoke this class's `GetSomeInformation()` method. The actual method invocation is a remote access call.

### Client-side Configuration File: HTTPRemotingClient.config

The contents of the `..\config\HTTPRemotingClient.config` configuration file is as follows:

```
<configuration>
  <system.runtime.remoting>
    <application>
      <client>
        <wellknown type="WXAPIToRemote.WXAPI,WXAPIToRemote"
                   url="http://10.0.0.111:8999/WXRemoteStuff" />
      </client>
    </application>
  </system.runtime.remoting>
</configuration>
```

The focus of our discussion of the previous configuration file centers on the `<wellknown>` element. This element indicates that a specific class will not be accessed locally but will instead be accessed remotely. The class is not local because it runs on the server and hence uses "server activation". The XML attributes associated with the `<wellknown>` XML element dictate the aforementioned server activation:

- `type` – specifies the type that will be accessed remotely. The data associated with this attribute takes the form of `"type,assembly"` where type is represented as `Namespace.ClassName` (`WXAPIToRemote.WXAPI`). The second part (just like in the sever-side case) is just the assembly name (`WXAPIToRemote`) without the `.dll` extension.
- `url` – specifies the URI referenced on the remote machine. Recall that the URI of the server was WXRemoteStuff. The URL indicates that the host on which the URI resides is `10.0.0.111`, the protocol is part of the URL (the `http://` prefix where `http` is the protocol and `://` is a separator). The `8999` in the URL specifies the port.

In the future, you can specify a different server or URI or access other remoted classes just by altering the configuration files. Furthermore, you could access `WXAPIToRemote.WXAPI` locally without using remoting; it is all the same to the WXClient application.

#### Location of Application Files

You might be wondering now that we've developed all these projects how you will get them on to the remote machine. The key to controlling this is the Output Path textbox on the Configuration Properties | Debugging page of the projects Property Pages dialog. When running a project locally (the default), the Output Path corresponds to the location on the local machine of the project's binary files. When running a project remotely (the Configuration Properties | Debugging property page specifies a remote host) the Output Path corresponds to the path (on a remote machine) of the project's binary files. This need not even be a path on the local machine.

> **Under the remoting case, it is important to be careful when rebuilding. The remote executable could reside on a drive letter that is unknown on the localhost and the build could fail. If the build does succeed, it might place the file in some location on the local machine. This non-standard location might not be the directory that contains the requisite class libraries and application configuration files required to run the application on the client host.**

The suggestion made to avoid the above gotcha is to ensure that the build path on the local machine is identical to the execution path on the remote machine.

# Initiating Per-Solution Debugging

The context menu displayed by right-clicking on the solution within Solution Explorer contains a key debugging menu item, Set Startup Projects. Selecting this menu item displays the following dialog:

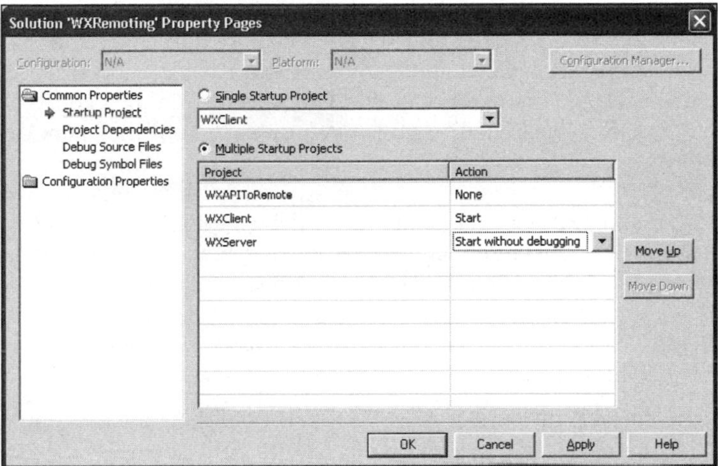


The menu item that displays the previous dialog is a plural not a singular, Set Startup Projects. In the screenshot above, there are two radio buttons (only one can be checked at a time):

- Single Startup Project – specify the lone startup project. The drop-down list below the Single Startup Project radio button provides a list of candidate projects.
- Multiple Startup Projects – run one or more projects at start up.

It is completely acceptable to debug a client-server application by debugging both the client and the server at the same time within one instance of Visual Studio .NET. Next to each project listed underneath the Multiple Start Projects radio button is an Action column. The permissible actions are:

- None – the project is not launched when debugging is initiated.
- Start – the project is launched when debugging is initiated and the project is run under control of the debugger.
- Start without Debugging – the project is launched when debugging is initiated but the project is run separately from the debugger.

If we just want to debug the WXClient application, the client project's action could be set to Start while the server (not being debugged) could be set to Start without Debugging, the action for WXAPIToRemote is set to None, as we don't need to start this project.

# Per-Project Debugging with WXClient and WXServer

Per-solution debugging is a way to have two start-up projects within the same solution. However, this approach does not always work with the client-server solutions where the client application depends on the server application. `WXServer.exe` must be running and hence exposing `WXAPI` as a remoted class before launching `WXClient.exe`. This is because when `WXClient.exe` runs, it expects there to be a remoted instance of `WXAPI` to be found at the URL specified in the client-side remoting configuration file (namely http://10.0.0.111:8999/WXRemoteStuff). If the client cannot find the server, it throws an exception.

If `WXClient.exe` and `WXServer.exe` are to be debugged in the same instance of Visual Studio .NET, per-project debugging is a better option. The steps required to initiate per-project debugging with the aforementioned application are as follows:

- Display either the Solution Explorer or the Class View window. Within either of these windows, highlight the WXServer project.
- Right-click on the WXServer project and from the context menu displayed, select Debug | Start new Instance. Since WXClient depends on WXServer, it is now possible to debug WXClient.

Although we can debug the client (WXClient), the server (WXServer) is running on the same host as the client. To allow the client and server to run on the same machine, you need to tweak the `HTTPRemotingClient.config` file, the client's remoting configuration file. Modify the `url` XML attribute of the `<wellknown>` XML element:

```
<wellknown type="WXAPIToRemote.WXAPI,WXAPIToRemote"
           url="http://localhost:8999/WXRemoteStuff"/>
```

In the previous XML snippet, the host in the `url` XML attribute was changed from `10.0.0.111` to `localhost`. The `localhost` can also referred by IP address, `127.0.0.1`. Both `localhost` and `127.0.0.1` simply mean access the host on which the application is presently running. After the host name is changed from `10.0.0.111` to `localhost` in the configuration file, `HTTPRemotingClient.config`, the steps required to debug the client within the same instance of Visual Studio .NET in which the server is running are as follows:

- Highlight the WXClient project within either the Solution Explorer or Class View window.
- Right-click on the WXClient project and from the context menu displayed, select Debug | Start new Instance or Debug | Step Into new instance.

At this stage, client and server are running in the same Visual Studio .NET instance.

## Start Action Configuration

Recall from Chapter 1 that the Start Action region of the Configuration Properties | Debugging property page specifies how the project will start. For example, if the project is an executable (Windows Forms application, console application, etc.) or an application that behaves like an executable (ASP.NET application) the Start Action is set to Start Project. This means simply run the executable associated with the project.

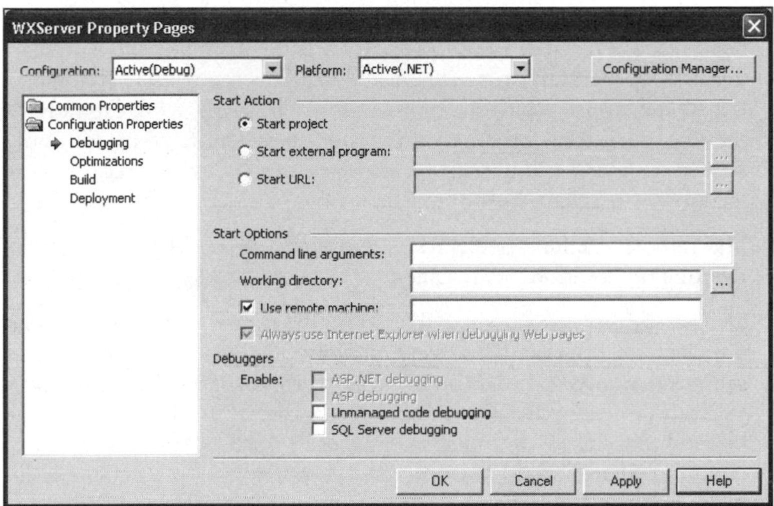


**Example: Use remote machine**

The steps required to debug a server such as `WXServer.exe` on the client machine are as follows:

- On the client machine bring up an instance of Visual Studio .NET and load the solution which contains the sever project (the WXServer project).
- In either the Solution Explorer or Class View window, highlight the WXServer project.
- Select the Project | Properties menu item.
- Select the Configuration Properties | Debugging property page.
- Checking the Use remote machine checkbox enables the textbox to the right so you can specify the remote machine on which an application runs.
- Inside the Use remote machine textbox enter the name of the remote machine on which the server will be run. For our purposes, the remote machine is 10.0.0.111.

How the server, WXServer, is launched in the debugger can be accomplished a variety of ways. If the WXServer project is the start up project for the solution, F5 will start debugging WXServer where `WXServer.exe` will be run on host 10.0.0.111 but Visual Studio .NET is running on the client host (IP address, 10.0.0.32).

In order to get remote debugging to work there are a few things to pay attention to:

- The location of the `WXServer.exe` on host, 10.0.0.111 (the remote machine) must match the value of the Output Path property found on the Configuration Properties | Build properties page. To make life simpler, make the executable path on the client the same as the server. This way the Output Path will not have to be reset for debugging with a remote host and then set back to its original value when the client is going to rebuild the source code associated with `WXServer.exe` (which would be a different location if the client host and server host paths were not identical).
- The remote machine needs to have Visual Studio .NET or Remote Debugging components installed.
- The `WXServer.exe` (executable to be debugged) must be in a shared directory on the remote (server) machine. One the simplest ways to handle this restriction is to build the client-server executable in a directory shared by both the client and server hosts. This directory can be specified via Project | Properties | Configuration Properties | Build | Output Path. Using a common, shared build location the client machine can act as the lone build machine. It is a little disconcerting to have the server code on the client host but the server running on the server host. To prove it is actually working (the server is running on its own host), you check the `WXServer.exe`'s dialog is running on the server machine rather than the client machine.
- The user of the client machine (the machine on which Visual Studio .NET debugging takes place) must be in the Debugger Users or the Administrators group of the server machine.

This last requirement can take a bit of effort. When a Windows NT domain or Active Directory domain is deployed then the user names of different hosts and the groups to which those users belong are identical across machines (provided the machines are in the same domain). It is easy under this deployment regime to assign the appropriate permissions to a user to enable remote debugging (assuming the systems administrators at your location do not put up a bunch of roadblocks.

When the environment deployed under is a workgroup (not a domain) each machine should contain an identically set up user. The user on the client machine should be IvanSmith with password ShhSecret. A similar user should be set up on the server machine (same user name, same password). The complexity with a workgroup is that user accounts must be set up per-machine manually but on the plus side, there is typically no cumbersome administration bureaucracy slowing down development.

User management is very operating-system and network-deployment dependent. The following is a brief overview of where to look to ensure that you are included in the appropriate group (Debug Users or Administrators):

- Windows 2000 without Active Directory or an NT Domain: Control Panel | Administrative Tools | Computer Management and from the dialog select Local Users and Groups
- Windows 2000 or Windows XP with Active Directory: Control Panel | Administrative Tools | Active Directory Management
- Windows XP without Active Directory or an NT Domain: Control Panel | User Accounts

With the server (`WXServer.exe`) running on the server machine (debugged on the client host), the client (`WXClient.exe`) can be launched. This is a matter of bringing up a second instance of Visual Studio .NET on the client machine. The following diagram illustrates the process:

**Figure 2**

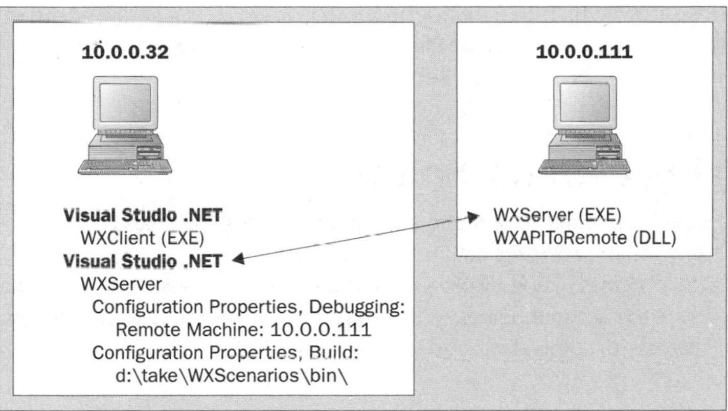


This example demonstrates debugging the client and server in separate instances of Visual Studio .NET. Whether the client and server are debugged in lone or dual instances of Visual Studio .NET is a 'lifestyle' choice of the developer. Hint, using separate instances of Visual Studio .NET is simpler than using a lone instance of Visual Studio .NET.

**Example: Start External Program**

The server (`WXServer.exe`) ultimately loaded a class library, `WXAPIToRemote.dll`. What would happen in the case of a developer working on `WXAPIToRemote.dll` and the developer only having the release build version of `WXServer.exe`? This pre-built version of the `WXServer.exe` Windows Forms application is built for release (non-debug), so it contains no project that can be used to build the executable and no source code to be rebuilt. How can the `WXAPIToRemote.dll` class library be debugged under this circumstance?

The answer is easy: the Start External Program option on the Configuration Properties | Debugging page of the Property Pages dialog. The steps for setting `WXServer.exe` to be the external project used to launch `WXAPIToRemote.dll` in the debugger are:

- In either the Solution Explorer or Class View window, highlight the WXAPIToRemote project.
- Right-click on the project and from the context menu, click on Select as Startup Project.
- Select the Project | Properties menu item.
- Select the Configuration Properties | Debugging property page.
- Select the Start External Program radio button. This enables the browse button (...) next to the Start External Program textbox.
- Using the browse button, navigate the folder hierarchy and select the `WXServer.exe` as the program that will start `WXAPIToRemote.dll` externally.

Once the previous steps have been followed, `WXAPIToRemote.dll` can be debugged by hitting the F5 key (which initiates debugging) or by right-clicking on the class libraries project in Solution Explorer or Class View and therefore displaying the context menu that contains the Debug menu item.

## Debugging with no Solution

Recall from Chapter 3 that the Tools menu contains the Debug Processes menu item. This menu item allows one or more processes that are currently running to be debugged by Visual Studio .NET. The Processes dialog displayed by Tools| Debug Processes is also displayable using the Debug menu's Processes menu item. When either of the aforementioned menu items is invoked, the Processes dialog is displayed, similar to the following:

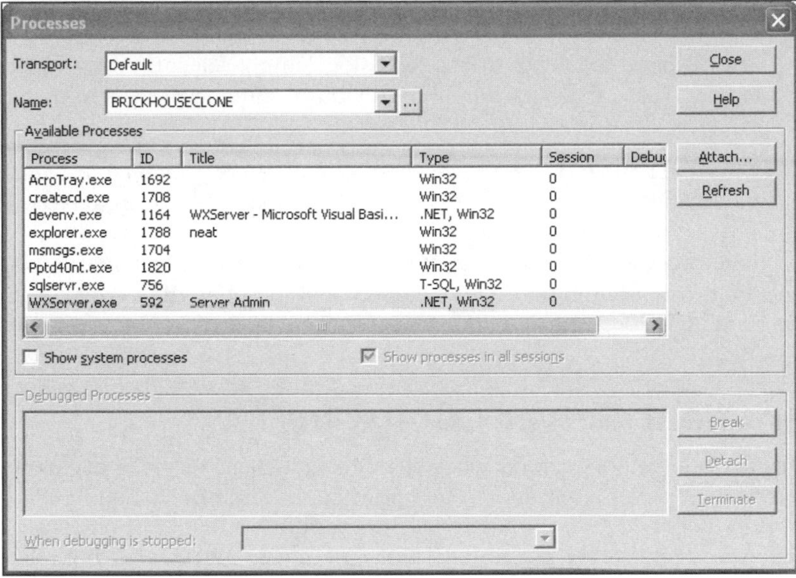


Notice in the screenshot above, that the hostname is BRICKHOUSECLONE. Actually, the value `10.0.0.111` was entered and when the return key was clicked, the hostname filled itself in. So, using the Processes dialog it should be possible to debug a previously running server (WXServer) residing on host `10.0.0.111` from the client machine (IP address, `10.0.0.32`, which is where the client will ultimately run).

### Debugging Running Applications Remotely

The steps required to perform this task are:

- Load the solution that contains the project used to build the remotely running application. It is possible to attach a process to Visual Studio .NET without a solution but under this circumstance Visual Studio .NET has no knowledge of how to build the application being debugged. At the same time, it is harder to get to source code since windows such as Solution Explorer and Class View are not available without the solution.

- From the Tools menu, select the Debug Processes menu item (or Debug, Processes). This displays the Processes dialog.

- Within the Name textbox of the Processes window, enter the name of the remote host or its IP address (for example `10.0.0.111`). Once this value is entered, hit the enter key and the processes on this host will be displayed under Available Processes.

- If the process is a Windows service, click on the Show system processes checkbox.

- Select the process, for example `WXServe.exe`, and click the **Attach** button.
- This displays the **Attach to Process** dialog; simply select **OK** in the **Attach to Process** dialog thus attaching the previously running process to the current instance of Visual Studio .NET.
- Once the remote process is attached to the presently running instance of Visual Studio .NET, the process will appear under the **Debugged Processes** lists.

With the remote process (`WXServer.exe`) being debugged, you can merrily place breakpoints in the application thus allowing the client to debug the server (even if the server was running before Visual Studio .NET was launched).

## Better Client-Server Debugging

The worst thing a developer can do when debugging a client-server application is to debug it as a client-server application. The application should be as bug-free as possible before deploying it on separate machines. This is a matter of practicality. Once running in a true client-server situation the bugs are not so much code, but related performance, system administration, and setup issues. This previous statement is true provided you do the brunt of the code debugging before client-server deployment. The system administrative issues faced include network setup, security management, web server configuration, and database administration.

To rid an application of bugs before launching it on multiple machines, take the following steps:

- Debug the client (for example `WXClient.exe`) directly against the class library (`WXAPIToRemote.dll`). This means that the DLL and the executable will run in the same address space.
- Debug the client and server on the same machine. If the server is ultimately to be a Windows Service, first debug the server when running as a server (just a process running and not running under the service control manager).
- Debug the client and server on the same machine with the server running as a service. When a server application is running as a service, the working directory changes, the user profile loaded in the registry changes (depending on the account the service logs in as) and security setup changes (depending on the account the service logs in as). Debug all these issues before deploying client-server on separate hosts.
- Debug the client and server running on separate machines with the server running as a process and not running as a Windows service. This approach works provided the server would ultimately run as a Windows service.

- Debug the client and server running on separate machines with the server running as a Windows service. This represents the final and most complicated deployment. By this stage, you should have eliminated most of the non-administrative bugs from the application.

The server (`WXServer.exe`) is a Windows Forms application, which means the application, interacts with the screen. A Windows service does not usually interact with the desktop (a.k.a. the screen) so it does not make sense to develop a server that runs as a service using Windows Forms (especially since Visual Studio .NET has a stock project of type Windows Service).

## Client Loading Class Library Directly

Thus far WXClient has always accessed the `WXAPI` class's `GetSomeInformation()` method courtesy of remoting provided by WXServer. Recall that the WXClient project references the `WXAPIToRemote` class library and the only thing causing the contents of this class library to be accessed remotely is the `..\config\HTTPRemotingClient.config` configuration file. It is possible within an XML document (the configuration file is an XML document) to include comments. Comments are prefixed by `<!--` and suffixed by `-->` and hence the take the form `<!-- comment here -->`.

Using this bit of extra XML knowledge, the specific line in the configuration file that specifies remoting can be commented out:

```
<configuration>
  <system.runtime.remoting>
    <application>
      <client>
        <!-- <wellknown type="WXAPIToRemote.WXAPI,WXAPIToRemote"
                   url="http://10.0.0.111:8999/WXRemoteStuff" /> -->
      </client>
    </application>
  </system.runtime.remoting>
</configuration>
```

When WXClient now runs, the configuration file does nothing. It now contains no XML elements with XML attributes that configure remoting. The text between the `<client>` start tag and the `</client>` end tag is all just comments. This simple change allows the `WXAPIToRemote` class library to run in the same address space as the `WXClient` Windows Forms executable.

## Client and Server Running on the Same Host

This was already demonstrated and was simply a matter of changing the WXClient's remoting configure file from:

```
<wellknown type="WXAPIToRemote.WXAPI,WXAPIToRemote"
           url="http://10.0.0.111:8999/WXRemoteStuff" />
```

to a URL the uses the local host rather than a remote host:

```
<wellknown type="WXAPIToRemote.WXAPI,WXAPIToRemote"
           url="http://localhost:8999/WXRemoteStuff" />
```

An alternative way to do this would be to use `127.0.0.1` as this is equivalent to `localhost`. You could also use the client's IP address, `10.0.0.32` in this case. Finally, you could also use the name of the localhost rather than the local host's IP address.

### Client and Server Running on Separate Hosts

Two approaches were demonstrated that achieve this style of debugging:

- Selecting Project | Settings using the by Configuration Properties | Debugging property page and specifying the remote host on which to launch the application to be debugged in the Use remote machine textbox after the corresponding checkbox has been checked.
- Selecting Tools | Debug Processes and specifying the name of the remote in the name textbox of the Processes dialog.

# Threads and VB6 InterOp

One of the biggest misconceptions when it comes to threads is that they will speed up an application. Spawning five threads in a single CPU environment does not increase the speed by a factor of five. In fact, many applications will slow down if made multithreaded. Additionally, when an application is multithreaded, debugging becomes more difficult and errors become more likely. Add to this the possibility of deadlock and working with threads can be a bit daunting. Clearly, threading is an important and useful tool that makes applications more responsive but only use them when they are appropriate.

Before introducing how to debug multithreaded VB.NET applications, we need an application that uses multiple threads in order to solve some practical problem.

## *VB6 to VB.NET Interoperability Example*

The concept for this example comes from a real-world problem encountered an engineer named, Kathy. The current product was complex VB6 GUI to which we wanted to add some VB.NET functionality. The idea was to add all new features in VB.NET but still maintain legacy functionality in VB6 (a practical, long-term upgrade strategy). The application is composed of the following files:

- WXVB6Application.exe – a VB6 GUI application that displays a VB.NET modeless dialog.
- WXKathysForm – a VB.NET Windows Forms application that compiles to an executable or DLL depending on the context in which is it used. We'll see that this dual behavior (DLL and executable) is quite handy from a debugging perspective.

## Creating a Windows Form Executable

Create the `WXKathysForm` Windows Form executable by adding a new Windows Application project in Visual Studio .NET. The type of application created is therefore an executable that is not readily accessible by VB6. The reason we do not want VB6 interoperability is that it is simpler to debug `WXKathysForm` as an executable than as a .NET DLL called from a VB6 executable. It is easier to debug because the functionality can be debugged as a standalone project without having to rely on an external executable to exercise that functionality.

The `WXKathysForm` executable is simple in appearance. This assembly contains a button that closes the application (button Close) and a button that performs an action (button Do Something) where the action is displaying a message box:

Although the dialog is quite mundane, certain features merit discussion because they will ultimately require the creation of a thread. The Close button maps to tab stop 0 and the Do Something button maps to tab stop 1. This means that when the dialog is in focus, hitting the tab key toggles control focus between the Close and the Do Something buttons. Note also that there are mnemonics associated with the previous buttons namely if *Alt-C* is selected the Close button is clicked since the C in Close is underlined and if *Alt-D* is selected the Do Something button will be clicked since the D in Do Something is underlined.

The code associated with the application is not meant to be very exciting since the real excitement (tab order and mnemonics) is specified via properties in Visual Studio .NET's Windows Forms designer:

```
Private Sub CloseIt(ByVal sender As System.Object, _
                    ByVal e As System.EventArgs) _
                        Handles ButtonClose.Click, MenuItemExit.Click
 Close()
End Sub
```

```
Private Sub ButtonDoSomething_Click(ByVal sender As System.Object, _
                                    ByVal e As System.EventArgs) _
                                        Handles ButtonAction.Click
  MessageBox.Show("This is action?", "Dull action!")
End Sub
```

The `CloseIt()` method in the previous code snippet closes the dialog and subsequently the application if the `WXKathysForm` is built as an executable. The `CloseIt()` method is triggered when the File | Exit menu item is selected or Close button is clicked (or another approach is taken to closing the window). The `ButtonDoSomething_Click()` method is triggered when the Do Something button is clicked. This method performs the action associated with the dialog (displaying a message box).

> *When an application is a standalone executable it is simpler to debug than when it is a DLL. The reason is that no external dependencies are required in order to launch the assembly. At this stage, the application can be debugged and only when most of the bugs are gone, should you convert it into a DLL for use by the VB6 application.*

#### Converting a Windows Forms Executable into a DLL

Building the `WXKathysForm` project generates an executable. Converting the assembly to a DLL is simple. The steps required to perform this conversion are to select the Project | Properties menu item, Common Properties | General subfolder. From the drop-down list labeled Output type, change Windows Application to Class Library. With the `WXKathysForm` assembly now a DLL, we are now able to make this DLL accessible to VB6.

Once in DLL form you can convert the assembly back to an executable by changing Class Library to Windows Application. Always debugging the dialog as an executable before hooking up (in DLL form) to the VB6 application simplifies things greatly. Another reason to use this technique is if you're machine has limited RAM (256 MB or less). The performance when debugging managed and unmanaged code simultaneously can be poor so you might want to debug native and managed code separately.

#### Making a .NET Class Library (DLL) Accessible to VB6

When an assembly is in class library form, it can appear to be a COM server. Legacy (unmanaged) applications acting as COM clients can access the assembly.

The steps required to make a .NET class library accessible to unmanaged code involve using Visual Studio .NET as follows: select the Project | Properties menu item, and the Configuration Properties | Build subfolder. From the dialog displayed, enable the checkbox labeled Register for COM Interop. Henceforth, when you build the application a type library is generated (`WXKathyForms.tlb`) that lets VB6 applications view the assembly's metadata in a form they understand (a.k.a. as a type library). Additionally, enabling this checkbox causes the build process to create the registry entries that specify WXKathysForm as a COM server.

## Creating a VB6 Application that calls a Windows Forms DLL

In order to demonstrate why we need to create a thread, we need to create a VB6 application that calls WXKathysForm treating the aforementioned assembly as if it is a COM server. Remember, we are not advocating creating VB6 applications from scratch. The scenario is that we are using a Windows Forms generated dialog with an existing VB6 application. To create this legacy VB6, bring up the Visual Basic 6 IDE and access the following File menu, New Project menu item, New Project dialog, and from this dialog select Standard EXE. Our WXVB6Application will contain a single form called FormOldToNew.

The VB6 FormOldToNew form is similar to the VB.NET Windows Form (click on icons in the Toolbox and hence place them in the IDE's forms designer). The FormOldToNew form when laid out appears as follows:

The buttons are fairly self-explanatory:

- Exit – exits the application by calling the VB keyword, `End`.
- Launch in Same Thread – launches the WXKathysForm dialog in the same thread in which the VB6 dialog is running.
- Launch in Different Thread – launches the WXKathysForm dialog in a different thread from that in which the VB6 dialog is running.

Laying out the previous buttons is a trivial matter. Note that each button represents a tab stop. When the previous dialog is in focus, hitting the tab key moves the currently selected control on the form from Exit to Launch in Same Thread to Launch in Different Thread. It should also be clear from the previous screenshot that each button is associated with a mnemonic that allows the button to be clicked automatically (*Alt-X* clicks the Exit button, *Alt-S* clicks Launch in Same Thread, and *Alt-D* clicks Launch in Different Thread). To repeat we are focusing on tab stops and mnemonics because they are going to cause an interoperability issue that we can solve by spawning an additional thread.

With the buttons laid out courtesy of VB6's Toolbox and Properties windows, what remains is to hook the VB6 application up to the `WXKathysForm` assembly.

**Making VB6 Application talk to a COM Server (a.k.a. our .NET assembly)**

It is misrepresentation to say that our VB6 application must perform a special step in order to access our .NET assembly. All the VB6 application needs to do is to access a COM library. This is something VB6 applications merrily did long before .NET was born. So to access WXKathysForm, select the Project | References menu item and in the References dialog displayed click the checkbox associated with the WXKathysForm COM Server (our .NET assembly).

Once the reference is specified, the dialog with the WXKathysForm assembly can be displayed. There is nothing spectacular about the code that does this (the Launch in Same Thread button code) and the code associated with the Exit button. This code is as follows:

```
Private Sub CommandExit_Click()
  End
End Sub

Private Sub CommandLaunchSame_Click()
  Dim showItSame As New WXKathysForm.WXSimpleDialog
  Call showItSame.Show
End Sub
```

In the previous code snippet the `New` keyword creates the VB.NET Windows Form and after this, the `Show()` method of the Windows form is used to show the dialog in a modeless manner.

## The Rational for Multithreading

When the Launch in Same Thread button is clicked, the VB6 and VB.NET windows are displayed simultaneously. The problem is that the tab stops and mnemonics in the VB.NET dialog do not work.

Knowing a bit about the Windows platform is helpful even in this era of .NET. Clearly, the VB6 dialog is acting as a parent to the VB.NET child dialog. The parent is not forwarding the tab stop and mnemonics messages (Windows messages) to the child window. Therefore, we have to launch the VB.NET dialog in such a way that it is not a child window of the VB6 dialog.

All Windows run in an execution thread; launching the VB.NET window in a separate thread should sever the parent-child relationship between the windows and the VB.NET dialog should henceforth handle its tab stops and mnemonics.

Within the VB.NET assembly, we need to create a new class, `WXLaunchInThread`, that: creates a thread that then creates an instance of the dialog.

In order to create this multithreaded application, take the following steps. First, `Import` the types within `System.Threading` namespace:

```
Imports System.Threading
```

The assembly in which the `Thread` class resides is `mscorlib.dll`. This assembly is automatically referenced by all managed applications and therefore there are no special references required of the WXKathysForm assembly in order to make use of multithreading.

The `WXLaunchInThread` class that spawns a thread and creates a dialog creates a data member for containing the thread class and another for the dialog:

```
Public Class WXLaunchInThread
  Private _simpleDialog As WXSimpleDialog = Nothing
  Private _dialogThread As Thread = Nothing
End Class
```

Create a method, `Launch()`, that will be the entry point for launching the thread. This method creates the dialog (if it doesn't exist) and does a `ShowDialog` in order to show the dialog as modal. Fear not that the dialog is modal in nature. This dialog is running in a separate thread so in relation to the VB6 form, the VB.NET form appears modeless. The code associated with `Launch()` is as follows:

```
Private Sub Launch()
  If _simpleDialog Is Nothing Then
      _simpleDialog = New WXSimpleDialog()
  End If
  ' Since we are a separate thread, we are modal but appear modeless
  ' with respect to the VB6 dialog running in a separate thread
  _simpleDialog.ShowDialog()
  SyncLock Me
  _simpleDialog = Nothing
  _dialogThread = Nothing
  End SyncLock
End Sub
```

Notice that the previous method uses `SyncLock` to serialize access to the `_simpleDialog` and `_dialogThread` data members; this means that only one thread can enter this piece of code at any one time. The dialog is closed either by the user closing the VB.NET dialog or by the VB6 program calling close. This means that either the VB6 thread or the VB.NET dialog thread can manipulate these data members after the dialog is closed. The `SyncLock` method ensures only one thread, per-`WXLaunchInThread` object instance (hence the `Me` keyword as in `SyncLock Me`) at a time gains access to these data members.

The `Show()` method is exposed by the `WXLaunchInThread` class in order to create the thread that launches the Windows Form dialog. The `Show()` method is implemented as follows:

```
Public Sub Show()
  SyncLock Me
  If _dialogThread Is Nothing Then
      _dialogThread = New Thread(AddressOf Launch)
      _dialogThread.Start()
      ' wait for new thread to launch
      While _simpleDialog Is Nothing
          Thread.Sleep(100)
      End While
  Else
      ' ignore if dialog is already displayed
  End If
  End SyncLock
End Sub
```

The `Show()` method uses `SyncLock` to ensure that each instance of type `WXLaunchInThread`, is serialized with respect to creating the thread that in turn creates the dialog. There is a while loop in the `Show()` method that stalls this method until after the spawned thread creates its dialog.

A `Close()` method is implemented so that the VB6 application has a means by which to close the Windows Forms dialog. The `Close()` method uses `SyncLock` to ensure each `WXLaunchInThread` instance only closes the dialog once (one thread at a time has access to this call). The implementation of the `Close()` method is as follows:

```
Public Sub Close()
  Dim copyDialogThread As Thread

  SyncLock Me
  If _simpleDialog Is Nothing Then
    Return ' Nothing to do here
  End If
  _simpleDialog.Close()
  copyDialogThread = _dialogThread
  _dialogThread = Nothing
  End SyncLock

  ' This must be outside the lock so we do not race against our own
  ' thread
  If Not copyDialogThread.Join(5000) Then
    Throw New Exception("The thread should have ended by now")
  End If

End Sub
```

Yes, the `Close()` method could do a better job of error handling with respect to the unlikely case of the thread not exiting in a timely fashion, but that not necessary for this demonstration.

**Tab Stops and Mnemonics Restored**

The VB6 dialog exposed a button, Launch in Different Thread that makes use of the .NET assembly's `WXLaunchInThread` class. In order to create this class and call its method, create a data member in the VB6 application (`showItDifferent`) so that the VB.NET dialog instance still exists after the Launch in Different Thread button click is handled. The method that handles this button click and the data member of type `WXLaunchInThread` is as follows:

```
Dim showItDifferent As WXKathysForm.WXLaunchInThread

Private Sub CommandLaunchDifferent_Click()

  If showItDifferent Is Nothing Then
      Set showItDifferent = New WXKathysForm.WXLaunchInThread
  End If

  Call showItDifferent.Show
End Sub
```

There is no need to perform any locking in the previous code because the VB6 application is single threaded. The lone GUI thread cannot simultaneous handle multiple Launch in Different Thread button clicks so there is no reason to perform any locking.

The purpose of the previous code snippet is to launch the VB.NET dialog in a separate thread, which should restore this dialog's tab stops and mnemonics. As it turns out this what happens. There might be an easier way to perform this task but given the time deadlines associated with Kathy's original project, this was the first solution that worked.

## Debugging Managed (VB.NET) and Unmanaged (VB6)

Visual Studio .NET is capable of debugging VB.NET independently, VB6 independently or VB6 and VB.NET jointly (managed and unmanaged code simultaneously). For the WXKathysForm application, the following approaches can be used to debug the application as a whole:

- Run WXKathysForm as an EXE from within Visual Studio .NET. Under this circumstance, there is no need to simultaneously debug unmanaged code and hence Visual Studio .NET will experience better performance.

- Run WXKathysForm as a DLL specifying the VB6 executable as an external program (Project | Properties, Configuration Properties | Debugging, Start external program). Under this circumstance the VB6 portion of the application can be debugged at the same time as the VB.NET portion of the application by specifying Visual Studio .NET Project | Properties, Configuration Properties | Debuggers section, and then enabling Unmanaged code debugging.

# Debugging VB.NET to Unmanaged C++

This section presents the following practical debugging scenarios that make use of some of the following Visual Studio .NET features:

- Debugging from managed code to unmanaged code:
- Debugging from unmanaged code to managed code
- Debugging across multiple languages
- Debugging applications built originally with Visual C++ 6.0.

We'll demonstrate these scenarios using the WXAppDomainDemo solution.

## *WXAppDomainDemo Example*

The WXAppDomainDemo solution consists of a Windows Forms application (WXAppDomainDemo) and a legacy in-process COM Server (WXBelowTheSurface written in unmanaged C++). The functionality exposed by this combination of projects includes displaying all currently running processes. This can display modules associated with a process or the application domains running within the process.

## *WXBelowTheSurface*

Although this is a VB.NET text, there are just times when VB.NET will not deliver the functionality required. For example, how can a list of all managed processes be retrieved, and for such processes, how can their application domains be retrieved? The answer to this question is by accessing a legacy COM API exposed by the inner workings of the .NET Framework. Remember the .NET Framework is (presently) built on top of unmanaged code. For this reason the API's exposed by .NET's internals include legacy COM interfaces and C-style functions.

The API for accessing managed processes and their application domains is in corpub.h. This is a C/C++ header file and not a type library, which means that VB.NET applications (managed applications) cannot access the requisite COM objects. For this reason, we'll use an unmanaged C++ application to access these objects.

Include the .NET SDK facilities in the WXBelowTheSurface application courtesy of its stdafx.h header file:

```
#include <cor.h>
#include <corpub.h> // make sure we link to corguids.lib
```

There is a bit of documentation provided in the previous source code telling the developer to link with a specific library so that all the class and interface ID's are available to the application. The stdafx.h header file also contains a macro that can be used to check for an error and if one is detected for the execution of the method to return:

```
#define HR(val) if FAILED(hr = val) { return hr; }
```

The COM object exposed by the WXBelowTheSurface's unmanaged C++ code is WXManagedProcesses. As the name indicates, this retrieves the managed processes running on a system. This COM object exposes the IWXManagedProcesses interface. This interface implements a single method (Get) to determining what managed processes are currently executing on a system:

```
STDMETHOD(Get)(BSTR bstrPreTag,
               BSTR bstrPostTag,
               VARIANT_BOOL onlyProcesses,
               BSTR *pbstrProcesses);
```

The Get() method returns the list of processes and potentially their application domains via a parameter of type string, pbstrProcesses. This string contains serialized XML that is readable by a managed application; we could also reconstitute this into a managed object. This approach to returning data demonstrates how useful serialization to XML is. As XML text is both human and machine-readable, this makes VB.NET objects and objects created in other languages accessible for a variety of purposes including debugging.

The bstrPreTag and bstrPostTag parameters correspond to the text used to prefix and suffix the XML returned by the Get() method. The onlyProcesses parameter is a Boolean set to true (VARIANT_TRUE) if only processes are to be retrieved and set to false (VARIANT_FALSE) if processes and their application domains are to be retrieved.

## ICorPublish and ICorPublishEnum

The CorPublish object found in the corpub.h header file exposes the ICorPublish interface. This interface exposes the following methods:

- EnumProcesses() – returns an enumerator used to return a list of managed processes. This enumerator is exposed using the ICorPublishProcesssEnum interface.
- GetProcess() – given a process ID this retrieves an ICorPublishProcess interface corresponding to a CorPublishProcess object instance.

The ICorPublishProcesssEnum interface is an enumerator and hence it implements rather self-explanatory methods such as Skip(), Reset(), Clone(), and GetCount(). The method most germane to examining managed processes is the Next() method. This method returns the next process in the enumeration. The process is represented by a COM object that exposes the ICorPublishProcess interface.

The basic premise used to access managed processes is to:

- Create an instance of type CorPublish and expose this object's ICorPublish interface.

```
CComPtr<ICorPublish> spICorPublish;

HR(spICorPublish.CoCreateInstance(CLSID_CorpubPublish));
```

- Use the EnumProcesses() method of ICorPublish to retrieve the interface used to enumerate over the processes, ICorPublishProcesssEnum.

```
CComPtr<ICorPublishProcess> spICorPublishProcess;

HR(spICorPublish->EnumProcesses(COR_PUB_MANAGEDONLY,
                                 &spICorPublishProcessEnum));
```

- Loop calling the Next() method of the ICorPublishProcesssEnum interface. For each process retrieved by Next() an ICorPublishProcess interface is retrieved. Use the ICorPublishProcess interface to retrieve information about the processes.

```
while (true)
{
  spICorPublishProcess = 0;
  HR(spICorPublishProcessEnum->Next(1,
                                     &spICorPublishProcess,
                                     &elementsFetched));

  // Retrieve the pertinent values for the managed process using
  // the ICorPublishProcess interface retrieved
}
```

The WXGetManagedProcesses() method within the WXBelowTheSurface project iterates over the list of managed processes. The WXGetManagedProcesses() method is implemented as follows:

```
HRESULT WXGetManagedProcesses(VARIANT_BOOL onlyProcesses,
                              CComBSTR &bstrResults)

{
  HRESULT hr = S_OK;
  CComPtr<ICorPublish> spICorPublish;
  CComPtr<ICorPublishProcessEnum> spICorPublishProcessEnum;
  ULONG elementsFetched;
  CComPtr<ICorPublishProcess> spICorPublishProcess;

  HR(spICorPublish.CoCreateInstance(CLSID_CorpubPublish));
  HR(spICorPublish->EnumProcesses(COR_PUB_MANAGEDONLY,
                                  &spICorPublishProcessEnum));
  while (true)
  {
    spICorPublishProcess = 0;
    HR(spICorPublishProcessEnum->Next(1,
                                      &spICorPublishProcess,
                                      &elementsFetched));
    if (S_FALSE == hr)
    {
      break; // S_FALSE is a success case and we are done
    }

    // There is a bug; Next() does not return S_FALSE when the
    // enumerator is done so we double-check and make sure
    // spICorPublishProcess is set (not NULL)
    if (!spICorPublishProcess)
    {
      break;
    }

    bstrResults += L"<Process>";
    HR(WXDisplayProcess(spICorPublishProcess,
                        onlyProcesses,
                        bstrResults));
    bstrResults += L"</Process>";
  }

  return hr;
}
```

Within the code snippet above notice that the `WXDisplayProcess()` method returns a string containing all the processes. The actual sequence of code where this method is called is as follows:

```
bstrResults += L"<Process>";
WXDisplayProcess // parameters go here
bstrResults += L"</Process>";
```

This returns the string of processes within an XML element (the `<Process>` element). Later we'll se how to deserialize this in order to create a managed object with a VB.NET application.

## ICorPublishProcess and ICorPublishAppDomainEnum

The `WXGetManagedProcesses()` method calls the `WXDisplayProcesses()` method in order to access properties of a specific managed process. The process's properties can include that process's application domains provided the second parameter to `WXDisplayProcesses` is set to true (`VARIANT_TRUE`).

The `WXDisplayProcesses()` method receives a parameter of type `ICorPublishProcess`. This interface corresponds to the current process. The methods and properties exposed by this interface include:

- `IsManaged` – returns true (`VARIANT_TRUE`) if the process is managed and false otherwise (`VARIANT_FALSE`).
- `GetProcessID` – returns the ID of the process. The ID is a value that uniquely identifies the process on the system.
- `GetDisplayName` – retrieves the display name associated with the process instance. The `GetDisplayName` has the ability to return the size of the name before retrieving the name. Returning the size of the process name is achieved by specifying only a parameter that retrieves the name length (such as `nameLength` below) and after determining the size, an appropriately sized array to hold the name can be allowed using a function such as `malloc` (allocating unmanaged memory):

```
HR(spICorPublishProcess->GetDisplayName(0, &nameLength, NULL));

auto_ptr<wchar_t> apDisplayName((wchar_t *)
                     malloc(nameLength * sizeof wchar_t));
```

- `EnumAppDomains` – retrieves an `ICorPublishAppDomainEnum` interface. This interface can be used to enumerate over a process's application domains.

The `ICorPublishAppDomainEnum` interface returned by `EnumAppDomains` is another enumerator. As it is an enumerator, this interface exposes the same old methods: `Skip()`, `Reset()`, `Clone()`, and `GetCount()`. The `ICorPublishAppDomainEnum` interface also exposes a `Next()` method. This method returns a COM object corresponding to a specific application domain within a process. This COM object exposes the `ICorPublishAppDomain` interface. The approach used to return a process's application domains is as follows:

- Using the `ICorPublishProcesses` interface corresponding to a process, return the properties associated with the process including process ID, whether or not the process is managed:

```
HR(spICorPublishProcess->GetProcessID(&processID));
HR(spICorPublishProcess->IsManaged(&bManaged));
```

- The `ICorPublishProcesses` interface also allows the length of a process's display name to be retrieved, and memory to be allocated to hold this display name, before retrieving the actual display name:

```
// returns number of characters required include EOLN marker
HR(spICorPublishProcess->GetDisplayName(0, &nameLength, NULL));

auto_ptr<wchar_t> apDisplayName((wchar_t *)
                   malloc(nameLength * sizeof wchar_t));

HR(spICorPublishProcess->GetDisplayName(nameLength,
                                        &nameLength,
                                        apDisplayName.get()));
```

- Retrieve the enumerator (`ICorPublishAppDomainEnum` interface) used to iterate over a process's application domains:

```
CComPtr<ICorPublishAppDomainEnum> spICorPublishAppDomainEnum;

HR(spICorPublishProcess->EnumAppDomains(
                                      &spICorPublishAppDomainEnum));
```

- Then, loop through each application domain using the `Next()` method made available by `ICorPublishAppDomainEnum`. This method returns a COM object that exposes the `ICorPublishAppDomain` interface:

```
while (true)
{
  spICorPublishAppDomain = 0;
  HR(spICorPublishAppDomainEnum->Next(
      1, &spICorPublishAppDomain, &elementsFetched));
  // Handle each application domain here by utilizing
  // ICorPublishAppDomain
}
```

The `WXDisplayProcess()` method within the WXBelowTheSurface project accesses an individual process and iterates over that process's application domains. The `WXDisplayProcess()` method is written as follows:

```
HRESULT WXDisplayProcess(
                 CComPtr<ICorPublishProcess>& spICorPublishProcess,
                 VARIANT_BOOL onlyProcesses,
                 CComBSTR &bstrResults)
{
  HRESULT hr = S_OK;
  CComPtr<ICorPublishAppDomainEnum> spICorPublishAppDomainEnum;
  CComPtr<ICorPublishAppDomain> spICorPublishAppDomain;
```

```
BOOL bManaged;
ULONG32 nameLength = 0;
UINT processID;
ULONG elementsFetched;
CComVariant vConvert;
HR(spICorPublishProcess->GetProcessID(&processID));
// returns number of characters required include
// EOLN marker
HR(spICorPublishProcess->GetDisplayName(
    0,
    &nameLength,
    NULL));

auto_ptr<wchar_t> apDisplayName((wchar_t *)
                    malloc(nameLength * sizeof wchar_t));

HR(spICorPublishProcess->GetDisplayName(
        nameLength,
        &nameLength,
        apDisplayName.get()));
HR(spICorPublishProcess->IsManaged(&bManaged));
bstrResults += L"<Managed>";
bstrResults += bManaged ? L"true" : L"false";
bstrResults += L"</Managed>";
bstrResults += L"<Name>";
bstrResults += apDisplayName.get();
bstrResults += L"</Name>";
vConvert = processID;
vConvert.ChangeType(VT_BSTR);
bstrResults += L"<ID>";
bstrResults += V_BSTR(&vConvert);
bstrResults += L"</ID>";

if (VARIANT_TRUE == onlyProcesses)
{
  return hr;
}

HR(spICorPublishProcess->EnumAppDomains(
                  &spICorPublishAppDomainEnum));
while (true)
{
  spICorPublishAppDomain = 0;
  HR(spICorPublishAppDomainEnum->Next(1,
                                    &spICorPublishAppDomain,
                                    &elementsFetched));
  if (S_FALSE == hr)
  {
    break;
  }

  // There is a bug; Next() does not return S_FALSE when the
```

```
      // enumerator is done so we double-check and make sure
      // spICorPublishAppDomain is set (not NULL)
      if (!spICorPublishAppDomain)
      {
        break;
      }

      bstrResults += L"<AppDomain>";
      HR(WXDisplayAppDomain(spICorPublishAppDomain,
                            bstrResults));
      bstrResults += L"</AppDomain>";
    }

    return S_OK;
  }
```

Throughout the `WXDisplayProcess()` method there was a smattering of XML. For example, the whether or not a process is managed it is wrapped in an XML element as follows:

```
HR(spICorPublishProcess->IsManaged(&bManaged));
bstrResults += L"<Managed>";
bstrResults += bManaged ? L"true" : L"false";
bstrResults += L"</Managed>";
```

The attributes of each application domain are handled using the `WXDisplayAppDomain()` method. This method is called towards the bottom of the `WXDisplayProcesses()` method. The parameter passed to `WXDisplayAppDomain` contains information about the application domain in the form of the COM object that exposes the `ICorPublishAppDomain` interface.

## ICorPublishAppDomain

The `ICorPublishAppDomain` interface exposes some easily understandable methods, namely `GetName()` (name associated with the application domain) and `GetID()` (numeric ID associated with the application domain). Within the WXBelowTheSurface project the `WXDisplayAppDomain()` method that makes use of `GetName()` and `GetID()` is implemented as follows:

```
HRESULT WXDisplayAppDomain(
           CComPtr<ICorPublishAppDomain> &spICorPublishAppDomain,
           CComBSTR &bstrResults)
{
  HRESULT hr = S_OK;
  ULONG32 addDomainID;
  ULONG32 nameLength = 0;
  CComVariant vConvert;
```

```
    HR(spICorPublishAppDomain->GetID(&addDomainID));
    HR(spICorPublishAppDomain->GetName(0, &nameLength, NULL));

    auto_ptr<wchar_t> apDisplayName((wchar_t *)
                            malloc(nameLength * sizeof wchar_t));

    HR(spICorPublishAppDomain->GetName(nameLength,
                                       &nameLength,
                                       apDisplayName.get()));
    bstrResults += L"<Name>";
    bstrResults += apDisplayName.get();
    bstrResults += L"</Name>";
    vConvert = addDomainID;
    vConvert.ChangeType(VT_BSTR);
    bstrResults += L"<ID>";
    bstrResults += V_BSTR(&vConvert);
    bstrResults += L"</ID>";

    return hr;
  }
```

The information retrieved is wrapped in XML (quite consistent, aren't we?) as follows:

```
<Name>application domain name</Name><ID>application domain id</ID>
```

# XML Data Format

The above COM object returns the resulting list of processes as XML, which requires the appropriate prefixes and suffixes to make it well formed. This prefix and suffix correspond to the `WXAppDomain` class's following data members:

```
Private ReadOnly _preTag As String = _
  "<?xml version=""1.0"" encoding=""utf-16""?>" & _
  "<WXProcesses xmlns:xsd=""http://www.w3.org/2001/XMLSchema"" " & _
    "xmlns:xsi=""http://www.w3.org/2001/XMLSchema-instance"">"

Private ReadOnly _postTag As String = "</WXProcesses>"
```

The complete set of elements used use to return processes and application domains is as follows:

```
<WXProcesses>
  <Process>
    <Managed> true or false here </Managed>
    <Name> process name here </Name>
    <ID> process ID here</ID>
    <AppDomain>
      <Name> application domain name here </Name>
      <ID> application domain ID here</ID>
    </AppDomain>
  </Process>
</WXProcesses>
```

The previous XML fragment is generated by the `WXBelowTheSurface` in-process COM server using its `WXManagedProcesses` COM object and the object's `Get()` method.

# .NET Serialization

The ability to serialize objects to XML and de-serialize them from XML in .NET is part of the `System.XML.Serialization` namespace and the `System.Xml` assembly. Within the context of this text, XML serialization is a useful debugging technique because it represents the ultimate form of logging. Most developers view XML serialization as only relevant to web services, which use the SOAP protocol (an XML-based protocol that exchanges objects between web services and consuming clients). For further details on serialization, see the *Visual Basic .NET Serialization Handbook*, (Wrox Press 2002, ISBN 1-86100-800-7).

The `System.XML.Serialization` namespace exposes a variety of classes that support XML serialization. The focal point of these classes is `XmlSerializer`, which facilitates the serialization of an object to XML and the creation of an object from XML.

## XmlSerializer

The `XmlSerializer` makes the act of serializing an object to or de-serializing it from XML quite trivial. The basic steps to serialize are:

- Create an instance of `XmlSerializer` associated with the type being serialized. The following snippet is found in a method contained in the `WXProcesses` class and hence `Me.GetType()` returns the type associated with this class:

  ```
  Dim serializer As XmlSerializer = New XmlSerializer(Me.GetType)
  ```

- Create a stream into which the serialized object can be written:

  ```
  Dim resultWriter As StringWriter = New StringWriter()
  ```

- Associate the serialized object with the stream using the `XMLSerializer` class's `Serialize()` method in order to serialize the object. In the following code snippet `Me` is the present object that is being serialized to XML:

  ```
  serializer.Serialize(resultWriter, Me)
  ```

- Extracting the XML text in string form is now a matter of accessing the `StringWriter` instance's `ToString()` method:

  ```
  resultWriter.ToString()
  ```

The steps required to convert an XML document into a managed object are similarly simple:

- Create an instance of `XMLSerializer` associated with the type to deserialize. In the following code snippet the `GetType()` method retrieves the type information associated with the `WXProcesses` class:

```
Dim serializer As XmlSerializer = _
                      New XmlSerializer(GetType(WXProcesses))
```

- Associate the XML document containing the serialized object with a `StringReader` and pass it into the `XMLSerializer` class's `Deserialize()` method in order to de-serialize the object:

```
Dim procs As WXProcesses = _
                 serializer.Deserialize(New StringReader(xml))
```

The previously described steps for performing XML serialization and de-serialization seem too good to be true. Actually, they are too good yet true because they are precisely that simple to follow. The `WXProcesses` class in its entirety is as follows:

```
Public Class WXProcesses

  <XmlElement("Process")> _
  Public _processes() As WXProcess

  Public Function ToXMLString() As String
    Dim serializer As XmlSerializer = _
                          New XmlSerializer(Me.GetType)
    Dim resultWriter As StringWriter = New StringWriter()

    serializer.Serialize(resultWriter, Me)

    Return resultWriter.ToString()
  End Function

  Public Shared Function _
    Create(ByVal xml As String) As WXProcesses

    Dim serializer As XmlSerializer = _
          New XmlSerializer(GetType(WXProcesses))

    Return serializer.Deserialize(New StringReader(xml))
  End Function

End Class
```

The lone data member of the `WXProcesses` class is an array of `WXProcess` instances, `_processes`.

XML serialization serializes the public data members and read/write properties of a class. By default, each data member and property is represented by an element name with the same name as the variable or property name. Each WXProcess instance is serialized into a <Process> element as the XMLElement attribute associated with the _processes data member.

## XmlElementAttribute and XmlAttributeAttribute

The _processes data member in XML serialized form becomes the <Process> XML element. We did this by using the XmlElementAttribute class from the System.XML.Serialization namespace:

```
<XmlElement("Process")> Public _processes() As WXProcess
```

It turns out the custom attribute <XmlElement("Process")> corresponds to the XmlElementAttribute class. The XmlElementAttribute class informs the XML serialization process that each element in the _processes array is contained in an XML element named <Process>. The reasons for converting _processes to <Process> instead of the default <_processes> are:

- Well-formed XML elements cannot contain an underscore as their leading character.
- The default XML element name created was a plural (<_processes>) because the variable name was a plural. What we actually store is a set of singular elements such as the following:

```
<WXProcess>
  <Process>
    <Managed>true</Managed>
    <Name>D:\Wrox\WXAppDomainDemo.exe</Name>
    <ID>3512</ID>
  </Process>
  <Process>
    <Managed>true</Managed>
    <Name>D:\Wrox\WXApp1.exe</Name>
    <ID>3544</ID>
  </Process>
  <Process>
    <Managed>true</Managed>
    <Name>D:\Wrox\WXApp2.exe</Name>
    <ID>3266</ID>
  </Process>
<WXProcess>
```

Given the previous XML fragment it remains to be seen how each element in the array (elements type WXProcess) gets converted to the XML elements <Managed>, <Name>, and <ID>. The WXProcess.vb source file contains the definition of the WXProcess class:

```
Public Class WXProcess

  <XmlElement("Managed")> Public _managed As Boolean
  <XmlElement("Name")> Public _name As String
  <XmlElement("ID")> Public _id As Integer
  <XmlElement("AppDomain")> Public _appDomains() As WXAppDomain

End Class
```

The WXProcess definition further demonstrates how public data members (such as _managed) are mapped to XML elements (such as <Managed>) using the XmlElementAttribute class. When the previous XML fragment was displayed it contained the <Managed>, <Name>, and <ID> XML elements.

The previous XML fragment did not contain an XML element named <AppDomain> as no application domains were retrieved in this case. Every managed process contains at least one application domain but recall that the IWXManagedProcesses interface's Get() method allowed managed processes to be retrieved without (onlyProcesses parameter set to VARIANT_TRUE) or with (onlyProcesses parameter set to VARIANT_FALSE) information describing their application domains.

## XML Representation Application Domains and Application Domain

Within the WXProcess class the XMLElement custom attribute was used to ensure the XML elements used to represent each application domain were singular, well-formed XML (<AppDomain>) and not plural, malformed XML (<_appDomains>). The WXAppDomain class is used to represent each application domain returned by the IWXManagedProcesses interface's Get() method. The WXAppDomain class makes use of the XmlElement custom attribute:

```
Public Class WXAppDomain

  <XmlElement("Name")> Public _name As String
  <XmlElement("ID")> Public _id As Integer

End Class
```

## WXAppDomain

The WXAppDomain Windows Forms application appears as follows:

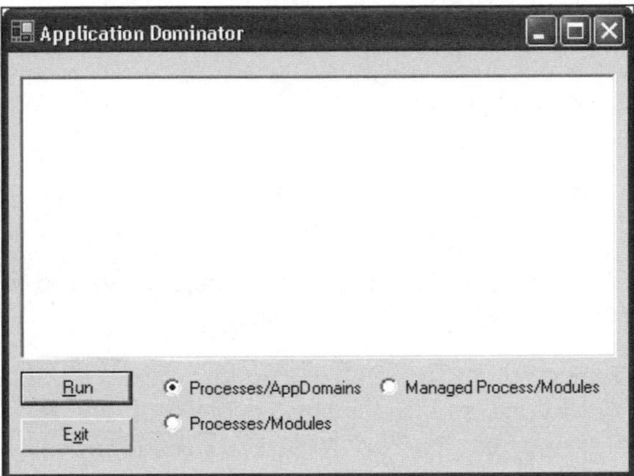


This screenshot shows what this application is designed to display:

- All managed processes and their application domains – shown in the `TreeViewResults` `TreeView` (the white rectangle) when the Run button is selected and the `RadioButtonAppDomains` `RadioButton` is checked
- All managed processes and their modules – shown in the `TreeView` when the Run button is selected and `RadioButtonManagedProcModules` is checked.
- All unmanaged processes and their modules – shown in the `TreeView` when the Run button is selected and `RadioButtonProcessModules` is checked.

The application itself consists of a Run button and a set of three radio buttons. The radio buttons are each associated with one of the previously bulleted options. Click on Run and display the information specified by the selected radio button.

The reason this application was chosen is that the aforementioned information is not provided by Visual Studio .NET. As we have already said, managed applications run within a Windows process. This process is associated with an executable while the managed application is associated with an application domain. The application domain can load assemblies that are executables. The disadvantage is that when Visual Studio .NET debugs processes, there is no way to look at a Windows process (using Visual Studio .NET's Processes window) and determine what assemblies that they are running are actually executables. This is the motivation for WXAppDomain, to determine where the assembly that needs debugging (potentially an executable) is running.

## Managed Applications Accessing COM Server

The WXAppDomain Windows Forms application makes use of the WXBelowTheSurface in-process COM server. The steps to access this COM DLL are quite simple because both WXAppDomain and WXBelowTheSurface are contained in the same solution. In order for WXAppDomain to access WXBelowTheSurface:

- Right-click on WXAppDomain project's References folder in order to displays a context menu.
- Select the Add Reference menu item from the context menu to display the Add Reference dialog.
- From the Add Reference dialog select the Projects tab and from the projects select the WXBelowTheSurface project.

The steps previously reviewed create a DLL that serves to provide interoperability between a managed application and unmanaged code (a COM DLL). The specific DLL created by the following steps is `Interop.WXBelowTheSurface.dll`. This DLL handles marshaling all data between the managed VB.NET code and the unmanaged C++ application.

## Retrieving Application Domains and Managed Processes

When the application's Run button is clicked and the `RadioButtonAppDomains` radio button is checked then the `WXProcessesAndAppDomains()` method is called. This method lives up to its name, in that displays all managed processes and their application domains. We retrieve this information by:

- Creating an instance of type `WXManagedProcesses` (a COM object from the `WXBelowTheSurface` DLL).

```
Dim managedProcesses As WXBelowTheSurface.IWXManagedProcesses = _
        New WXBelowTheSurface.CWXManagedProcessesClass()
```

- The `WXManagedProcesses` instance provides a `Get()` method and calling this method retrieves a string containing XML. The last parameter to the `Get()` method is `False` indicating that processes and their application domains will be retrieved:

```
Dim xml As String = _
              managedProcesses.Get(_preTag, _postTag, False)
```

- The XML string returned by `Get()` can be used to create an instance of type `WXProcesses`:

```
Dim processes As WXProcesses = WXProcesses.Create(xml)
```

- Once an instance of `WXProcesses` exists the processes within this instance can be enumerated over and for each process its application domains can be enumerated

The `WXProcessesAndAppDomains()` method in its entirety is as follows:

```
Private Sub WXProcessesAndAppDomains()
  Dim managedProcesses As WXBelowTheSurface.IWXManagedProcesses = _
    New WXBelowTheSurface.CWXManagedProcessesClass()
  Dim xml As String

  xml = managedProcesses.Get(_preTag, _postTag, False)
  Dim processes As WXProcesses = WXProcesses.Create(xml)
  Dim process As WXProcess
  Dim appDom As WXAppDomain
  Dim node As TreeNode

  For Each process In processes._processes
    node = TreeViewResults.Nodes.Add( _
              String.Format("{0} ({1})", process._name, _
              process._id))
    For Each appDom In process._appDomains
      node.Nodes.Add(String.Format("{0} ({1})", _
                     appDom._name, appDom._id))
    Next
  Next
End Sub
```

Within in the previous method there are some hints as to how the Windows Forms GUI displays processes and applications domains:

```
Dim node As TreeNode

node = TreeViewResults.Nodes.Add( _
          String.Format("{0} ({1})", process._name, process._id))
```

A Window Forms `TreeView` control is used to display the processes and their application domains. The basic idea is to create a `TreeNode` instance per process to the `TreeView` (`TreeView.Nodes.Add()`) and then add the application domains as child nodes of the per-process `TreeNode` (`TreeNode.Nodes.Add()`). An example of the managed processes and their application domains as displayed by WXAppDomainDemo is as follows:

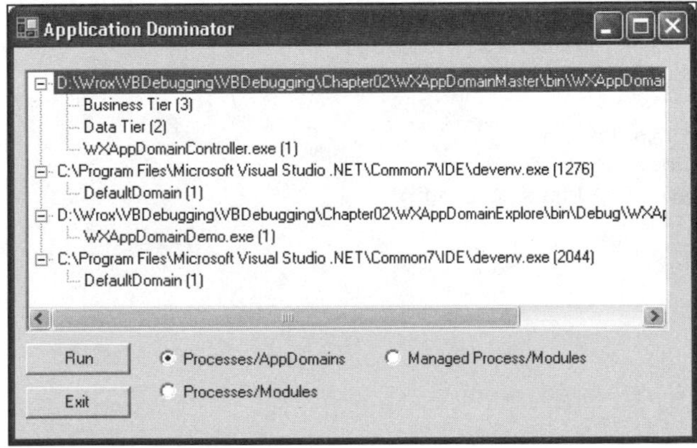

In the previous screenshot, the number displayed after each process is the process ID while the number displayed after the application domain entry is the application domain's ID.

## Retrieving Modules and Managed Processes

When the application's Run button is clicked and the RadioButtonManagedProcModules radio button is checked, the WXManagedProcessesAndModules() method is called. When this method calls the Get() method of the managedProcesses instance, it specifies True for the final parameter because only the managed processes are retrieved and not their application domains. Once the managed processes are known by calling unmanaged code, the Process class's GetProcessById() method can be called to retrieve an individual process. The Modules property of the process instance can be used to iterate through the modules associated with the managed process. The code for the WXManagedProcessesAndModules() method is as follows:

```
Private Sub WXManagedProcessesAndModules()
  Dim managedProcesses As WXBelowTheSurface.IWXManagedProcesses = _
    New WXBelowTheSurface.CWXManagedProcessesClass()
  Dim xml As String

  xml = managedProcesses.Get(_preTag, _postTag, True)
  Dim processes As WXProcesses = WXProcesses.Create(xml)
  Dim wxProc As WXProcess
  Dim proc As Process
  Dim procModule As ProcessModule
  Dim node As TreeNode

  For Each wxProc In processes._processes
    node = TreeViewResults.Nodes.Add( _
              String.Format("{0} ({1})", wxProc._name, _
                            wxProc._id))
    proc = Process.GetProcessById(wxProc._id)
    Try
      For Each procModule In proc.Modules
              node.Nodes.Add(String.Format("{0}", _
                             procModule.FileName))
      Next
    Catch ex As Exception
      node.Nodes.Clear()
      node.Nodes.Add(ex.Message)
    End Try
  Next
End Sub
```

### Knowing which Process contains a given Assembly

The WXAppDomain application's ability to display managed processes and their modules is crucial to debugging. Simply find the assembly that needs debugging from the applications tree view. The process ID and process name are then known, so you can initiate debugging using Tools | Debug Processes or the task manager.

### All Unmanaged Processes and their Modules

The WXAppDomain application can retrieve all unmanaged processes and their modules. This is achieved when the RadioButtonProcessModules RadioButton is checked and the Run button clicked. Here is the code for the WXProcessesAndModules() method:

```
Private Sub WXProcessesAndModules()
  Dim processes As Process() = Process.GetProcesses()
  Dim proc As Process
  Dim procModule As ProcessModule
  Dim node As TreeNode

  For Each proc In processes
    node = TreeViewResults.Nodes.Add( _
             String.Format("{0} ({1})", proc.ProcessName, proc.Id))
    Try
      For Each procModule In proc.Modules
        node.Nodes.Add(String.Format("{0}", procModule.FileName))
      Next
    Catch ex As Exception
      node.Nodes.Clear()
      node.Nodes.Add(ex.Message)
    End Try
  Next
End Sub
```

## Debugging Managed to Unmanaged Code

Using either Solution Explorer or Class View, it is possible to specify that WXAppDomainDemo is the project to start when debugging is initiated (context menu, Set as Startup Project). If this Windows Forms application is debugged (due to default project settings), it is not possible to step from the managed application into the unmanaged code. The highlighted line in the following code snippet is where the code steps into the unmanaged application (*F11* for Visual Studio-style developers) the debugger, however, will not step into but will instead step over:

```
Private Sub WXProcessesAndAppDomains()
  Dim managedProcesses As WXBelowTheSurface.IWXManagedProcesses = _
    New WXBelowTheSurface.CWXManagedProcessesClass()
  Dim xml As String

  xml = managedProcesses.Get(_preTag, _postTag, False)

End Sub
```

Given that it is possible for Visual Studio .NET to debug both managed and unmanaged code, shouldn't it be possible to debug managed and unmanaged code at the same time? The answer to this question is on the projects Property Pages (Configuration Properties | Debugging page):

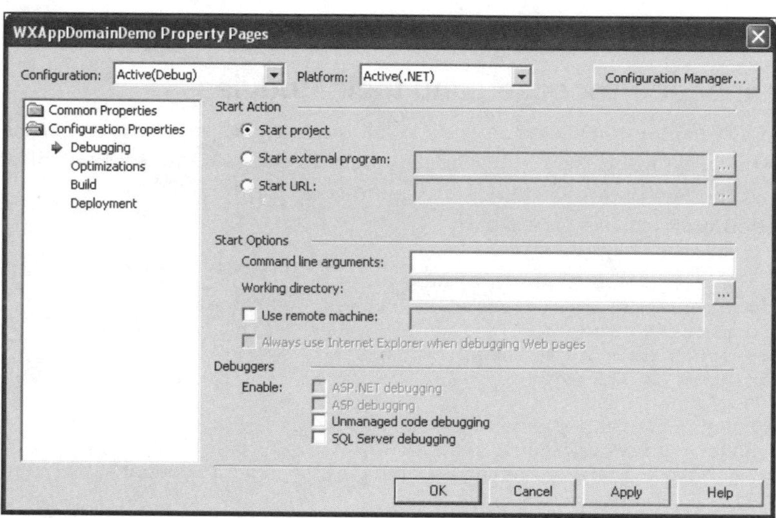


Notice underneath the Debuggers section in the screenshot above there is a column of checkboxes labeled Enable. By default, the Unmanaged code debugging checkbox is not checked. By checking this checkbox, it becomes possible to step from the realm of managed code (project, WXAppDomainDemo) into unmanaged code (project, WXBelowTheSurface). Checking this checkbox makes it possible to step into the following, infamous line of code:

```
xml = managedProcesses.Get(_preTag, _postTag, False)
```

## Debugging Unmanaged to Managed

Unmanaged code (for example written in C++) actually contains conceptually similar but still slightly different property pages. Within a C++ project such as the WXBelowTheSurface in-process COM server, the Property Pages are still displayed using the Project | Property menu item. It the previous section we used the Configuration Properties | Debugging Property Page. The analogous window for an unmanaged C++ project is as follows:

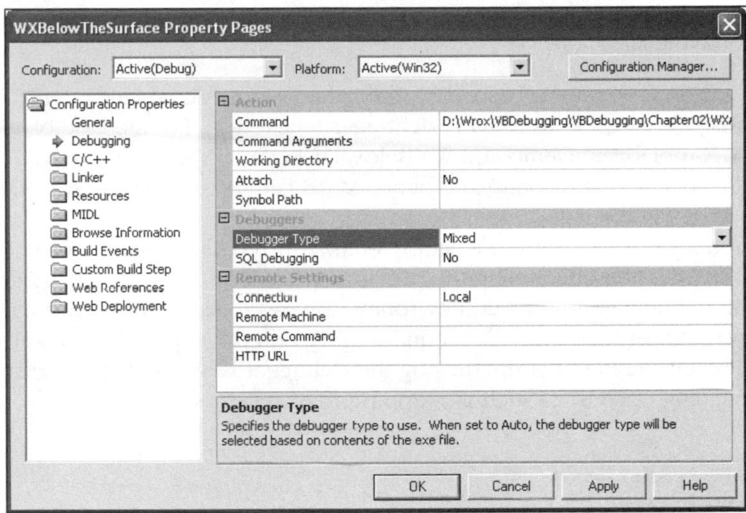


This screenshot does not display the default (out-of-the-box) setup for property page. The unmanaged C++ project, WXBelowTheSurface, is a DLL. For this reason, in the screenshot under Action the Command was set to point to WXAppDomainDemo (the executable that will load the WXBelowTheSurface dynamically linked library).

By default, breakpoints placed in the WXAppDomainDemo managed application would not be recognized when the executable was run and in fact, it would not be possible to step through WXAppDomainDemo code. The reason for this is that WXAppDomainDemo is a managed application being debugged from an unmanaged application.

By default, the previous dialog originally has Debugger | Debugger Type set to Auto. The Debuggers section specifies the supported debuggers for the application including SQL Debugging. In the previous screenshot, the Debugger Type is set to Mixed, indicating that both managed (WXAppDomainDemo) and unmanaged (WXBelowTheSurface) code can be debugged.

The permissible values for Debugger Type include:

- Native – debugging is only possible for unmanaged C++ code.
- Managed Only – debugging is only possible for managed code. Given that WXBelowTheSurface is an unmanaged DLL, this would not be the wisest of settings to choose. Setting this would allow the WXAppDomainDemo VB.NET to be debugged even though the unmanaged C++ module, WXBelowTheSurface, was the project started at the time the debugger was launched.

- Mixed – specifying this makes is possible to debug both managed and unmanaged code.
- Auto (default setting) – specifying this option lets Visual Studio .NET make a reasonable guess as to what debugger type to use. For the case of WXAppDomainDemo and WXBelowTheSurface, Visual Studio .NET chooses incorrectly (native only) and hence Mixed had to be explicitly specified.

The question does remain, "Why not simply enable mixed all the time?" The answer is likely speed. Even when developing the previous project on PIII 1.2 GHz machine with 1 GB of RAM, debugging in a mixed environment was still slow. It was not painfully slow but it was slower than normal. To quote MSDN on this topic, "In a mixed-mode application, the evaluation of properties by the debugger is an expensive operation. As a result, debugging operations such as stepping may appear slow."

# Summary

Visual Studio .NET can debug remote applications. It can launch applications remotely. It can attach to applications when they are running remotely. Debugging from VB.NET to/from VB6 or from VB.NET to Visual C++ 6.0 simply works (with the help of a managed/unmanaged debugging checkbox). Although not fully applicable to VB.NET developers, it can also debug standalone Visual C++ applications.

What remains to be shown it what Visual Studio .NET cannot do. It cannot edit and continue (as we saw in a previous chapter) but for a version 1.0 of a development tool there is nothing in this world like Visual Studio .NET, it is the state of the art when it comes to debuggers.

VB.NET

# Debugging

Handbook

Appendix A

# Application Configuration Files

The application configuration files are XML-based and can contain all sorts of configuration information security settings, remoting settings, database connection strings, and so on.

The relevance to debugging is that they are a good way for developers, testers, and technical support to enable various logging flags – as mentioned in Chapter 4. This appendix is intended to give those unfamiliar with application configuration files a quick run down on where they need to be placed and how to create them

## Configuration File Locations

For a .NET executable, the configuration file must be in the same directory as the executable and its name have the form `AppName.exe.config`. We were very explicit with the terminology here meaning that a configuration file is associated with an executable. If an assembly of type DLL is loaded by an executable assembly, the DLL uses the application configuration settings associated with the executable. The name "*AppName*" just refers to the application associated with the configuration file. Make sure to include the `.exe` extension in the name of the file, otherwise it will not be recognized at run time.

For ASP.NET applications, the configuration file is always `Web.Config`. In the ASP.NET world, it is possible for an application to be spread over a directory hierarchy. For example, an application might be found at a URL such as www.wrox.com/Level0/Level1. The actual directory, `Level0`, would contain a `Web.Config` application configuration file. The `Level1` sub-directory could also contain a `Web.Config` file. The application configuration settings for the application specified by the previous URL are a combination of the settings in `Level1/Web.Config` and `Level0/Web.Config files`. The local (`Level1/Web.Config`) application configuration settings take precedence over those further up the directory hierarchy (`Level0/Web.Config`).

Applications hosted in Internet Explorer (such as Windows Forms controls) can also use application configuration files. These files are specified within the application's HTML as follows:

```
<link rel="ConfigurationFileName" href="ConfigFileLocationURL">
```

The name of the configuration file is specified by the `rel` attribute while the `href` attribute specifies the URL corresponding to the configuration files location. The web site behind the Internet Explorer application must be the same as the web site on which this application's configuration file is located.

## Creating Application Configuration Files

There is no need when creating a Windows application, console application, or Windows service to actually create an application configuration file named *`AppName.Exe`*`.Config`. Visual Studio .NET natively supports a generic application configuration file with the name `App.config`. When such a file is included within a project, it is copied to the directory where the executable is placed and renamed *`AppName.Exe`*`.Config` when the project is built.

To create an `App.config` file, display a project in Solution Explorer and right-click on the project. From the context menu select Add | Add New Item to display the Add New Item dialog and from this select the file type, Application Configuration File:

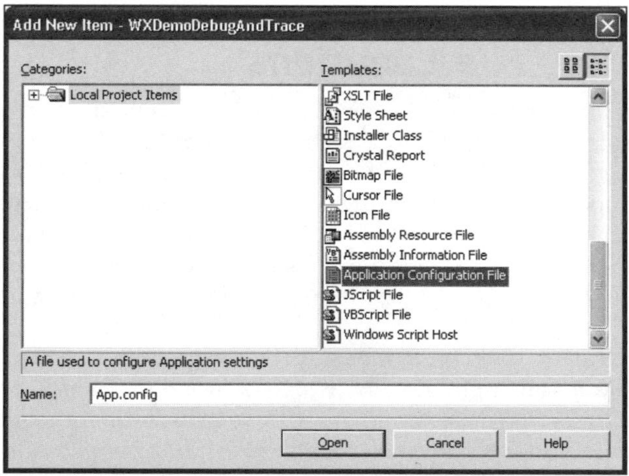


The `App.config` file shown is associated with the WXDemoDebugAndTrace project as can be seen from the title of the dialog displayed in the screenshot. Since the `App.config` file is associated with the aforementioned project, after the project is built the application configuration file used by the executable, `WXDemoDebugAndTrace.exe.config`, will be found residing in the same directory as the executable.

When created the `App.config` file just contains the shell that will ultimately be filled in with application configuration information such as trace listeners, switches, and other debug settings:

```
<?xml version="1.0" encoding="utf-8" ?>
<configuration>
</configuration>
```

We have covered the settings relevant to debugging in Chapter 4; for a complete run down on the possible settings refer to the .NET Framework documentation.

VB.NET

# Debugging

Handbook

Appendix B

# B

# Debugging Unmanaged Code

While this book is primarily about debugging managed Visual Basic .NET code, there are a number of features available in Visual Studio .NET that are only useful for debugging unmanaged applications and legacy code.

## *Improvements in Breakpoint Usability*

In Visual Studio 6.0, you could not place breakpoints in code that had not been loaded (for instance a COM DLL is only loaded when an object from it created). Even if the DLL had breakpoints, loading the DLL did not enable them. Visual Studio .NET has the ability to load DLLs (even unmanaged COM DLLs). However, if a DLL has breakpoints associated with specific lines of code those breakpoints are automatically restored and re-enabled by Visual Studio .NET.

Visual Studio .NET is so much better as a debugging environment that many developers use it while debugging their Visual Basic 6.0 and Visual C++ 6.0 applications. One reason for this is the ability to detach processes from the debugger. The other major reason is that during debugging the breakpoints associated with COM DLLs are enabled when the COM DLL is loaded. Of course, the fact that ASP.NET code written in VB.NET can be debugged in conjunction with the legacy C++ and VB6 code is another major reason to use Visual Studio .NET even though it is not used as part of the build process.

## Data Breakpoints

Even though Data breakpoints are only available for unmanaged code they are worth understanding due to their raw power and the simple fact that a great deal of initial VB.NET development will be done in conjunction with legacy unmanaged code. It is possible to associate a data modification condition with a breakpoint associated with a specific line within a source file (a breakpoint set using the File tab). A Data breakpoint is more powerful because it is triggered whenever and wherever the data is modified. A Data breakpoint is not associated with a specific line of code.

In unmanaged C++, such as the following code from the WXDataBreak solution, a Data breakpoint can be associated with the abc variable:

```
int abc = 0;

int _tmain(int argc, _TCHAR* argv[])
{
  abc = 999;
  printf("This is the line after the change so we will break here\n");

  return 0;
}
```

Data breakpoints can be set using the New Breakpoint dialog's (Debug | New Breakpoint) data tab.

There is no red dot in the source code indicating that there is a breakpoint associated with the abc variable. This makes sense since you might change a variable a thousand times in a file and hence your application would look like chickenpox. The Breakpoint window shows all the breakpoints associated with an application including Data breakpoints. Using the Breakpoint window (Debug | Windows | Breakpoints) you can view the properties associated with the abc breakpoint, and the Breakpoint Properties dialog is available from the context menu's Properties item:

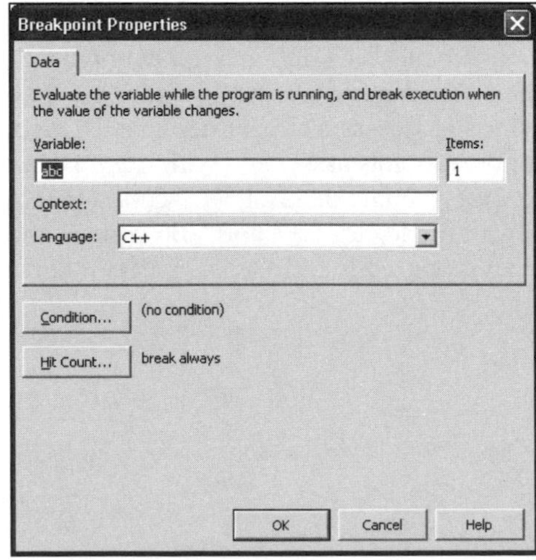

The Breakpoint Properties dialog can be used to modify the breakpoint (variable, items, context, condition, hit count, etc.):

- The Variable textbox in the previous screenshot contains the variable monitored, `abc`.
- The Items textbox is only useful when the variable is an array or a dereferenced pointer (a way to point to a region of memory in C++). Since an array or dereferenced pointer refers to a range of data, the number of items in the range is specified in the Items textbox.
- The Context textbox allows you to monitor variables outside of the current context. An example of a context would be data that is currently out of scope such as data residing in a separate module, file, or function.

Specifying C++ contexts is well beyond the scope of this text (we're VB gurus!) but for those interested see the MSDN section entitled, "Context Operator (C/C++ Language Expressions)": ms-help://MS.VSCC/MS.MSDNVS/vsdebug/html/vchowcontextoperator.htm

## Unmanaged Code and the Watch window

The `String.Format()` method was used in Chapter 2 to show off the flexibility of the Watch window. In the unmanaged world (C++), even more facilities are available using the Watch windows.

The first is the `err` pseudo-register. In an unmanaged application, a per-thread error value is typically set when Win32 functions experience an error. The value for this per-thread error value is retrieved using `GetLastError`. The pseudo-register `err` can be placed just like a variable in the watch Window (in the case of unmanaged code) and `err` will display the value corresponding to Win32's `GetLastError`..

Managed and unmanaged C++ allows format specifiers to be associated with items displayed in the Watch window. A subset of these format specifiers includes:

- `VariableName,x` – displays the variable's value as hexadecimal. A classic case for using this was in displaying COM style errors (HRESULT values) since such errors are broken down into hexadecimal chunks for easier interpretation as to what part of the code generated the error and what the specific error code was.
- `VariableName,su` – displays the variable's value as a Unicode string.
- `VariableName,s` – displays the variable's value as an ANSI string.
- `VariableName,hr` – interprets the variable's value as an error code such as would be passed to the Win32 function, `FormatMessage`. The string text associated with this error code is displayed by the `hr` format specifier.

The format specifier (`err,hr`) where the last error value is displayed as an error string is particularly useful, as can be seen by comparing the lines err,hr and err in the screenshot below:

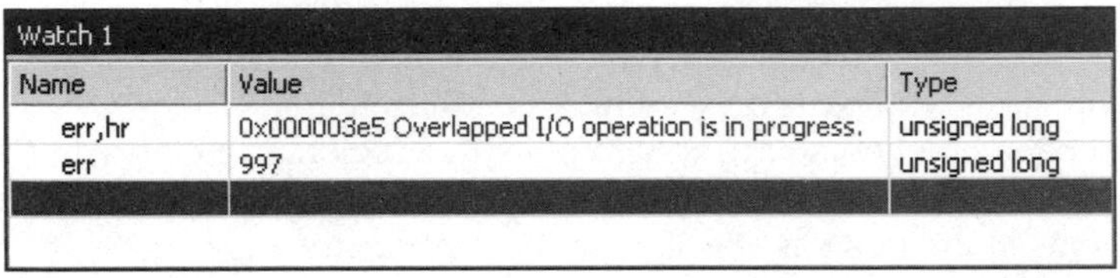

Watch 1

| Name | Value | Type |
|---|---|---|
| err,hr | 0x000003e5 Overlapped I/O operation is in progress. | unsigned long |
| err | 997 | unsigned long |

## Unmanaged Code and the Memory Window

When coding in unmanaged C++ or unsafe C# code it is possible to view the address of an unmanaged variable and hence the specific memory associated with that variable. To understand the importance of this, consider the following bit of unmanaged C++ from `WXManagedProcesses.cpp`. This code returns an extremely long XML string (courtesy of `pbstrProcesses`):

```
STDMETHODIMP CWXManagedProcesses::Get(BSTR bstrPreTag,
                                      BSTR bstrPostTag,
                                      VARIANT_BOOL onlyProcesses,
                                      BSTR *pbstrProcesses)
{
  HRESULT hr = S_OK;
  CComBSTR bstrResults = bstrPreTag;

  HRXGetManagedProcesses(onlyProcesses, bstrResults));
  bstrResults += bstrPostTag;
  *pbstrProcesses = bstrResults.Detach();

  return hr;
}
```

The Watch window displays an annoyingly small snippet of the string returned (`*pbstrProcesses`) but the Memory window really provides insight by displaying significant amounts of the string at once:

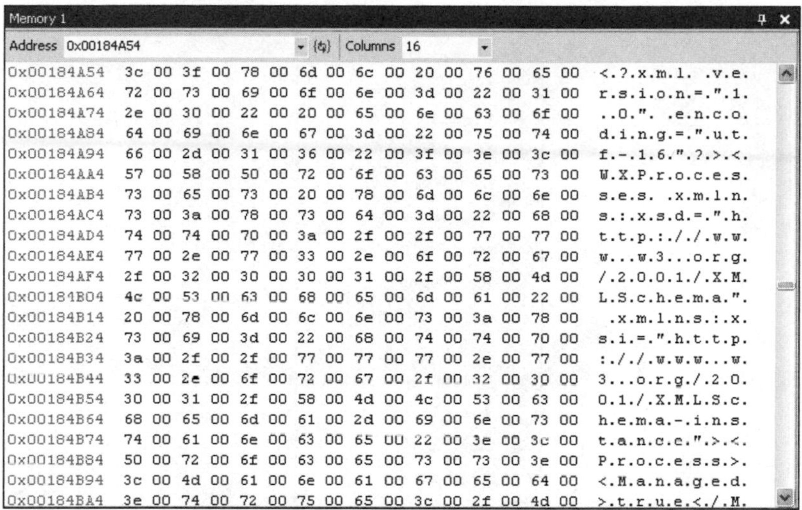

There are up to four separate Memory windows that can be displayed under Debug | Windows | Memory (Memory 1 through Memory 4).

The value `*pstrProcesses` was initially specified in the Address listbox above. Visual Studio .NET translated the variable into the corresponding memory address (`0x00184A54`). The number of columns was set to 16 meaning that sixteen columns of hexadecimal bytes at a time were displayed (since that fits nicely on a page).

Actually, the previous screenshot is unsatisfying in that it only shows only a portion of the data returned. To be completely candid, the hexadecimal bytes add nothing to string on the right of the Memory window. Remedying the format used to display data in the Memory window is a matter of right-clicking on the Memory window, which displays a context menu:

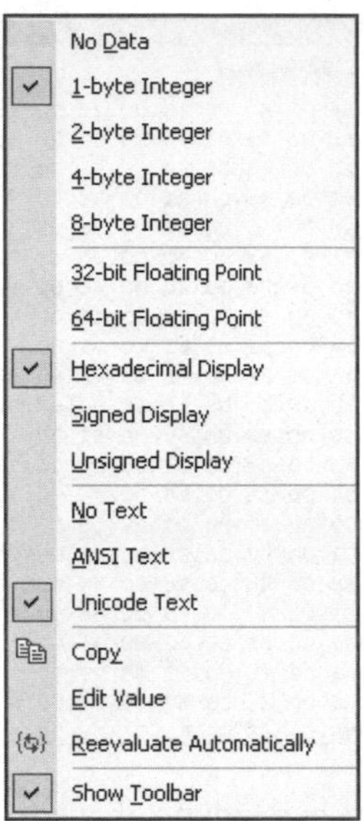


The hexadecimal values displayed in the previous Memory screenshot correspond to the data displayed in numeric form. In the Memory window's context menu, the data can be displayed as integer (one byte, two bytes), floating point (32-bit or 64-bit) or not at all. When displaying data in numeric form, it can be viewed as hexadecimal, signed, or unsigned decimal.

The data is also displayed in character form (the columns to the right side of the Memory screenshot) and as the context menu specifies this data can be displayed: not at all (No Text), as ANSI Text, or as Unicode Text (two bytes per character). If you're displaying ANSI text in a lot of cases you'll get something that looks like "X . Y . Z", which usually means that the text is Unicode. A better way to view the previous data is to specify No Data, Unicode Text:

```
Memory 1
Address 0x00184A54                               Columns 48
0x00184A54   <?xml version="1.0" encoding="utf-16"?><WXProces
0x00184AB4   ses xmlns:xsd="http://www.w3.org/2001/XMLSchema"
0x00184B14    xmlns:xsi="http://www.w3.org/2001/XMLSchema-ins
0x00184B74   tance"><Process><Managed>true</Managed><Name>D:\
0x00184BD4   Wrox\VBDebugging\VBDebugging\Chapter02\WXAddDoma
0x00184C34   inExplore\bin\Debug\WXAppDomainDemo.exe</Name><I
0x00184C94   D>632</ID><AppDomain><Name>WXAppDomainDemo.exe</
0x00184CF4   Name><ID>1</ID></AppDomain></Process><Process><M
```

Even though the Memory window's context menu contained an Edit Value menu item, this value is somewhat superfluous; to edit the Memory windows simply type over a value in the window.

**Do not try to use backspace or delete when editing the memory window. What you are changing is memory; it is not possible to delete a byte or bytes of memory. You can only overwrite a byte or bytes with a different value.**

In the world of managed code, it is not legal to directly determine the address of a specific variable. However, using the scrollbar to the right of the Memory window, the specific location at which the managed heap resides can be found. Once the managed heap is found (by manually looking for data values stored in this heap), the memory associated with any managed type can be viewed. Of course, when garbage collection kicks in, all the managed types may be shuffled as the managed heap is compressed.

## Practical Disassembly and Registers

The Registers window (Debug | Windows | Registers) shows the registers associated with the natively compiled code. This Registers window certainly cannot show the registers associated with Intermediate Language (IL) since the underlying language of .NET is stack-based and hence has no registers (this facilitates IL's platform-generic approach). It is the JIT compiler's job to convert IL to native machine code.

In order to demonstrate a practical reason for viewing the registers, consider the following snippet of C++ from the WXAssemblyLanguage unmanaged console application. This bit of C++ generates a exception because it attempts to assign a value to a region of memory (`*pBuffer = 'a';`) assigned to `NULL` (C++ `NULL` is `Nothing` in VB.NET lingo); an exception arises because you cannot point a pointer at nothing:

```
DWORD WXTryAndFix(DWORD dwExceptionCode, char* &pBuffer)
{
  if (EXCEPTION_ACCESS_VIOLATION == dwExceptionCode)
  {
    pBuffer = reinterpret_cast<char *>(malloc(256));
    return EXCEPTION_CONTINUE_EXECUTION;
  }

  return EXCEPTION_CONTINUE_SEARCH;
}

void WXCannotFixThis()

{
  char *pBuffer = NULL;

  __try
  {
    *pBuffer = 'a'; // This will generate an exception
  }
```

```
        __except(::WXTryAndFix(::GetExceptionCode(), pBuffer))
        {
        }
    }
```

The `WXTryAndFix()` function in this code snippet assigns a value to the `pBuffer` variable (`pBuffer = reinterpret_cast<char *>(malloc(256));`). This futile attempt to fix the code generates an exception due to an assignment to an invalid memory value. In order to see why it is futile, consider the following screenshot from the Assembly window that demonstrates what is going one below the high-level language (at the assembly level, not the C++ level):

```
                    *pBuffer = 'a';
00413256  mov          eax,dword ptr [pBuffer]
00413259  mov          byte ptr [eax],61h
```

What the previous assembly snippet shows is that a memory address is copied into register `EAX` (instruction at byte offset `413256`). After this address is set up, an attempt is made to copy a value to the memory reference by the `EAX` register (instruction at byte offset `413259`). If the memory location is invalid, an exception is raised (which is handled by the `__try`/`__except` construct in the code snippet). In order to determine if `EAX` contains a valid value, use the Registers window (Debug | Windows | Registers):

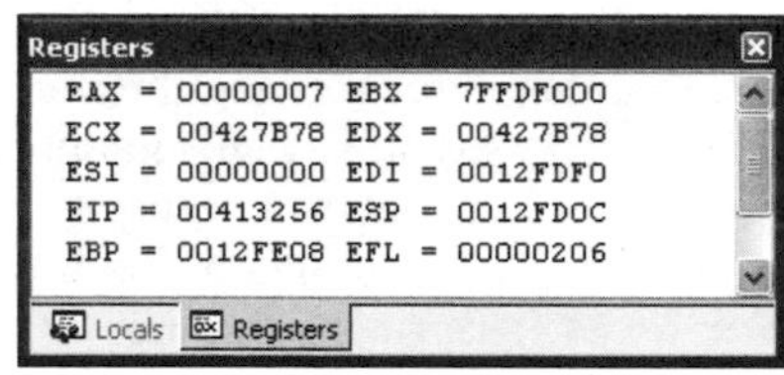


Developers who have worked with Win32 for a while know that the memory range `0x00000000` through `0x0000FFFF` is invalid. The `EAX` register contains a value of `0x00000007` that is clearly invalid and will hence continually generated an exception. The `EAX` register is never fixed because the line that should allocate a buffer (`pBuffer = reinterpret_cast<char *>(malloc(256))`) works to fix what is wrong at the C++-level but does nothing to fix the assembly-level code and register `EAX`. There is no simply or intermediate way to fix this issue using a high-level language.

The point of this example is to show that, even though assembly and registers are not the norm, there are just times when they are worth exploring. The example (project, WXAssemblyLanguage) is actually an infinite loop because the exception keeps being raised again and the code that attempts to fix the exception returns `EXCEPTION_CONTINUE_EXECUTION` thus starting the whole process repeatedly. If the infinite loop was left running, the memory associated with the process will be exhausted because the unmanaged memory allocated using `malloc` is never freed using the `free` function. There is no garbage collection in unmanaged code so an infinite memory leak is death to the running processes and under worst case scenarios can bring a machine to a halt.

## Adding User-Defined Win32 Exceptions

The Add button on the Exceptions dialog (Debug | Exceptions) can add Win32-style user-defined exceptions. Such exceptions are thrown using Win32's `RaiseException()` method and such exceptions are identified by a four-byte number whose format is specified on MSDN or can also be found in the `winerror.h` header file. When the new exception dialog is displayed, this numeric value is specified since there is no named exception corresponding to the Win32 exception. .NET developers will likely never create Win32 style exceptions but .NET developers may find it useful to add certain Win32 exceptions to the Exception windows when working in a mixed managed/unmanaged environment.

VB.NET

Debugging

Handbook

Appendix C

C

# Support, Errata, and Code Download

We always value hearing from our readers, and we want to know what you think about this book and series: what you liked, what you didn't like, and what you think we can do better next time. You can send us your comments, either by returning the reply card in the back of the book, or by e-mailing us at feedback@wrox.com. Please be sure to mention the book title in your message.

## How to Download the Sample Code for the Book

When you log on to the Wrox site, http://www.wrox.com/, simply locate the title through our Search facility or by using one of the title lists. Click on Download Code on the book's detail page.

The files that are available for download from our site have been archived using WinZip. When you have saved the archive to a folder on your hard-drive, you will need to extract the files using WinZip, or a compatible tool. Inside the Zip file will be a folder structure and an HTML file that explains the structure and gives you further information, including links to e-mail support, and suggested further reading.

# Errata

We've made every effort to ensure that there are no errors in the text or in the code. However, no one is perfect and mistakes can occur. If you find an error in this book, like a spelling mistake or a faulty piece of code, we would be very grateful for feedback. By sending in errata, you may save another reader hours of frustration, and of course, you will be helping us to provide even higher quality information. Simply e-mail the information to support@wrox.com; your information will be checked and if correct, posted to the Errata page for that title.

To find errata, locate this book on the Wrox web site (http://www.wrox.com/books/1861007299.htm), and click on the Book Errata link on the book's detail page.

# E-Mail Support

If you wish to query a problem in the book with an expert who knows the book in detail then e-mail `support@wrox.com`, with the title of the book, and the last four numbers of the ISBN in the subject field of the e-mail. A typical e-mail should include the following:

- The book title, last four digits of the ISBN (7299), and page number of the problem, in the Subject field
- Your name, contact information, and the problem, in the body of the message

We won't send you junk mail. We need the details to save your time and ours. When you send an e-mail message, it will go through the following chain of support:

- **Customer Support**

  Your message is delivered to our customer support staff. They have files on most frequently asked questions and will answer anything general about the book or the web site immediately.

- **Editorial**

  More in-depth queries are forwarded to the technical editor responsible for the book. They have experience with the programming language or particular product, and are able to answer detailed technical questions on the subject. Once an issue has been resolved, the editor can post the errata to the web site.

- **The Author**

  Finally, in the unlikely event that the editor cannot answer your problem, they will forward the request to the author. We do try to protect the author from any distractions to their writing (or programming); but we are quite happy to forward specific requests to them. All Wrox authors help with the support on their books. They will e-mail the customer and the editor with their response, and again all readers should benefit.

The Wrox support process can only offer support for issues that are directly pertinent to the content of our published title. Support for questions that fall outside the scope of normal book support is provided via our P2P community lists – http://p2p.wrox.com/forum.

# p2p.wrox.com

For author and peer discussion, join the P2P mailing lists. Our unique system provides Programmer to Programmer™ contact on mailing lists, forums, and newsgroups, all in addition to our one-to-one e-mail support system. Be confident that the many Wrox authors and other industry experts who are present on our mailing lists are examining any queries posted. At http://p2p.wrox.com/, you will find a number of different lists that will help you, not only while you read this book, but also as you develop your own applications.

To subscribe to a mailing list follow these steps:

- Go to http://p2p.wrox.com/
- Choose the appropriate category from the left menu bar
- Click on the mailing list you wish to join
- Follow the instructions to subscribe and fill in your e-mail address and password
- Reply to the confirmation e-mail you receive
- Use the subscription manager to join more lists and set your mail preferences

VB.NET

# Debugging

Handbook

# Index

# Index

## A Guide to the Index

The index is arranged hierarchically, in alphabetical order, with symbols preceding the letter A. Most second-level entries and many third-level entries also occur as first-level entries. This is to ensure that users will find the information they require however they choose to search for it.

## Symbols



## A

# D

# F



# G



# H

## W

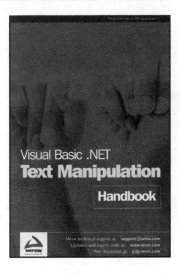

# Visual Basic .NET Threading Handbook

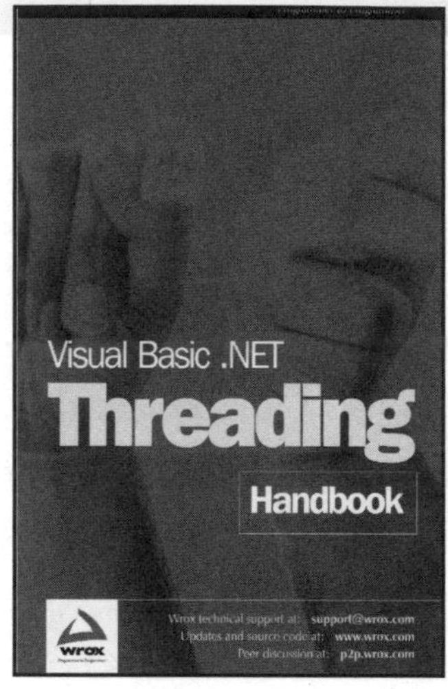


Authors: Ardestani, Ferracchiati, Gopikrishna, Redkar, Sivakumar, Titus
ISBN: 1-861007-13-2
US$ 29.99
Can$ 46.99

All .NET languages now have access to the Free Threading Model that many Visual Basic Developers have been waiting for. Compared to the earlier apartment threading model, this gives you much finer control over where to implement threading and what you are given access to. It also provides several new ways for your application to spin out of control.

This handbook explains how to avoid some common pitfalls when designing multi-threaded applications by presenting some guidelines for good design practice. By investigating the .NET threading model architecture, you will be able to make sure that your applications take full advantage of it.

**What you will learn from this book**

- Thread creation
- Using timers to schedule threads to execute at specified intervals
- Synchronizing thread execution - avoiding deadlocks and race conditions
- Spinning threads from within threads, and synchronizing them
- Modeling your applications to a specific thread design model
- Scaling threaded applications by using the ThreadPool class
- Tracing your threaded application's execution in order to debug it

# Visual Basic .NET Class Design Handbook:
## Coding Effective Classes

Authors: Andy Olsen, Damon Allison, James Speer
ISBN: 1-861007-08-6
US$ 29.99
Can$ 46.99

Designing effective classes that you do not need to revisit and revise over and over again is an art. Within the .NET Framework, whatever code you write in Visual Basic .NET is encapsulated within the class hierarchy of the .NET Framework.

By investigating in depth the various members a class can contain, this handbook aims to give you a deep understanding of the implications of all the decisions you can make at design time. This book will equip you with the necessary knowledge to build classes that are robust, flexible, and reusable.

**What you will learn from this book**

- The role of types in .NET
- The different kinds of type we can create in VB.NET
- How VB.NET defines type members
- The fundamental role of methods as containers of program logic
- The role of constructors and their effective use
- Object cleanup and disposal
- When and how to use properties and indexers to encapsulate data
- How .NET's event system works
- How to control and exploit inheritance in our types
- The logical and physical code organisation through namespaces and assemblies